The Peyote Effect

The Peyote Effect

From the Inquisition to the War on Drugs

Alexander S. Dawson

UNIVERSITY OF CALIFORNIA PRESS

University of California Press, one of the most
distinguished university presses in the United States,
enriches lives around the world by advancing scholarship
in the humanities, social sciences, and natural sciences. Its
activities are supported by the UC Press Foundation and
by philanthropic contributions from individuals and
institutions. For more information, visit www.ucpress.edu.

University of California Press
Oakland, California

Library of Congress Cataloging-in-Publication Data

Names: Dawson, Alexander S. (Alexander Scott),
    1967- author.
Title: The peyote effect : from the Inquisition to the War
    on Drugs / Alexander S. Dawson.
Description: Oakland, California : University of
    California Press, [2018] | Includes bibliographical
    references and index. |
Identifiers: LCCN 2017059947 (print) | LCCN 2017061379
    (ebook) | ISBN 9780520960909 (ebook) |
    ISBN 9780520285422 (cloth : alk. paper) |
    ISBN 9780520285439 (pbk. : alk. paper)
Subjects: LCSH: Peyote—Law and legislation—United
    States. | Peyote—Law and legislation—Mexico. |
    Indians of North America—Drug use. | Indians of
    North America—Religion. | Indians of North
    America—Social life and customs.
Classification: LCC RS165.P44 (ebook) | LCC RS165.P44
    D39 2018 (print) | DDC 362.29/308997—dc23
LC record available at https://lccn.loc.gov/2017059947

27 26 25 24 23 22 21 20 19 18
10 9 8 7 6 5 4 3 2 1

For Nina, Maia, and Alejandra

Contents

Acknowledgments

Twenty-five years ago, when I was just learning how to be a scholar, I was almost pathologically reluctant to ask for help. I am lucky that I overcame some of that fear by the time I started this project, as this work is far better than it would have been without the advice and criticism of a wide community of friends and colleagues. During my years in Vancouver I had the great fortune to benefit from the kind and critical words of Jerome Bacconnier, Courtney Booker, Max Cameron, Jeff Checkel, Susan Cho, Liz Cooper, John Craig, Greg Feldman, Bill French, Chris Gibson, Gaston Gordillo, John Harriss, Eric Hershberg, Mark Leier, Jack Little, Tamir Moustafa, Kathleen Millar, Shaylih Muehlmann, Gerardo Otero, Elodie Portales-Casamar, Judy Rein, Lisa Shapiro, Jen Spear, Dorris Tai, and Ellen Yap. Jon Beasley-Murray, with whom I have been arguing about peyote, affect, race, and history for more than a decade, has had an incalculable impact on this book. Roxanne Panchasi, my longest friend in the SFU history department, provided critical advice as I was writing the book.

I have also benefited enormously from the help and advice of Javier Barrera, Roteleo Carrillo, Shane Dillingham, Erika Dyck, Andrew Feldmar, Higinio González, Luis González-Reimann, Matthew Kent, Bia Labate, Brooke Larson, Eligio López, Francisco López, Martin Nesvig, Gabriel Parra, Ricardo Pérez Montfort, Pablo Piccato, Scott Robinson, Janine Rodiles, Norma Roquet, Richard Yensen, Annie Zapf, and Eric Zolov. Paul Gootenberg and Isaac Campos have been constant sources of knowledge and useful critique throughout the process. Barbara Weinstein has been mentor, friend, and impossibly fine role model all these years. At every step of the way I also have benefited from the dedicated work of archivists, at the US National Archives (Washington, DC), the Smithsonian's National Anthropological Archives, the Archivo General de la Nación (Mexico City), the Archivo Histórico de la Secretaría de Salud Pública (Mexico City), the Archives of the Comisión Nacional para el Desarrollo de los Pueblos Indígenas (Mexico City), and the Archivos Económicos of the Biblioteca Miguel Lerdo de Tejada (Mexico City). At the UC Press I have had the great fortune to work with Kate Marshall and Bradley Depew. Many thanks also to Holly Bridges, for her copy editing, and Andy Christenson for the index.

Research for this project was funded by an SSHRC Standard Research Grant, as well as grants from the Faculty of Arts and Social Sciences at Simon Fraser University. Portions of chapters 7 and 10 are drawn from material previously published in the *Hispanic American Historical Review.*

It remains impossible for me to fully express my gratitude to my parents and sister, who remain the steady forces they have always been in my life, dear friends, sources of comfort and support, and playmates for my children. I am fifty as I write these words, and am acutely aware of just how young Rick and Janet were when they lost their own parents. Their continued presence in my and my children's lives is a gift that they were denied. Maia and Nina, who now know more about peyote than your average teen, have also been critical sources of support and inspiration. The questions they asked when I tried to explain my interests to them, their occasional incomprehension, and the interest they showed when I managed to tell the story in an interesting way, can be seen the ultimate form of this book. Most of all, though, I am impossibly indebted to Alejandra Bronfman, who has always been my most careful reader. I strive each day to meet the standards she sets. Most days I fail.

1833

The Cholera Epidemic

As cholera ravaged the small Mexican town of Monclova during the summer of 1833, Dr. Ignacio Sendejas took desperate measures. His neighbors had turned to a variety of local cures in their efforts to stem the epidemic, mixing water, lime, and a root called *nejayote,* but nothing they tried had been effective. Sendejas hoped that a better solution to the crisis might lie with peyote, a cactus root that had until recently been illegal but that was, he wrote, "well known for its narcotic effect" and said to be less dangerous than opium. Peyote had been used by indigenous and nonindigenous curers in the region for centuries, and, given the desperation of the times, it seemed reasonable to see if this powerful cactus might save the day.

Modern medical knowledge tells us that cholera is an infectious disease caused by the bacterium called *vibrio cholera,* typically transmitted through fecal contamination of water sources, and that peyote is an unlikely cure. Sendejas did not know this, however, and when the patients he treated began to recover, he was convinced that he had found the right treatment for a public health crisis. Within eight days of the outbreak, his peyote-based medicine (it was mixed with orange leaves and six drops of laudanum) evidently cured more than two hundred people in nearby Monterrey, along with preventing any further deaths. Heartened by these results, the city government of Monclova ordered that Sendajas's formula be widely disseminated.[1]

Such an edict would have been unimaginable just a decade earlier, under a colonial regime that viewed the peyote cactus as diabolical—a source of superstition at best and congress with the devil at worst. Banned by the Inquisition in 1620, peyote was implicated in over eighty religious trials during the colonial period.[2] While this ban did little to affect indigenous use of the cactus (both because those groups for whom peyote was sacred, like the Huichols, lived largely outside colonial control and because the Inquisition had no authority over Indians), it did place people like Sendejas in a difficult position. The Spaniards and *castas* who came into contact with peyote risked punishments that ranged from prison, to the lash, to banishment. And yet, as Sendejas's comment on the "well-known" properties of peyote reminds us, the banned cactus circulated in those worlds throughout the colonial period, for the most part quietly, used as a purgative, a source of energy, and a hunger suppressant, and even to quell what were sometimes obliquely described as disturbances of the mind. It should be unsurprising, then, that peyote continued to circulate in the newly independent Mexico. Freed from the stigma of the Inquisition and not yet subject to the regulations that state and federal governments would later impose to control the national market for medicines, peyote disappeared from the view of the carceral state, and Sendejas was free to experiment with it in the hope of solving a public health crisis.[3]

In some ways this made Sendejas a model of the nineteenth-century man of science: willing to experiment with locally known medicines, interested in turning them into specific pharmaceutical cures, untroubled by the anxieties that informed the Inquisition's persecution of peyote users. He was one of many Mexican men of science who would work during the nineteenth century to create modern public health agencies and drug purity laws, and to develop new drugs and treatments, sometimes basing their own therapies on long-standing folk remedies.[4] To Inquisitors, peyote represented a threat to what was essentially a project committed to purifying and disciplining Christian bodies. Bodies under the influence of peyote were brave, strong, and beyond the control of the state. Those bodies saw things that the church insisted were not there and revealed their secrets without regard to proper comportment. They shook, danced, chanted, and howled and escaped the discipline of even their own minds. They spoke with angels and conspired with the devil (or at least they thought they did).[5] Sendejas, however, was not afraid of the Inquisition's devil and was uninterested in disciplining the flock. Instead, he hoped that there might be scientific value in peyote. He wanted to make that value legible to the modern world, to experiment with the cactus so that it might become a medicine that could cure sick bodies.

Sendejas's experiment in some ways represented the triumph of scientific inquiry over superstition, a victory made possible by the departure of the Inquisition. And yet it was only a partial victory. The end of the Inquisition did not signal the end of deep and often ugly conflicts over peyote. In the nearly two centuries since Sendejas published his curative method, the tensions between what was once an Inquisitional concern over peyote and what we might call scientific curiosity about the effects of the drug have played out again and again. No longer quite so closely associated with the devil, peyote nonetheless has managed to elicit a great deal of anxiety among missionaries, teachers, health officials, and other representatives of modernizing states. For those attempting to build citizens out of Indians, peyote has long been associated with degenerated, infirm bodies, its origins in the dirt closely linked to the indigenous filth that modernizing states sought to eradicate. Against these disgusted voices, indigenous peyotists have again and again defended the cactus as sacred, while men and women of science have repeatedly questioned its actual effects, experimenting in their laboratories and with their patients and observing indigenous uses of the plant in an effort to uncover what they hoped would be powerful cures—cures in which peyote itself would be purified, synthesized, and made into an industrially manufactured drug. Others too, ranging from English poets to North American hippies, have found themselves enchanted by peyote, drawn by its seeming capacity to offer powerful insights into human consciousness.

. . .

For much of the past century, scholarly accounts of indigenous peyotism have tended to treat it as a legitimate medicinal and spiritual tradition among groups as diverse as the Huichols of western Mexico and the Native American Church in the US.[6] These same accounts tend be less sympathetic toward the non-Indians who found peyote irresistible. In our age of essentialist identity politics, Euro-Americans (and Mexicans) who desire both the effect of the drug and to be part of the indigenous ritual surrounding its use cross a line. These *white shamans* risk condemnation not just from the agents of modernity but from scholars intent on finding and defending the authentic, and from indigenous activists who claim that their heritage has been stolen and their lifeways put at risk by rapacious outsiders.

These claims about the inauthentic use of peyote by non-Indians underpin the curious place that peyote now occupies within the Mexican and US legal systems. Despite reams of scientific evidence attesting to its relative harmlessness,[7] peyote is today illegal (a Schedule I drug in the US), classified as without therapeutic value, and subject to a high potential for abuse. That is, it is illegal unless one is a member of the Native American Church in the US (members must also have one-quarter Indian blood) and members of groups with a history of traditional use in Mexico (the most notable being the group historically known as the Huichols). Aside from being overtly racist (as is explicit in the US's blood quantum rule), these prohibitions effectively erase a long history in which nonindigenous peoples have been attracted to peyote, drawing an arbitrary distinction between those who supposedly venerate the cactus as a god and those who are said to use it as a drug. Though often couched in the language of particularity—indigenous tradition is specific, safe, rooted in natural history, whereas non-Indian users simply treat it as a drug and use it in a decontextualized fashion[8]—these arguments mask legal regimes in which the sine qua non of licit peyote use is Indian blood. Just as troubling, they align with a long-standing tradition in which peyote—its unadulterated origins in the dirt being something quite distinct from modern drugs like mescaline, which, while derived from peyote, are produced in laboratories—stands in for the Indian. It, like the Indian, is nature and exists in stark opposition to culture (read civilization, or modernity). Indeed, this version of the Indian in nature helps to give modernity its very form.[9]

This is the dilemma that animates this book. After four centuries of change, we have arrived at the beginning of the twenty-first century to a point where our laws concerning peyote resonate uncomfortably with the laws promulgated by the Spanish Inquisition. The justifications are different, and in part these similarities seem like a quirk of history, but I am nonetheless left wondering if laws the Mexican and US governments have created in the twentieth and twenty-first centuries in some ways repeat a colonial tradition in which indigenous bodies were made incommensurable with nonindigenous bodies through the legal and social proscriptions enacted around peyote. Given that we live in a moment when the class of drugs to which peyote belongs is once again under serious consideration for use treating any number of ailments, it seems particularly salient that we understand how peyote came to be so closely identified as an Indian thing even as other plants and animals native to the Americas lost their indigenous essence.[10]

. . .

Peyote's long association with Indianness aside, it is also a thing—a small cactus that grows close to the ground, with discrete physical properties. Botanists describe it as a mild hallucinogen, containing about sixty different alkaloids. Extremely bitter to the taste, when consumed orally it generally produces nausea, even vomiting. In small quantities it raises the blood pressure, lowers the pulse, increases energy, eliminates fatigue, and reduces hunger. Applied topically it seems to have an effect on joint and muscle inflammation, as well as having a mildly antibiotic effect. In larger doses it can significantly affect perception without impairing cognition. Narratives about peyote that involve vivid and brilliant colors, fire, depersonalization, and auditory hallucinations can be found over long periods of time and in a variety of cultural contexts, ranging from Mexican shamans to English poets.[11]

Bodily effects, or at least the way they are described, are in some ways contextual. The vocabularies we use for describing pain, illness, feeling, and emotion, even what constitutes these phenomena, are rooted in specific milieus and often do not translate well from one setting to another.[12] This is certainly the case for the effects caused by peyote, especially the hallucinations caused by the cactus, which have been understood in widely divergent ways over time and space. Colonial castas may have been visited by the devil, while Huichol peyotists communicated with their ancestors and the spirit world. Nineteenth-century men of science thought that the peyote effect took place entirely within their minds and bodies, while later psychonauts[13] would believe that they had gained the capacity to perceive a world that was hidden to the naked eye. Invariably these moments reveal the way that the peyote effect is specific to time and place.

Still, that does not tell the whole story. In texts from the colonial period to the present, written by voices as divergent as Spanish friars, nineteenth-century scientists, Native American activists, and 1960s hippies, peyote is described as something with the capacity to overwhelm the user. Over many centuries those who consumed peyote have described forms of depersonification, a sense that they are somehow outside of their bodies, that the world around them has shifted, that they are in a dreamlike space. They have long described their bodies under the influence as unusually connected to other bodies. The boundaries between body and mind, and self and other, seem to collapse, and the illusion that the world can be understood wholly through the five senses becomes untenable.[14] In some instances the body itself dissolves, its boundaries melting as it becomes connected to others. This represents a loss of control, but in a very particular way. It is not dull and clumsy, nor is it entirely euphoric (though peyote intoxication often involves a euphoric stage). Indeed, the perceiving body feels somehow sharpened, even as one's domination over that body is suddenly placed in doubt.

In this sense peyote is one of a group of hallucinogens (similar to psilocybin, LSD, and MDMA) whose effects are unlike alcohol, marijuana, or opium. The latter substances have historically been associated with drunken bodies, and as such present a problem for modern civilization, which relies on the sober worker in order to ensure industrial discipline and safety.[15] By contrast, peyote is more closely associated with the body that is beyond control of the mind or external authority, even as the mind under the influence of peyote is said to possess an acute clarity—much greater clarity than the sober mind. As with other hallucinogens it is a mind that lacks the will or desire to conform to social rules, a mind that is unable to dissemble. Peyote produces bodies that are preternaturally brave, often exceptionally strong, able to endure privations, defiant. They are also bodies that reveal truths, whether or not the mind wants those truths revealed. This is the nature of the body under the influence of peyote, and the source of its greatest threat. Peyote reveals what the body and mind would otherwise conceal.[16]

In some ways this claim describes a physiological experience produced by the drug. The hallucinating body, overwhelmed by sensation, finds it difficult to dissemble and conceal. It is the mind possessed by the body as the antithesis of the body controlled by the mind.[17] It is also a body that is less inclined than it otherwise might be to bow down before authority, especially when the desires of the mind and body do not perfectly align. In colonial and postcolonial settings, where physical obedience is required but the disciplined body does not necessarily indicate willing acquiescence, peyote has the power to disrupt the performance of power.[18] This presents a distinct kind of threat to colonial and postcolonial states, and for these reasons the forces of order have long responded to peyote with visceral disgust, translating that affect into an argument that peyote is disordering, dangerous, and destructive.[19]

. . .

The Inquisition hangs over this book, reminding us that drug prohibitions that differentiate indigenous bodies from white bodies are nothing new. Nonetheless, this is not a book about the Spanish Inquisition. The Inquisition left Mexico in 1820, and with its retreat Mexican officialdom effectively forgot about peyote to the extent that at the turn of the twentieth century the most important botanists in the country could not identify the cactus accurately. Peyote was rediscovered by the Mexican state at the end of the nineteenth century, and only after it was discovered by ethnographers and scientists in the US, Germany, and England. During these same years peyote use expanded considerably in the US, principally through a loosely affiliated series of groups that came to be known as the Native American Church (NAC). Over time peyote also gained a small but devoted following among nonnatives. This book, then, is principally the story of how in the process of rediscovering peyote and developing their systems of classifications and proscriptions, twentieth-century men and women of law and science wound up in a place that is oddly reminiscent of the world created by the Inquisition. As such, this book is focused less on peyote cultures as systems unto themselves and more on the ways that over a long period peyote has been tied to the mutual constitution of indigeneity and whiteness. In exploring moments in which both whiteness and indigeneity were being contested, I hope to suggest that historical processes through which indigenous peyotism was naturalized while other forms were pathologized offer us important insights into the ways that racial identities were reinscribed over time.

One of the things that seems to tie the world of the Inquisition to the present day is the way that peyote has long been linked to three particular affective responses: disgust, enchantment, and curiosity (some would call the latter a minor affect, or as Sianne Ngai might say, "mere interest").[20] Ever since the sixteenth century the "authorities"—that is, those charged with maintaining order and disciplining bodies—have registered their displeasure with peyote through vivid language in which they seem to physically recoil at the very thought of the cactus. Others, some of them indigenous and some of them not, have long harbored a view of the cactus that was diametrically opposed to this affect, seeing in peyote a portal to other worlds, a magical means of expanding their consciousness, medicine to heal their souls, an answer to the problems they faced in everyday life. And alongside these enthusiasts stood those who simply wondered, who like Sendejas thought that peyote might be something useful, an important source of healing sick bodies and minds, but who were not quite sure. They remained uncertain as to whether peyote belonged in the realm of the licit or the illicit and were forever attempting to make it legible either as useful medicine or dangerous drug.

I believe that the long history in which peyote has been intertwined with the making of racial categories is best understood through these distinct but intersecting affective responses. It is, I believe, the interplay of these affects that ultimately gave rise to systems in both Mexico and the United States in which peyote can be legal (because it is not actually dangerous), but only for indigenous bodies. Organized around a loose chronology, the book explores twelve discrete instances from the late nineteenth century to the present, in which scientific, religious, and legal authorities, along with indigenous and other peyotists, shaped the terrain of licit and illicit peyote use. The history of peyote does not allow for a seamless argument or one that suggests linear change over time, because the history of peyote, race, the border, science, and the law is neither linear nor seamless. Rather that history is jarring, often contradictory, and at times includes multiple, seemingly incompatible phenomena existing in overlapping times and spaces. At times it seems as if the logics that animated the Inquisition resonate to this day, or that the same visceral anxieties that animated early twentieth-century prohibitionists persist in the twenty-first century. And yet this is also a story of great change, of investigation, accumulated knowledge, and transformed legal regimes. It is, I believe, this collection of disparate experiences that has produced the outcomes we see today, and I attempt to reproduce some of that complexity in the structure of the book. It is also for this reason that the text repeatedly moves back and forth across the US-Mexican border. We see in these crossings the way that this boundary remains important, marking discrete systems of law and states with significantly different capabilities. And yet, we also see in these crossings the way that an emphasis on the border obscures processes that unfold in eerily similar ways on both sides, especially when it concerns the articulation of the racial categories that inform peyote's place in contemporary North America.

Chapters 1 and 2 consider a series of "discoveries," first in the US and Europe and then in Mexico. We see in these moments the ways Euro-Americans and Europeans attempted to make sense of peyote and its derivative, mescaline, in the late nineteenth and early twentieth centuries. In chapters 3 and 4 we move to a more ominous story, as we see early efforts to eradicate peyote as its use spread in Native American communities. Chapters 5 and 6 shift the focus to the growing community of peyotists in the US during the first half of the twentieth century, considering both those who sought to carve out a licit space for peyotism within US law and those who sought to use antidrug laws to stop the spread of this new religion in their communities.

In chapter 7 we return to Mexico and move into the era of psyche-delic psychiatry. Mescaline (a peyote derivative) and later LSD prom-ised to transform the practice of mental health on a global level in the 1950s, and Mexicans took a keen interest in these innovations, espe-cially where they utilized peyote and psilocybin mushrooms. Both were native to the country and seemed to offer Mexicans a unique opportu-nity to contribute to modern psychiatric methods. More than this, the indigenous knowledge associated with these plants suggested that Mex-icans might already have within their midst unique forms of knowledge about mental health.

We see here and in the following chapters the ways that peyote was sometimes subsumed within a burgeoning curiosity about hallucino-genic drugs. Starting in the 1950s, psychedelics captured the attention of a variety of actors in the US and Mexico and were sometimes posi-tioned as the key to human enlightenment and at other times lumped in with other drugs that were presumed dangerous. Nonethless, peyote did not simply become another psychedelic drug, as mescaline seems to have become, measured largely in terms of its bodily effects. Peyote instead managed to remain a plant, somehow distinct from mescaline and associated with the wild desert, indigenous peoples, hippies, and, later, new agers. In the final six chapters of the book we see how peyote was simultaneously embedded in four distinct phenomena: a taxonomic project concerned with making sense of psychedelic substances as drugs, a countercultural movement that saw in peyote an opportunity to embrace alternative forms of consciousness, a conservative movement that understood peyote as one of a number of existential threats to civilization, and burgeoning movements for indigenous self-determina-tion that saw in peyotism a powerful expression of indigenous alterity.

Finally, a brief note on language. Racial categories are produced over time at least in part through the shifting language of classification, shifts that are reflected in the changing terminology one finds in archival texts. In this book I seek to consider the importance of those shifts by using, for the most part, the terminologies in circulation at any given moment. That is, for instance, why at a certain point in this text *Huichol* becomes *Wixárika* (though the shift is not nearly as straightforward as this might make it seem, as today terms like *Huichol, Wixárika,* and *Wixáritari* continue to circulate). I have found it even more difficult to come to terms with the use of the term *Indian* in the North American context. It is a term that the regulatory state continues to use, and is alternately mobilized and despised by different actors to whom the label is applied. In some ways we can go beyond this dilemma by using the language of ethnic or national affiliation, though the fact that "Indian" remains a salient political category seems relevant here. Given that this book is in part the story of the ways that the colonial past resonates with the present, it seems important that the persistence of this language be reflected in this text.

CHAPTER ONE

1887

Dr. John Briggs Eats Some Peyote

It seemed to me my heart was simply running away with itself, and it was with considerable difficulty I could breathe air enough to keep me alive. I felt intoxicated, and for a short time particularly lost consciousness.

—John Briggs, May 1887

Peyote was well known in Ignacio Sendejas's world, used within a variety of Indian communities from west-central Mexico into what is today the southwestern United States as a sacrament, and used by curers and botanists in the borderlands for any variety of ailments. Outside of the borderlands, however, Euro-Americans had scant knowledge of the cactus. The doctors and scientists in Mexico City who were then endeavoring to create a modern state had little interest in things tainted by indigeneity, and most could not have identified peyote or discussed its properties in any detail. Beyond Mexico the classificatory challenges were even greater, in part because the name *peyote* had long been associated with at least three different plants. Early in the colonial period, Bernardino de Sahagún classified two plants as peyote, one identified with Xochimilco and the other with Zacatecas. Decades later Francisco Hernández coined the scientific term *peyotl zacatensis* to describe the cactus that we know today as peyote. Later still, when nineteenth-century North American and European botanists began to classify the myriad cacti found in Mexico, they identified no less than four species of cactus that went by the name *peyote*. Probably the first to correctly identify the cactus associated with indigenous ritual life was the French botanist Charles Antoine Lemaire, who in 1840 introduced the name *Echitiocactus Williamsii* for reasons that remain in dispute to this day (it was probably named for C. H. Williams, a British official who was at one time ambassador in Bahia, Brazil).

During these same years the proliferation of colloquial names for peyote signaled its growing use in the United States. *Bartlett's Dictionary of Americanisms* reports it as "whisky root" in its 1860 edition, indicating that "the Indians eat it for its exhilarating effect on the system, it producing precisely the same [effect] as alcoholic drinks."[1] Traveling through south Texas in the late nineteenth century, the Norwegian ethnographer Carl Lumholtz was told that members of the Texas Rangers used mescal buttons (the local term for peyote) to stave off their hunger and fatigue when taken prisoner during the Civil War, soaking the buttons in water and calling them "white mule." Others reported that residents of the border regions where peyote grew abundantly used it for headaches, open sores, and rheumatism.[2]

Peyote entered North American pharmacology in May 1887, when Dr. John Raleigh Briggs, a doctor living in Fort Worth, published an account of his experiment with the cactus in *The Medical Register*. His article, "'Muscale Buttons'—Physiological Effects—Personal Experience," describes symptoms that would be repeated again and again as medical researchers experimented with peyote.[3] After taking the "mescale button," Briggs's pulse rate jumped from 60 to 90, and he began to breathe more rapidly. His head began to ache and he felt dizzy as his pulse rate reached 160 beats per minute. He described his distress:

> The peculiar and dazed feelings I then experienced, together with alarm, prevented my taking notes on respirations, and therefore don't know the number, but they had certainly still further increased. It seemed to me my heart was simply running away with itself, and it was with considerable difficulty I could breathe air enough to keep me alive. I felt intoxicated, and for a short time particularly lost consciousness.

Briggs then rushed to the office of his friend, Dr. E. J. Beall, who prescribed large doses of smelling salts and whisky. After taking a long walk, he began to recover his senses, and within eight hours the only remaining symptom was a lingering depression, which was gone by the next day. Looking back, he was chastened by the experience. "I believe if prompt aid had not been given me I should have died."[4]

Briggs's account was momentous in two ways. First, it marked the beginning of a period in which the effort to identify peyote shifted from traditional botany (a system of classification in which the cactus was identified by its physical appearance and habitat) and toward chemistry (in which the key identifying markers would lie in the physical effects that peyote produced in bodies). Second, a reprint of the article in *The Druggists' Bulletin* caught the attention of George Davis, secretary and general manager of Parke, Davis and Company, who convinced Briggs to send him a cigar box filled with peyote buttons in June 1887. Frank Augustus Thompson, a chemist at the company, managed in July 1887 to prepare alcoholic extracts from the buttons, revealing numerous alkaloids. Over the next few years he and others in the company undertook numerous attempts to market peyote as a cardiac stimulant.[5]

As luck would have it, around this time a prominent German toxicologist named Louis Lewin visited the company's offices in Detroit. Either Thompson or someone else at the company gave a few buttons to Lewin, who took them home to Berlin. He in turn showed the buttons to Paul Cristoph Hennings, a botanist at the Berlin Botanical Garden, who identified them as a new species of anhalonium cactus. He named it *Anhalonium Lewinii* in honor of Lewin.[6] (The name would not stick. In 1894 US botanist John M. Coulter created the genus *Lophophora* and called peyote *Lophophora Williamsii*. This classification persists to this day.)[7]

Working in his Berlin lab with the samples from Detroit, Lewin extracted his first alkaloid in 1888. He called it *anhalonine,* and after testing it on animals, he and Henning penned the first scientific paper on peyote. They found that anhalonine had a strong effect, causing agitation and muscle cramps in the test animals. The same tests also suggested that it was toxic in large doses, similar to strychnine. Human tests indicated that it produced no visual hallucinations, which suggested there were other important alkaloids yet to be extracted from the cactus.

Working in fits and starts because of the irregular supply of peyote, over the next several years Lewin and his colleagues in Germany would slowly begin to unpack the botanical mysteries of the cactus. Arthur Heffter at the Pharmacological Institute of the University of Leipzig identified pellotine in what was probably *lophophora diffusa* in 1894. Anhalonine had shown no effect on human subjects, but fifty- to sixty-milligram doses of pellotine made them sleepy without seeming to produce side effects.[8] Still, subjects given the drug did not hallucinate, which meant that the researchers had still more work to do in identifying the most powerful alkaloids in the cactus.

In 1896, and this time definitely working with *Anhalonium lewinii/ Lophophora williamsii,* Heffter identified four distinct alkaloids (mescaline, anhalonine, anhalonidine, and lophophorine)[9]. After conducting some self-experiments with mescaline (measured out so that his dose was the equivalent of about five buttons), he concluded that it, and not anhalonine or pellotine, was the most important alkaloid in the peyote cactus.[10]

For his self-experiment Heffter made an extract residue by percolating the dried material with 95 percent alcohol and then evaporating the alcohol under vacuum. The extract was then placed on paper wafers to make it palatable. Heffter consumed the extract over half an hour between 10:15 and 10:45 in the morning. He experienced a series of common effects, including a change in pulse rate, nausea, a headache, dizziness, blurred vision, and clumsiness, but was particularly impressed by the visions, "richly colorful pictures . . . which consisted partly of tapestry patterns and mosaics, and partly of winding colored ribbons moving with the rapidity of lightning." Heffter also experienced auditory hallucinations and other visions, which included shooting lights like "fireworks," and "thick purple intertwined roots and fibers on a dark, glossy background." He reported that his intellect remained unimpaired during the experiment, but that he experienced "the loss of the sense of time: I estimated a few minutes as lasting 1/2 hour. The 10-minute-long walk from my house to the laboratory seemed endlessly long."[11]

Mescaline, denatured, purified, and distinct from peyote, was clearly a powerful drug. What remained was the question of whether this was something useful or merely interesting. It seemed obvious how one might position pellotine as a therapeutic drug, as its direct applicability as a sleep aid with no side effects was limited only by the rather high cost of extracting the alkaloid from *Lophophora diffusa* (the introduction of low-cost barbiturates in 1904 killed the market for pellotine). Heffter's mescaline visions, by contrast, did not portend obvious therapeutic uses. The specificity of his descriptions of the mescaline effect suggested that it was highly idiosyncratic, linked to the particular history and experiences of the person who took the drug. These types of experiences can be revelatory at an individual level but are not clearly useful when commercializing a drug. Pharmaceutical companies depend on a consistent effect from one patient to the next.

. . .

Back in the US, peyote research was faring no better. Working in laboratories that were inferior to their German counterparts, chemists at Parke Davis never made any progress in identifying the alkaloids in the peyote cactus. Peyote remained almost unknown among North American scientists until November 1891, when James Mooney, an employee of the Smithsonian Institution's Bureau of Ethnology, made a presentation at the Anthropological Association in Washington about a peyote ceremony he had witnessed the previous summer among the Kiowa Indians of Oklahoma. The ritual was relatively new to the community, having been introduced by proselytizers from the Comanche tribe, and Mooney was the first white man to observe it. At that point he had not taken any mescal buttons.[12]

His first personal experience with peyote came the following summer when, on the advice of his informants, he ate some buttons to remain alert through the all-night Kiowa ceremony. Wanting to understand its effect further, two years later he purchased a large quantity of peyote from Comanche purveyors and took it back to Washington for study. He gave about half to Harvey Wiley, chief chemist at the US Department of Agriculture, who promised to undertake chemical tests. Another large sample was given to D. W. Prentiss and Francis Morgan of the medical department of the Columbian University in Washington (now George Washington University), who promised to test the buttons on human subjects. Mooney also sent a few buttons to the famed Philadelphia neurologist Dr. Silas Weir Mitchell.[13]

Wiley tasked Ervin E. Ewell at the US Department of Agriculture with isolating and analyzing the active elements in the mescal buttons, but Ewell (seemingly unaware of the growing record of German publications on the cactus) decided to focus his energies on extracting resins from the buttons instead of isolating the alkaloids. The decision was misguided, but it may also have been strategic. He had the capacity to extract the resins, but his rudimentary equipment and poor technical skills made it impossible for him to isolate the alkaloids in his samples. In 1897, after three years of inconsistent results, the USDA abandoned the tests.[14]

Ewell did not abandon the project before he tried the buttons himself. Wiley, who tried to discourage him, recounted the experiment years later.

> So he took the buttons home with him and he chewed them in the manner described by Mr. Mooney as being practiced by the Indians; he chewed them until they formed a bolus, and then swallowing the bolus. . . . About 2 o'clock on Sunday morning the condition of Mr. Ewell became so alarming to his roommate that he came with Mr. Ewell to my residence and awakened me, the laboratory mate feeling he could not take the responsibility any longer. . . . It was 48 hours before he could sleep after he had taken these beans and after the excitement had gradually passed away. He was constantly talking and saying, "Oh, how beautiful; oh, how splendid; how magnificent." I was particularly struck with this expression. I knew something of

his views and that he was a great admirer of Robert G. Ingersoll. One of the things he said was, "Oh, I wish I could talk with Ingersoll just for a minute; I could convince him that there is a heaven. I see it. I see the angels in the streets of gold.[15]

Alarmed by Ewell's experience, Wiley concluded that the mescal buttons produced delusions, were a dangerous drug, and should be closely regulated.

Prentiss and Morgan took a somewhat more systematic approach in their study of the effect of peyote on humans, seeking to experiment in a way that was informed by the practices of the Kiowas. They believed that the Indians were "addicts" whose "tolerance" for significant quantities of peyote was "a result of both his own habitual use and of the hereditary influence received by him from his progenitors," yet they also believed that the rituals surrounding peyote use were important to understanding the effect. According to their 1895 report in the *Therapeutic Gazette,* they sought as much as possible to replicate those rituals (holding ceremonies at night, choosing only male subjects, and including drumming) over the course of their six experiments, but reduced the quantity of mescal buttons to what they felt was a reasonable level for white subjects. They found that between 3.5 and 7 (instead of the 10–12 taken in Kiowa ceremonies) could "produce a marked effect,"[16] including visions, colors, euphoria, lucidity, loss of conception of time, lowered heart rates without any effect on respiration, dilation of pupils, varying levels of muscular depression, partial anesthesia of the skin, and an inability to sleep. Prentiss and Morgan also found that the drumming enhanced the beauty of the visions that their subjects experienced.

That said, all the results were not entirely positive. One subject grew paranoid, thinking the others were trying to kill him. Another became unable to walk without assistance. Yet another reported a dual personality while under the influence. They also found that pleasure had an inverse relationship to muscular depression, and that some of the test subjects experienced headaches that persisted for some time after taking the mescal buttons. They did report that (as with the Kiowa rituals) there seemed to be no persistent aftereffects.[17]

The word Prentiss and Morgan used to describe the effect—*intoxication*[18]—reminds us of the conceptual limitations within which they worked. Lacking a vocabulary to describe what many today call psychedelic involvement, or a trip, they resorted to language that more easily aligned with drunkenness, even as they seemed to acknowledge the inadequacy of the term. Their tests suggested that peyote had some similarity to *Cannabis indica* (which was then in use for a variety of purposes), but while *Cannabis indica* was a hypnotic that led to sleep, mescal buttons produced neither effect. Also, while *Cannabis indica* created merriment, they described the mescal buttons as producing "wonder and admiration, but no merriment."[19] Peyote was thus unlike the drugs then increasingly facing prohibitionist pressures: opium, marijuana, alcohol.

Interviewed by the *Sunday Herald* in Boston in the aftermath of the experiments, Prentiss reiterated his ambivalence. The drug produced vivid, colorful dreams and had few aftereffects, but he and his collaborators did not know how they might put it to use. "It promises to be valuable medicine, but its alkaloids and resinoids must be examined separately to ascertain which are the active principles."[20] He doubted it could replace any drug then in circulation but offered that it "promises to become an important addition to the class of drugs known as nerve stimulants and tonics." When confronted with the concern that the "white man might become addicted to its use as an intoxicant," Prentiss equivocated. "The Indians are not addicted (no habit is formed) but we cannot say what will happen to Caucasians."[21]

A few months later Mooney published a detailed account of the Kiowa peyote ceremony in the *Therapeutic Gazette,* in which he insisted that "so numerous and important are its medical applications, and so exhilarating and glorious its effect, according to the statements of the natives, that it is regarded as the vegetable incarnation of a deity."[22] As far as Mooney could tell, the Kiowa used it to great effect for fevers, headaches, chest pains, hemorrhages, and consumptive diseases. Its power in curing the latter had made it very popular among students returned from eastern boarding schools "who almost inevitably acquire consumption in the damp eastern climate." They were "the staunchest defenders of the ceremony, having found by experience that the plant brings them relief."[23] In order to drive this point home Mooney told the story of his Kiowa interpreter, Paul Setkopi, who spent four years in New York but was eventually sent home to die among his people after contracting consumption. He was given a few mescal buttons for his coughing when he arrived home and felt immediate relief. Thirteen years later he was still alive and had largely recovered.[24]

Mooney also insisted in the article that the mescal buttons had no deleterious mental effect. To prove this point he invoked Quanah Parker (here called Zuanah), another figure he would return to over the years in his efforts to defend indigenous peyotism. Parker, he said, was the great high priest of the peyote rite among the Comanches and a mixed-race chief of the tribe. "Any who know him at home or in Washington will admit that there is no more shrewd or capable business man in the Southwest." During one ceremony Mooney had watched Parker consume thirty buttons. The next morning he was doing business with cattlemen, showing no effect. Others might eat as many as fifty buttons, with no ill effect. Their examples demonstrated that the buttons were a powerful stimulant that enabled those who consumed them to endure "great physical strains without injurious reaction."

For his own part, Mooney reported that the first times he had observed a ceremony without taking any buttons he finished the evening numb, exhausted, and hardly able to stand. Since he had adopted the habit of taking three to four buttons, he had found that he could stand all night and come out in the morning feeling refreshed. He had never consumed more than seven and believed that were he to take more, the disagreeable taste "would probably cause me to vomit." This was too few buttons to experience a "mental effect," which his informants indicated only came after eating ten buttons (they typically ate twelve to twenty).[25]

. . .

Weir Mitchell was the last of the recipients of Mooney's peyote to experiment with the buttons, waiting until after he read Prentiss and Morgan's report in the *Therapeutic Gazette*. Wanting to concentrate the power of the buttons, he made an alcoholic extract, in which each drachm of alcohol represented one button. At noon on 24 May 1896, he drank one and a half drachms of the extract, followed by another drachm an hour later. His initial symptoms included a flushed face, a sense of exhilaration, and a tendency to talk, while his reflexes remained unimpaired. At two o'clock he ventured out for his consultations with his patients and noticed that he had much more endurance than usual, making a four-story climb two steps at a time without experiencing any shortness of breath. He commented that "this is akin to the experience, as I learn, of the mescal eating Indians, and to that of many white men." At this point he noticed that colors were shifting, and after returning home and taking some more of the extract (to a total of six and a half drachms), he noticed that "a transparent, violet haze was about my pen point." He began to feel especially confident in his abilities and experienced a number of visual hallucinations. Lying down, he saw bright lights, "such as I find it hopeless to describe in language which shall convey to others the beauty and splendor of what I saw." The effect, he said, was in some ways similar to an ophthalmic megrim (migraine).[26]

Splendorous as the visions were, the experience left him with an ominous feeling.

> I predict a perilous reign of the mescal habit when this agent becomes attainable. The temptation to call again the enchanting magic of my experience will, I am sure, be too much for some men to resist after they have once set foot in this land of fairy colours where there seems to be so much to charm and so little to excite horror or disgust.

Published in the *British Medical Journal*, this deeply ambivalent account attracted the attention of Henry Havelock Ellis, who managed to buy some mescal buttons at Potter and Clarke, a London apothecary. As he reported in the *Lancet* in June 1897, in his first experiment he took three buttons at intervals of one hour each. The doses immediately caused a headache to disappear, followed by unusual energy and intellectual power, which also passed quickly. After that he experienced a variety of hallucinations, including kaleidoscopic colors, with no impairment of his intellectual judgment. The world around him glowed, had a polished quality, was fibrous, and everything he cast his sight on was in a constant state of change. Impeded motor coordination and cardiac and respiratory depression were the only unpleasant symptoms he suffered, though he was disturbed by the fact that during the experience his "body felt unfamiliar to the touch."[27] Mescal buttons had produced an intoxication of the senses and nerves, overloading the brain with sensory experience, but the cognitive brain remained remarkably clear through the experience (unlike with hashish, marijuana, alcohol, and opium). "The mescal drinker remains calm and collected amid the sensory turmoil around him; his judgment is as clear as in the normal state; he falls into no oriental condition of vague and voluptuous reverie."[28]

Ellis did have some concern about the effect of the drug, as he recounted in the *Contemporary Review*. While his experience had been rather benign, in an artist friend peyote brought on "paroxysmal attacks of pain at the heart and a sense of imminent death."[29] The sudden illumination of the world around terrified his artist friend, as it

> seemed like a kind of madness beginning from inside me. . . . My speedy dissolution, I half imagined, was about to take place. . . . At another time my eye seemed to be turning into a vast drop of dirty water in which millions of minute creatures resembling tadpoles were in motion.[30]

Shortly thereafter the friend's right leg became "heavy and solid," carrying the entire weight of his body. He reported that "the rest of my body had lost all substantiality." After that "the back of my head seemed to open and emit streams of bright colour; this was immediately followed by the feeling as of a draught blowing a gale through the hair of the same region."[31]

Most terrifying was the fact that his mind remained lucid as the world around him dissolved. "Pressing my fingers accidentally against my temples, the fingertips became elongated, and then grew into the ribs of a vaulting or of a dome-shaped roof. . . . My arm separated from my body." He described a biscuit passed to him erupting in blue flame. When he touched his trousers with the biscuit, they were set on fire. He then put the biscuit into his mouth, creating a fire inside his mouth. His skin then grew as thin as tissue paper.[32] Describing this as an out-of-body experience, he said:

> During the period of intoxication, the connection between the normal condition of my body and my intelligence had broken—my body had become in a manner a stranger to my reason—so that now on reasserting itself it seemed, with reference to my reason, which had remained perfectly sane and alert, for a moment sufficiently unfamiliar for me to become conscious of its individual and peculiar character. It was as if I had unexpectedly attained an objective knowledge of my own personality. I saw, as it were, my normal state of being with the eyes of a person who sees the street on coming out of the theatre in broad day.[33]

Coupled with an account of William Butler Yeats fearing that his weak heart would give out under the effect of peyote, these stories did not exactly amount to a ringing endorsement of the new drug. Nonetheless, Ellis did not think it should be prohibited, and argued that others would be attracted to it for good reason. It was "the most purely intellectual" of the drugs, and for this reason posed little threat of abuse. What was more, "unlike the other chief substances to which it might be compared, mescal does not wholly carry us away from the actual world, or plunge us into oblivion; a large part of its charm lies in the halo of beauty it casts around the simplest and commonest things."[34] He suspected it would become popular, believed it was very promising for those who "cultivate the vision-breeding drugs," and was certain that it would be of great interest to psychologists and physiologists.[35]

. . .

Ellis wrote with a certainty that the drug acted on the body, producing a physiological effect. Peyote did not have the powers attributed to it by indigenous users and the colonial subjects who were drawn to the cactus. It did not allow users to see something that was normally hidden, to speak with God, the devil, the ancestors. It instead distorted the body's capacity to sense itself and the world around it. Time did not change. The body did not fly. If the body became unfamiliar to the touch, or if the physical boundaries of the body in its normal state seemed to dissolve (the out-of-body experience, or depersonalization), it was because the drug had affected cognition, not because the drug had reshaped reality or enlarged the user's capacity to perceive the world. It was the trick performed by the drug, a trick that later scientists would use to classify peyote as a psychotomimetic—a drug that mimics psychosis. It was up to modern science to determine if this effect was significant enough to undertake a process in which they could transform peyote into a useful drug.

That task would not be easy. Reading Ellis's work as subjective, unscientific, and superficial, the editors of the *British Medical Journal* excoriated Ellis for his essay in the *Contemporary Review*. His mescal paradise would be better phrased as a new inferno, not so different from that caused by opium, and his "eulogy" to the drug represented "a danger to the public."[36] Aside from highlighting the terrifying visions experienced by his artist friend, and the fact that Yeats could have died because of his weak heart, they were particularly alarmed by Ellis's claim that a healthy person who takes it once or twice will have an "unforgettable delight" and an educational experience. Their response:

> Surely this is putting temptation before that section of the public which is always in search of a new sensation; and this temptation to mescal drugging is enhanced when Mr. Ellis "explains" that the taking of this substance can never degenerate into a habit.

Noting that some people might even be killed by their first dose, they also disputed Ellis's claim that there was no danger of a "mescal mania." People might begin for intellectual reasons but could easily become addicted because of the pleasure it brings. As for the reports of Kiowa mescal ceremonies, they dismissed Kiowa rituals as "mescal orgies" and reminded their readers that these rites had been suppressed by the US government (this claim was only partly true). In a classic display of late nineteenth-century racism, they also derisively noted that "we have yet to learn that the Kiowa Indians are the most intellectual of the inhabitants of the sister Continent."[37]

The journal's sarcastic, casual dismissal of the Kiowa relied on a commonplace but circular logic, in which Indians were degenerate because they were peyotists, or peyotists because they were degenerate

Indians. Perhaps the modern men of science and Christian morals could rescue them, but given the degeneracy-peyote cycle, it was unlikely. By extension this logic suggested that civilized folk had much more to lose should they fall prey to the drug, and that the differences between their bodies and indigenous bodies made them more vulnerable to the dangers of peyote. It did not really matter whether Indian bodies were different because of an essential distinction between whiteness and indigeneity or because of their peyote use. Their bodies were fundamentally, essentially different.[38]

CHAPTER TWO

1899

The Instituto Médico Nacional

It may be supposed that the peyote produced effects in dogs similar to those described in Indians taking the drug in its natural form: excitation of the central nervous system, particularly the brain, as it appeared that the animals had visual hallucinations

—*Estudio Relativo al Peyote, 1913*[1]

Given the interest in peyote seen elsewhere in the 1890s, it is curious that it took until 1899 for Mexican researchers to turn their attention to the cactus; more curious, because a decade earlier the country's liberal dictator Porfirio Díaz had created just the sort of institution one would expect to be at the forefront of peyote research. Founded under the direction of Dr. Fernando Altamirano in 1888, Instituto Médico Nacional (IMN) was the brainchild of a regime that saw research into Mexico's natural riches (especially its botanical wealth) as a means for promoting economic development. Indigenous plants offered a rich source of material for a modern pharmaceutical industry, and Mexican researchers had been undertaking limited efforts to test the efficacy of those drugs for some time at the National Preparatory School and College of Mines (consider also Dr. Sendejas). But prior to the founding of the IMN, botanical research in Mexico had been dominated by foreigners.[2] It was up to the IMN to reclaim the national pharmacopoeia.

By the turn of the century the IMN had collected 17,000 plant samples, classified 6,000 by genus, and analyzed the chemical makeup of 177 plants and 700 extracts.[3] It was not enough, however, to simply identify and analyze the component elements of the plant-drugs that could be found growing naturally in Mexico. Doctors employed by the

IMN also administered solutions prepared at the institute to patients in the San Andrés Hospital, treating over two hundred with products created in the institute.[4] Testing these drugs in what they saw as a controlled, scientific context, these experiments were part of the IMN's larger effort to supplant traditional herbal markets (and an associated tendency of curers in these markets to focus on the supernatural causes of illness) in favor of a closely regulated pharmaceutical industry, in which drugs would be administered based on a clearly understood therapeutic effect on the body, established through rigorous experimentation.[5]

The IMN was informed by a theory of the human body and the cure that sought precision and predictability. Empirical study and experimentation demanded that the active elements of approved drugs be isolated, controlled, and purified so that the effect could be regularized, repeated, and understood through written description—this last act being critical to the constitution of both modern medicine and the modern self. Knowledge had to become an abstraction, knowable far and wide, universal, and applicable in any place and any setting. It had to be separated from the knower.

As far as peyote was concerned, this would not be an easy task. Though researchers at the IMN were only vaguely familiar with the cactus, they were heirs to a long tradition in which peyote had been marked as inescapably Indian. In the colonial period Indians were so intimately associated with the power of the cactus that Spaniards often did not take it themselves but contracted an Indian to consume peyote and then tell them what it had revealed. These practices made peyote part of a very particular world, unknowable to the Spaniards yet available to any Indian, whether or not they had previous knowledge of peyote.[6]

This suited the social and racial hierarchies of a colonial society, as it reminded both those who were enchanted and those who were disgusted by peyote of the chasm of difference between the Spaniard and Indian, but it was a version of particularity that was inimical to the world of twentieth-century medicine. If peyote was to be medicine, it would need to enter the world of the universal cure, applicable to specific illnesses and available to anyone who suffered. And if it was dangerous, barbarous, or primitive, it would need to be eradicated. Indeed, if it posed a threat to the bodies that consumed it, peyote would need to become illicit for all Mexicans, including its principal devotees (by the end of the nineteenth century this would include the Huichol, Cora, and Tepehuán of the western sierra, and the Tarahumara of Chihuahua), who as citizens of a modern nation did not occupy the distinct caste categories they had during the colonial period.

. . .

The classification of peyote within a modern system of public health regulation did not need to obey a stark distinction between designating it as dangerous or medicinal to the human body. Even as the IMN was endeavoring to sort out this classification, other scientific experts were beginning to explore peyote as something much more interesting—as a substance that offered an opportunity to explore a system of beliefs and practices that differed in fundamental ways from the value systems of the West. Unimpressed by the dark renderings of Mexico's peyotist peoples they could find in colonial texts, these researchers traveled into the western sierra in search of the Huichols, whom they believed to be one of the last truly pre-Colombian civilizations in the Americas.[7]

Beginning with Carl Lumholtz and León Diguet, and later Konrad Theodor Preuss and Robert Zingg, the ethnographers who traveled to the region that came to be known as the Sierra Huichola produced an extensive record of a society untouched by the outside world.[8] They drew on observations in the sierra to create images of a truly remarkable community, unlike any other in the Americas, possessing forms of knowledge that offered a powerful contrast to the alienated industrial societies of the West.[9] It was a world that was not organized hierarchically or systematically. Most of the few thousand residents of the sierra lived dispersed among four hundred small ranchos spread throughout the area, in communities of a few families connected by kin, at some distance from the three principal Huichol ceremonial centers (San Sebastián Teponahuastlán [Wautüa], Santa Catarina Cuexcomatitlán [Tuapuri], and San Andrés Cohamiata [Tatei Kié])[10]. Each rancho had its own distinct traditions, as local shaman/singers (sometimes called *mara'akámes*) rendered Huichol myths and histories in their own ways.

That said, there were a number linguistic, cultural, and religious traditions that marked communities as Huichol and that acted as signifiers of a profound and profoundly important system of knowledge in the writings of the ethnographers. Ceremonial centers were organized around a temple, known as a *tuki,* with adjacent *xirikis* or ancestor-god houses.[11] The tukis were built according to the cardinal directions, with the openings positioned to indicate summer solstice, winter solstice, and the fall and spring equinoxes—all of it intended to keep the cosmos in balance. Tukis were built and maintained by rotating groups of community members and replaced according to a complex set of requirements every five years when cargo responsibilities shifted. Cargo holders cared for each community's sacred objects (crystals, arrows, other fetishes) and were in turn connected to a complex system of religious and civil authority, in which local political authorities changed each year, as determined by a council of elders (*kawiterutsixi*).

Religious ceremonies marked all the critical moments of Huichol life, often revolving around the cultivation of maize, the deer hunt, and pilgrimages to sacred sites, the most important being the five principal sacred sites of the Huichol world.[12] These included the Tee'kata (Santa Catarina, Jalisco), Huaxamanaka (Cerro Gordo, Durango), Tatei Haramara (San Blas, Nayarit), Xapawiyeme-Xapawiyemeta (Isla de los Alacranes, Lake Chapala, Jalisco), and Wirikuta (near Real de Catorce, San Luis Potosí). The most important of these was Wirikuta, where the sun first appeared and where the peyote grew.

Shaman-singer-healers were themselves highly specialized and divided their responsibilities between the dry season and the rainy season. Most apprenticed for years, traveling to Wirikuta several times before declaring themselves authorities (a designation that, while informal, required general agreement among their neighbors). This pilgrimage, which was allegorically described as the Peyote Hunt (*Tatei Hikuri*), took place between December and start of spring and involved a four-hundred-kilometer return journey, on foot, between the sierra and Wirikuta. The journey was organized around connecting to and winning the goodwill of the ancestors. Peyote was said to create the ability to perceive the ancestors, creating sacred insight that allows one to pass through a portal and enter a different realm of perception.

In the sierra annual ceremonies were divided between rainy season and dry season, and, aside from the pilgrimage to Wirikuta, included a vast array of ceremonies and purification rituals, most of which centered around the agricultural calendar. New kernels of corn could not be consumed until the Dance to Our Mother was performed and the blood of a sacrificed deer or bull offered. At the end of the dry season, just before the planting of the maize, communities in the sierra would perform the Peyote Dance (*Hikuri Neixa*), a special ceremony that lasted two days and two nights, drinking peyote that had been dried, ground to powder, and mixed with water.

Free of any civilizing imperative, and untroubled by the devil, nineteenth century ethnographers (most notably Lumholtz and Diguet) were much more inclined than earlier interlopers[13] to record these rituals with a sense of wonder. These events were merely the most spectacular acts in lives characterized by carefully scripted invocations of the sacred in a host of daily acts, in which peyote had a place alongside the deer and maize as central to Huichol cosmovisions. Lumholtz was particularly taken with the idea that Huichols made no distinction between the sacred and the profane, that they occupied a landscape in which animals, trees, rocks, rivers, and canyons all carried sacred connotations and possessed a life force, and that peyote played a principal role in this cosmovision. According to Lumholtz, "Religious feeling pervades the thoughts of the Huichol so completely that every bit of decoration he puts on the most trivial of his everyday garments or utensils is a request for some benefit, a prayer for protection against evil, or an expression of adoration of some deity."[14]

. . .

Lumholtz was deeply impressed by the way that peyote formed a central part of Huichol pharmacopoeia, though he noted that the notion of medicine deployed within these contexts did not have easy analogues to the Western tradition. Peyote was used as a poultice for wounds, scorpion bites, for body aches, and to calm intestinal distress, and seemed quite effective. Still, the Huichols did not explain its effects through reference to Western notions of physiology. They instead saw evil spirits, witchcraft, and additional otherworldly causes of illness, sometimes attributing illness to the personal failings of the victim, and at other times to the malicious intent of others. This made for a rendering of the Huichols as deeply knowledgeable but otherworldly, completely cut off from Western civilization.[15]

This may have been why researchers at the IMN largely ignored Lumholtz even as they sought information on indigenous uses of peyote as a part of the effort to understand the cactus. Though they were quite content to render the Huichols as otherworldly, they preferred sources (like the eighteenth-century Franciscan José Arlegui and the then political boss of Tepic, General Mariano Ruiz) that treated Huichol uses of peyote as somehow serendipitous and backward, and rendered Huichol rituals in ways that suggested that their use of peyote was intemperate (they used "excessive amounts") and linked to madness (they used it to "go crazy").[16] In these texts the Huichols were said to explain peyote's effects (for instance, as a hunger suppressant) as rooted in magic. They believed that it imparted oracular power, that it could protect them from witchcraft, and that they should trust the visions produced "through the drunkenness."[17]

What in Lumholtz is a community that does not distinguish between the sacred and the profane becomes in these texts a community that is simply backward, that lacks the capacity to understand the power of the cactus. True, Indians used peyote as an ointment for their wounds, as a salve for rheumatic pain, and as a hunger and thirst suppressant, but the historical chronicles and contemporary informants that the IMN relied upon suggested that the they had no proper understanding of the effect of the drug. In these texts Indians are said to use peyote indiscriminately for all ailments—against snakebites, burns, wounds, and rheumatism, to fortify the body to resist illness, as a preservative, and as an aphrodisiac.[18] Derived from a deep faith in the power of the cactus to address all needs, these practices represented polar opposites to the forms of scientific knowledge that interested researchers at the IMN.

Indigenous worship of the cactus thus became superstition, tied to fortune-telling, the belief that it gave them special powers, and the secret worship of ancient gods (including peyote itself), reproducing much of the colonial posture toward peyote.[19] In contrast to Lumholtz's description of the Huichols as a "nation of shamans," the IMN zeroed in on drunkenness, superstition, and savagery. Peyotism produced a "primitive poisoning,"[20] a form of "intoxication with traces of madness,"[21] with "the same effect as marijuana" (which in this passage indicated a risk of temporary madness and violence).[22] Those who abused it were "shattered" by the experience.[23] Frequent usage also resulted in a buildup of tolerance for the drug—Indian bodies degenerated by peyote but that were also better able to control the effects of the drug because they were so used to it.[24]

What in Lumholtz is an inspiring, mystical sensibility was in the eyes of the IMN mere delusion. After a few days of peyote intoxication, of hearing voices, the Indians "emerged, convinced that they had been in relationships with some alien being they considered a god."[25] Of course, "the revelations, or rather the hallucinations, seldom coincided with the truth." Instead, innocent victims found themselves blamed for crimes they did not commit, causing discord in families and within and between tribes, hate, and "innumerable disastrous acts of vengeance."[26]

. . .

If these (highly selective) renderings of Huichol peyotism served as something of a cautionary tale, they nonetheless did suggest that peyote had some real power. It simply needed to be harnessed properly, in a way that discarded the delusions and superstition of the Indians for a modern, scientific approach to the cactus. And in order to do this, they needed something that also looked like a modern drug, a product that was consistent, carefully measured for dosage, and looked less like something one finds on the desert floor and more like something made in a laboratory. It was the sort of task the IMN was founded to undertake. Responsibility for this endeavor fell to Dr. José Ramírez in Section Two (Chemistry).

Unfortunately, while he was guaranteed a ready supply of peyote, Ramírez had nothing like the kinds of laboratory equipment or skills possessed by his colleagues in Germany and was unable to extract alkaloids with any significant degree of purity.[27] In his first efforts he produced a powder (*sacaruro de peyote*) by soaking the buttons in an alcoholic solution and then drying and pulverizing the residue, but this concoction was largely unsuccessful in tests. The animals given the powder tended to vomit the drug before enough had been administered to have an effect. Efforts to inject the powder also failed, because the crystals in the solution would not pass through syringes. Their first successes did not come until D. Altamirano, the lead chemist on the project, created a solution extracted directly from macerated peyote, which he then successfully injected into the veins of test animals.[28]

Little in this process resembled the work then being done in Germany or the US. North of the border, researchers saw no need to transform their peyote into something that distanced the cactus from its origins (they even sometimes sought to reproduce the sounds and sights of a peyote ceremony in their experiments), while in Germany peyote was increasingly being transformed into mescaline. Researchers at the IMN lacked the ability to transform peyote into mescaline (a failing they would later claim as a virtue, insisting that the greatest therapeutic effect was produced by peyote as a whole, and not its component alkaloids)[29], but they could at least create something that bore no resemblance to the peyote consumed by the Indians in the sierra. Their injectable solution had the look and feel of something that could be tested for consistent effects and toxicity, and that the regulatory state could approve for sale in pharmacies instead of herbal markets.[30]

Their tests began with a variety of preparations of peyote, administered to small animals to measure the physiological effects of the drug.[31] Early tests showed that even small doses caused an immediate changes in the heart rate, increased energy, and elevated blood pressure. In one case a frog that suffered from poor coloration (*negruzca*), an arrhythmic heart, and the general appearance of being moribund was injected with a small amount of extract dissolved in water and immediately experienced a significant increase in the strength and speed of its heart rate, producing a healthy infusion of blood into the heart. The doctors were unable to produce this effect in frogs they artificially or incompletely asphyxiated but concluded that peyote had acted as a heart tonic on the frog that had a preexisting arrhythmia.[32]

Other frogs were injected with increasingly larger doses until Dr. Vergara Lope determined that three grams of peyote injected into a frog of between eighty and ninety grams caused an initial muscular excitement followed by muscular paralysis and death.[33] Further experiments with pigeons, rabbits, and dogs were all used to establish the toxic doses of peyote to create a clear relationship between the size of an animal and the amount of peyote required to cause death. Toxic doses also produced other alarming results, including paralysis, nausea and vomiting, loss of bladder control, uncontrolled movements of the limbs, depression of the cerebral function, and cyanosis.[34]

More generally, these tests suggested that peyote had several predictable bodily effects. It acted as a vasoconstrictor, and in small doses it accelerated respiration without causing irregular breathing. At higher doses it accelerated breathing somewhat more and caused paralysis about an hour after injection. It also increased secretions of saliva, but not of urine.[35] Along with these observations, the researchers concluded that peyote produced "depression of the cerebral faculties, cutaneous anesthesia, exaltation of the reflexes, muscular paresis, and cardiac and respiratory paralysis, probably originating in the nervous system."[36]

As their test animals grew larger, the researchers believed that they also detected mental effects in their test subjects. They observed what they thought were hallucinations in the dogs, who ran around, hid, seemed to think they were being chased, and experienced convulsions and dilated pupils after being dosed. Twenty minutes after injecting a small dog with a liquid extract (five ccs to a dog weighing nineteen hundred grams):

> The animal grew clumsy; It wailed constantly, wandered around, seeking darkness. Later, he found it difficult to move, especially his hind quarters. . . . He threw himself from one side to the other, began sneezing, and was continually wailing.

They brought the dog's mother in to calm it, but that did not work. The dog kept screaming. "His movements slowed further, he grew very shaky and he was unable to get up" for the following two hours. Later, as the dog seemed to be recovering his motor skills, it vomited a great deal of mucus. Five hours after the injection it began to shake and "produced a yellowish, foul-smelling stool that was repeated 10 minutes later." Only then did the dog begin to recover. The following day he showed no signs of the experience.[37]

In an effort to repeat these results researchers then injected the peyote solution in the brother of the first dog, though this time with ten ccs of the solution. The dog had the same response, only more violent, and died after three hours.[38] From this they deduced the toxic level of the solution in dogs but also speculated that "it may be supposed that the peyote produced effects in dogs similar to those described in Indians taking the drug in its natural form: excitation of the central nervous system, particularly the brain, as it appeared that the animals had visual hallucinations."[39]

Having demonstrated the lethal doses in dogs, the researchers then turned to human subjects. But here, rather than testing the drug on themselves (as was common in Europe and the US), they turned to Section Four (Clinical Therapy) to test peyote's effects on patients in the Therapeutic Clinic of the Hospital General de San Andrés. Their focus concerned whether peyote could be considered a nervous system stimulant in ways that were analogous to strychnine, and thus useful in the treatment of dipsomaniacs (alcoholics). Using hydro-alcoholic extract of peyote, they administered ten to twenty centigrams per adult patient, every twenty-four hours.[40]

By May 1901 Dr. Juan Noriega, head of Section Four, was treating patients with a collection of solutions, including tepozán leaves, red mangrove, and peyote. Peyote was tested on a patient suffering from neurasthenia, who reported feeling quite good after taking the peyote but then woke up the next morning with ringing in his ears. A day later the patient was given the same dose, and it had no effect whatsoever, so the doctors increased the dose. Two hours after receiving the larger dose the patient experienced a level of excitement that his nurse described as comparable to drunkenness, which then lasted until the patient fell asleep at midnight. Upon awakening the next morning, the patient reported a headache. Later experiments on the same patient with somewhat smaller doses did not produce similarly intense experiences.[41]

In another experiment, Drs. Orvañanos and Cosío treated patients suffering from various types of paralysis with peyote for seven-day periods. Whether given a tincture of peyote or simply some mescal buttons to masticate (fifty grams, chewed for two hours), all but two of these treatments showed no effects.[42] Those who reported improvements (a patient named Desiderio Ortiz and another named Pedro Miranda) indicated that their paralyzed limbs felt stronger, though the doctors concluded that they had not actually recovered any strength or movement.[43]

Tests of peyote as a heart tonic overseen Dr. Antonio A. Loaeza produced significantly more promising results. Loaeza treated several patients over ten days with a tincture of peyote and concluded that it had produced a significant effect as a heart tonic.[44] After further tests in 1901 and 1902, Loaeza determined that a dose of twenty drops, administered three times a day to a person suffering from pulmonary congestion and decreased arterial flow increased the amount of urine they produced, improved breathing, and had a generally positive impact on the patient's general state. Loaeza thus declared that peyote possessed "a marked tonic action."[45]

By 1903 peyote was being used in several therapeutic studies under the direction of the IMN.[46] Their work over the next several years suggested that aside from its power as a heart tonic, it also had a positive therapeutic effect on patients with emphysema, though studies on other conditions treated with peyote did not yield significant improvements.[47] Researchers in Section Two, including Juan Noriega and Manuel Urbina, concluded that this therapeutic effect was because peyote produced "a direct stimulation of the intra-cardiac ganglia, a slowing of cardiac contractions, increased blood pressure, direct stimulation in the brain of the motor centers, [and] increased reflex excitability."[48] As such, peyote might be marketed as a heart tonic, and be included along with marijuana and strychnine in a class of drugs known as "nervous modifiers."[49] For his part, Urbina also hoped it would be useful in treating general nervousness, nervous migraines, nervous irritability, abdominal pain due to colic, hysteria, neurasthenia, hypochondria, melancholia, mania, insomnia caused by pain, and as a substitute for opium.[50]

These were hopeful claims, though they remained speculative, in part because of the small sample size that Noriega and Urbina had tested and because the effects of peyote seemed to lead them all over the place—there seemed to be no simple effect that could be made easily legible to the modern state (and the pharmaceutical industry). More than this, the negative effects, including nausea and vomiting, diarrhea and bloody stool, paralysis and death (these latter effects present only in very large doses), left the potential value of peyote in doubt. As for the effects on cognition, these were of little interest to researchers at the IMN. They tended to privilege the physical effects on the body over the less easily categorized effects on the mind, and saw little therapeutic value in the cognitive effects. Talkativeness, excessive brain activity, hallucinations, blurred visions, delirium, and crying fits were among the negative side effects of this drug. They were of no value to their version of science.[51]

In retrospect, it seems striking that the researchers at the IMN never evinced much interest in the hallucinogenic effects of the cactus. Unlike their colleagues elsewhere—in the US, in England, in Germany—who regularly consumed both peyote and mescaline and offered lengthy treatises on the effect, there is no evidence that any of the researchers at the IMN experimented personally with peyote. Furthermore, while most of the researchers outside Mexico believed that the visual and other hallucinations they experienced were the most important (and potentially therapeutic) effect, the Mexicans seem to have counted these as unfortunate side effects of the drug. We resort to speculation if we attempt to explain why the Mexicans took this route, but certain observations are pertinent. Scientists at the IMN treated the madness/drunkenness associated with Indigenous use of peyote with disdain, and associated it with ignorance, with backwardness. They were far more interested in discrete bodily effects that fell short of hallucination and treated experiences that went to this stage as evidence of the toxicity of the drug. The delirium they associated with primitive indigenous peyote use obviated the possibility that such an effect might be cast as meaningful for the moderns.

. . .

Further research into the therapeutic uses of peyote still seemed possible when the IMN published its study of the cactus in 1913, but both the research and the IMN were overtaken by Mexico's civil strife shortly thereafter. Undone by the Revolution, the IMN closed its doors on 6 September 1915, and by the time Mexico's institutional life began to take on a semblance of stability in the early 1920s, peyote research would face a new set of challenges.[52] New international treaties placed restrictions on the global flows of opium, cocaine, and marijuana, and north of the border peyote was increasingly being cast in the same light as these now dangerous drugs. The social conservatism of Mexico's new elites only exacerbated matters, as the image of the racially degenerated body produced by peyote—of the primitive Indian whose use was a sign of his backwardness—foreclosed an institutional interest in resuming peyote studies in Mexico.

Peyote intoxication was like drunkenness, and the new Mexican state was committed to eradicating this evil from the nation in the interest of progress. By the mid-1920s the country's new Department of Public Health, which was designed to police the "sanitary" habits of the people, left little room for significant scientific experimentation with peyote.[53] During the following two decades most of the research done on peyote in Mexico would be undertaken by foreign researchers living in the country.[54]

For the most part, however, peyote did not raise the ire of antidrug moralizers in ways that were entirely analogous to other drugs.[55] In the first major antinarcotics laws (1924), sanitary codes (1926), and anti-trafficking laws (1926) of the postrevolutionary period, a number of substances—including opium, cocaine, heroin, morphine, and cannabis—were either severely restricted or banned, but peyote was not among them.[56] Around this time several Mexican states passed laws intended to restrict the circulation of drugs, enshrining the concept of "crimes against health." This new category of crime was meant to address what medical professionals believed was a growing problem of *toxicomanía* in the country, a term that delineated between the intoxicated state and physical dependence on intoxicants, which health officials considered a true illness and threat to national progress. Increasingly, certain drugs (opium and cannabis) were labeled *enervantes,* a direct allusion to the way these drugs sapped the life force of both the individual and the social body, causing degeneration, encouraging homosexuality.[57] Peyote was first mentioned in the 1930 sanitary code, when the commission revising the code expanded its definition of enervantes to include peyote, along with several other "dangerous medicinal herbs."[58]

The timing of the ban was odd and likely obeyed the logic of a US-led international antinarcotics campaign rather than domestic pressure, because two years earlier Mexico's own Superior Health Council had declared that peyote was not an enervante, and that it had not produced any *intoxicaciones* (overdoses).[59] This may be why peyote was nowhere to be found in the subsequent revisions of the sanitary code in 1934.[60]

Small-scale research projects would resume in Mexico during the 1930s, though by this time the limited number of Mexican researchers working on peyote were as likely to purchase synthetic mescaline from abroad as they were to use peyote itself, using it in psychological tests for what was said to be its power as a psychotomimetic—that is, a drug with the power to induce temporary psychosis and that might deepen our understanding of the psychotic state. The researchers undertaking this work in the postrevolutionary period increasingly worked within a global community of mental health professionals and drew from the work of their colleagues in the US, Britain, and continental Europe to understand how peyote/mescaline might be mobilized in the treatment of nervous and mental diseases. And mostly they did this on the margins, sufficiently removed from debates over Indian drunkenness (especially when they experimented with synthetic mescaline) as to attract relatively little attention. Peyote use would be largely ignored by the Mexican state and research on peyote/mescaline little commented on until the 1960s, when the psychiatrist Salvador Roquet made national headlines with his novel psychedelic therapy (he will be discussed in chapter 7).

As for its other medical uses, after the Revolution peyote was largely left behind by a medical establishment that was both growing more sophisticated in its treatment of disease and more reliant on industrial pharmaceuticals and surgical intervention. While it continued to circulate in Mexico's herbal markets (and would do so at least into the 1960s) as a remedy for any number of ailments, and would even have a brief life as a miracle cure in Europe in the 1930s,[61] peyote never managed to gain as much traction as barbiturates, analgesics, amphetamines, and antibiotics among medical professionals. In comparison to these powerful drugs, it was merely a folk cure, a trace of the primitive past that modern, urban Mexicans hoped to leave behind.

CHAPTER THREE

1909

Poison

Nature has provided [it] with a poison to protect it from being eaten by stock.

—Special Agent, Rosebud, South Dakota, to Commissioner Indian Affairs, 21 August 21 1909[1]

Alarmed at the flood of mescal beans (the local term for peyote) flowing into American Indian reservations in Oklahoma, Iowa, Nebraska, and elsewhere, in early 1909 the US Commissioner of Indian Affairs tasked Special Investigating Officer (and noted prohibitionist) William "Pussy-foot" Johnson to investigate the source of the problem.[2] Johnson made his way to Laredo, Texas, where he learned that most of the peyote consumed in the region did not even originate in the US. Rather, it was gathered by Mexican pickers in secret locations south of Laredo, brought across the border by mule, and sold to one of two wholesalers (L. Villegas & Co. and Wormser Bros.), who in turn shipped it north by express mail. The trade had been growing robustly for several decades and was entirely legal.[3]

There was little Johnson could do about the Mexicans, but the wholesalers were businessmen, upstanding individuals who clearly did not understand the damage they were doing. According to Johnson's account, after alerting them to the evils of the cactus, he first elicited promises from both firms that they would cease the trade altogether. He then spent $443 buying all the available peyote in Laredo (this amounted to 176,400 buttons) and set it on fire. Johnson also secured a promise from the Mexican consul in Laredo that he would discourage Mexicans from further participating in the trade.[4] In subsequent months Johnson reported a dramatic decline in the trade, and a concurrent drop in the membership of peyotist groups in the US. The peyote business was "now practically everywhere as dead as the Pharaoh's mother," and it was only a matter of time before peyotism disappeared.[5]

His prediction was dead wrong. Johnson's plan was a classic supply-side attempt to curtail a consumer market, not unlike later twentieth-century efforts to choke the flow of other (by now illicit) comestibles from Latin America. And like those later efforts, he faced two critical challenges: a demand for the product that was not nearly as elastic as he supposed, and a limited supply of resources. While his efforts at inter-diction involved the purchase of a licit product and not a militaristic intervention in the market, he simply did not have the resources for a sustained and successful campaign. Johnson was running short of resources even in 1910, by which time another Texas company (Aguilares Mercantile) was rapidly picking up where Villegas and the Wormser Brothers had left off. By May 1911 the trade was once again as robust as it had been before Johnson hatched his scheme.[6]

Johnson significantly underestimated the resourcefulness of his foes. Working with the help of James Mooney and a collection of lawyers in Washington, DC, peyotists repeatedly pushed back against legal and legislative prohibitionist maneuvers. Some claimed that those who took part in the peyote cults had given up alcohol. Others insisted that the peyote cults were genuine religions, preaching moral uprightness and even Christianity, and that they were protected by the Constitution. Indian lobbyists repeatedly presented themselves to elected officials proclaiming that peyote had been a godsend to the Indians, improving their lives and making them more productive (proto)citizens. Their performances repeatedly won over enough congressmen to make a ban a nonstarter. Government agents might confiscate peyote they found in the mail, but they found it impossible to establish a legal basis to punish those who introduced peyote into a growing number of indigenous communities.

. . .

This stalemate did not sit well with Johnson and his ilk, for whom the spread of peyote represented an existential threat. Johnson, who was otherwise famous for his temperance work—employing tactics similar to those he did with peyote, smashing whisky bottles and destroying saloons in Oklahoma Indian Territory in highly symbolic fashion—represented the cutting edge of hardline prohibition in the United States, and he was joined by a chorus of missionaries and Indian agents in denouncing peyote.[7] In their view peyote was a narcotic, like opium, cocaine, hashish (often said to be more powerful than cannabis). Situated as a foreign menace, a Mexican drug damaging Indian bodies in ways that recalled the effect of the "oriental" drug opium on white bodies, peyote was intoxicating, produced drunken subjects, which were the opposite of the sober, disciplined bodies the missionaries idealized.[8] "Exceedingly injurious," peyote caused an "abnormal awakening of the imagination, during which the brain runs with fierce rapidity and is out from under control." It was an experience that "saps the nervous energy and will power."[9] And yet, unlike other foreign drugs, whose flow into the US would be strictly contained under the 1912 Hague Convention (originating in the 1909 Shanghai Conference, which aimed at stemming the flow of opium and cocaine, and was negotiated largely at the behest of the US government)[10], peyote could still flow across the border in unimpeded fashion.

The failure of federal government agencies to take action against peyote only inflamed the passions of the prohibitionists. Visceral, powerful, and largely impervious to reason, the anxieties peyote produced spoke to a sort of physical repulsion. When peyotists claimed that it helped them to give up whisky-drinking, the missionaries scoffed. Walter Roe, one of the leading opponents of the peyote religions, insisted that peyote was merely a "dope drug among all the Indians who use it."[11] Pussyfoot Johnson responded in similar fashion, insisting that the Indian who takes up peyote may stop drinking whisky, but that this was equally true of the Indian who takes up cocaine or opium.[12]

Repeatedly classifying peyote (erroneously) as a narcotic, the critics insisted that peyote was habit forming and destroyed the morals and the bodies of those who used it. Schoolboys were said to run away from school to attend meetings and to return in a state that left them "incapable of study, even mentally deficient, for several succeeding days."[13] Worse still, the superintendent of the Shawnee Indian School (Shawnee, OK) claimed that peyote had "deceived" the Indians through its "physical sensation or feeling," ultimately leading to numerous suicides. Others did not kill themselves directly, but under its influence had "grown weaker and weaker in their bodies, until some disease has taken them away."[14]

Relying on the tests performed by chemists in a variety of states, missionaries asserted that peyote was toxic, its alkaloids poisonous (the nausea and vomiting produced by peyote being a signal of its toxicity), and that it had a dangerously powerful effect on the human body. For that reason it was even more dangerous than whisky.[15] Like the latter it destroyed bodies, but unlike whisky its deleterious effects on the body were masked by the fact that it produced a blissful feeling of "happiness and peace. Thoughts of care, trouble and enmity disappear. The impression is created that everything is harmonious in the world, and that all is good and pure." Their religious tendencies energized, peyotists were inclined to continue using the drug, which in turn

> results in an increasing lassitude and inactivity, with a weakening of the will power to a marked degree, disinclination to exertion, a disinclination on the part of its victims to lead normal lives, and a loss of the normal power of resistance to disease. After one or two debauches it is difficult to break away from its continued use.[16]

This language is so rich, so disgusted, as to signal pure contempt. There could be no legitimate opposing point of view.[17] Bodies sapped of their vital energies were dulled, weakened, degenerated, no longer the productive citizens the Indian Agents and missionaries hoped to produce.[18] More alarmingly, indiscriminate use of peyote was said to lead to repeated overdoses , blindness, and death (one man supposedly died after eating seventy-five beans).[19]

> The Indian takes this supernatural remedy by the pound instead of by the grain. . . . No need to wonder that frequently an emaciated, anemic, helpless, dying patient will, under this powerful stimulation, rise from his bed, walk about, gather his relatives and friends together, make a most wonderful speech concerning the things he has seen, shake hands, bid farewell, and then lie down and in a few minutes die?[20]

If that were not enough, peyote was causing deep divisions among the Indians. Some tribal members complained about the "drunkenness and debauchery" that their neighbors were partaking in because of the spread of peyote.[21] They reported orgies at the peyote meetings, which were said to be run by young, good-looking males who were using the drug to enrich themselves and secure their own sexual conquests at the expense of their neighbors. During the rituals "animal passions are aroused [and] . . . many bad things are done." "Women seem to lose all the[ir] ashamedness, sometimes tearing their clothes and pulling out their hair."[22]

According to the prohibitionists, peyotists were not above using deception to hide these practices. George Hoyo, superintendent of the Otoe Agency (OK), reported attending a nighttime meeting on 4 November 1916, which took place in a tipi around a fire. Participants took eight buttons each, singing, praying, and talking through the night in an orderly ceremony. The following morning everything was orderly and quiet, and there were no signs of change in the Indians. "They did not seem stupid." Sometime later, however, a number of "anti-peyote Indians" visited his office and claimed that he had been the subject of a con, that the real ceremonies were nothing like what he had witnessed. In authentic ceremonies the participants ate twenty to fifty buttons, saw all sorts of visions, and were "very stupid" the following morning.[23]

This type of account fueled the skepticism of the critics, who rejected peyotist claims that their ceremonies adhered to the highest moral standards. Indeed, the very claim that peyotism was a religion irked the critics, who insisted that "a 'religion' that requires drug stimulation . . . is of no value"[24] and attributed their failures to get legislative action to "fanatical Indian enthusiast[s]" working under "the sad illusion of having found a panacea for all the ills of body and soul."[25] Though rooted in mysticism, critics insisted peyotism was simply a form of superstition that resonated among the Indians because of their predispositions.

> The old medicine superstitions no longer appeal. Here is something new and wonderful. It retains enough of the old to make it Indian, and it adds what he has superficially learned and observed in our civilization and religion. It appeals to his craving for leadership and the lusts of the flesh. And today we have a new, semi-religious movement among our Indian People, with peyote as a fetish that is worshiped as something extraordinarily supernatural.[26]

Peyotism, then, represented a regression to forms of ancient, mystical backwardness. Though often shrouded in Christian iconography, it was in fact inimical to Christianity, with "roots deep in the historic past of the red race."[27]

. . .

Peyote here comes across not as an ancient scourge to be eradicated (as it might in Mexico) but as something novel, an emerging threat to decades of work undertaken by missionaries and the state. Their visceral responses were often translated in the language of racial degeneration—a language that was particularly well suited to the battle to restrict the flow of dangerous drugs across the US-Mexican border in these early years of the twentieth century. Peyote became legible to US missionaries and government officials through this language, which expressed a fear not so much of the contamination of white bodies (that would come later) as of the further weakening of an already degenerated native body. Rooted in the Mexican indigenous past and linked to an autonomous space of religious expression that openly challenged the Christian churches, peyote was the perfect foil to the civilizing project of the Bureau of Indian Affairs (BIA) and the missionaries.

In this, the critics of peyotism in the US echoed the fears of their Mexican counterparts, though to somewhat different ends. Mexican nationalists feared that racial degeneration threatened the viability of their nation. Indians and a racially suspect mestizo underclass degenerated by peyote, marijuana, and alcohol constituted a majority of the national population (the exact numbers were invariably fuzzy). By contrast, in the US the problem of indigenous peyotism was not so much a crisis concerning the viability of the nation as it was a crisis confronting the civilizing project. It was a tragedy, but not a national calamity. It was also a tragedy characterized by a pernicious foreign influence. Mexico, in all its weakness, moral turpitude, and backwardness, was threatening to undermine a project in which upstanding Protestant missionaries would rescue Native Americans from their misery. In a way, by establishing their capacity to vanquish peyote, they were also reasserting American domination over Mexico.[28]

Though they were astoundingly off in their assessment of the impact of peyote on the bodies of their charges, there was some truth to the claims that peyote was new to North American Indian communities. Peyotism on a large scale was a relatively recent phenomenon in the early twentieth century. According to J. S. Sloktin, the ceremony Mooney first witnessed among the Kiowa was less than a decade old, though at the time some form of peyotism was also practiced among the Mescalero Apache, Comanche, Kiowa Apache, Wichita, Caddo, and Tonkawa.[29] The origins of these ceremonies, however, are still a matter of dispute. Though some believe that peyotism may have ancient roots in these communities,[30] it seems more likely that prior to the nineteenth century peyotism was very limited in its reach, and that it expanded significantly during the dislocations of the latter half of the century. One informant told Morris Opler that peyote had spread from the Carrizo (accounts of their peyote ceremonies date to 1649) to the Tonkawa and Lipan Apache in the early nineteenth century, when the latter lived along the Texas Gulf Coast and before warfare and epidemics forced them to move north. In this account the Lipan Apache then introduced peyote to the Comanche and Kiowa, who had also been forced to relocate from the border regions to the Oklahoma Indian Territories in 1859. Members of these groups took it up at some point in the 1880s.[31]

What does seem clear is that among those groups that had been forcibly relocated to Oklahoma, various and possibly diverse traditions rapidly consolidated into more formal religious practices during the 1880s. Peyotism then began to grow more rapidly after the collapse of the 1890 Ghost Dance. Within a few years peyote use could be found in more than fifty tribes, including Cheyenne, Shawnee, Pawnee, Arapaho, Chippewa, Blackfoot, Crow, Delaware, and Sioux. Often, the sites of diffusion were Indian boarding schools, where students would gather clandestinely and introduce their compatriots to the new "medicine."[32] Peyotists also built new networks of collectors, traders, and shippers, who could move peyote from its traditional growing areas to Oklahoma, where most peyotists now lived. One of the most important early peyotists, Quanah Parker, made his name in part because of his ability to make deals with cattle ranchers, government officials, and others to move peyote from the border to Oklahoma.[33]

By 1916 BIA officials estimated that there were 3,763 peyote users in the US, concentrated mainly in Oklahoma.[34] Within these communities peyotism tended to attract young men who were excluded from age-based power hierarchies. They joined the cults in search of a language that at once embraced healing—from alcoholism, tuberculosis, malnutrition—and could express their discontent with the forms of colonial rule to which they were subjugated. For them, peyote played dual roles as sacrament and medicine, a cure not just for wounds (a result of its antibiotic effects) but for coughing, pain, rheumatism, and a general illness of the spirit.

Tied as it was to efforts to heal both sick bodies and souls, and undertaken in secret in Indian boarding schools, peyotism's appeal was in some ways overdetermined. Young men could take peyote as medicine for the illnesses they contracted through their exposure to the pathogens that circulated in their communities and schools. Its seeming efficacy would have only enhanced its allure. On top of this, in a world characterized by white impositions—the school, the missionaries, the racial hierarchies enforced everywhere—peyote was truly an Indian thing, something shared within secret networks, hated by their white overlords, which offered the promise of escape, if only a temporary one, from the vicissitudes of everyday life.

. . .

It does not take much imagination to see how the strength of that appeal, and the fact that it was rooted in a direct challenge to the institutions the missionaries and BIA cherished so deeply, hardened the opposition of the missionaries, Indian Agents, and school superintendents to peyote.

Even though the peyotists claimed to be religious, even Christian, their cult flew in the face of the civilizers, who sought whatever means they could to curtail their rituals. Repeatedly reminded that they had no legal right to arrest peyotists or confiscate their peyote,[35] government officials nonetheless repeatedly did so, using their connections at the postal express offices in several states to "capture" shipments (they usually came in twenty-pound boxes from the Aguilares Mercantile Company) and detaining those who came to pick them up. Nothing came of the arrests, as no less than three times the courts ruled that peyote was perfectly legal.[36] In spite of this, the confiscated peyote was never returned.[37]

Slowly, however, the campaign against peyote gained ground. In 1912 the Board of Indian Commissioners (the citizen advisory board for the BIA that tilted heavily toward evangelical interests)[38] began to lobby for a federal prohibition.[39] The board relied on affidavits from Winnebago Indians and declarations by white farmers, missionaries, psychologists, and chemists decrying the dangers of peyote. Efforts to ban peyote through a new federal prohibition failed in 1912, but in March 1913 the US House of Representatives added "peyote" to the Indian Affairs Appropriations Bill that financed efforts to suppress the traffic in "intoxicating liquor." After aggressive lobbying on the part of Oklahoma peyotists, the Senate struck this language from the final version of the bill.[40]

In October 1914 the Board of Indian Commissioners voted unanimously to request that Congress outlaw the importation of peyote from Mexico and prohibit its use and sale on Indian reservations. They also asked that peyote be included as an intoxicant on the next Indian bill.[41] Other efforts, largely coordinated by the BIA, included a successful initiative in 1915 to have the Department of Agriculture ban peyote imports under the authority of the Pure Food and Drug Act. Shortly thereafter, the US Post Office banned the shipment of peyote through the mail.[42] It seemed that it would be only a matter of time before peyote was outlawed entirely.

CHAPTER FOUR

1917

The Ban

*The effect of peyote on the morals of these Indians is
beginning to be decidedly noticeable. Especially is this true
with regard to sexual matters. Several recent separations of
husband and wife who had lived contentedly together for
years may be traced to the use of this drug. . . . . A number of
young girls, some of whom had been attending school, have
gone to the bad under the influence of peyote. . . . The
pretense of religious rite connected with its use is a travesty.*

—Doctor from the Uintah and Ouray Agency, Fort Duchesne, Utah, 1917[1]

In late April 1917 Peter Phelps (an Indian from the Pine Ridge Reservation, also known as Cactus Pete and Henry Lone Bear) was arrested just
across the Colorado border from the Uintah and Ouray Reservation and
charged with peyote possession. He was not the first Indian to have his
peyote confiscated or to be arrested for possessing the cactus. He was,
however, the first to be arrested under a new state prohibition, passed in
March 1917 (Utah passed a similar law at the same time).[2] Unlike previous defendants, he could not count on a sympathetic judge to dismiss the
case because peyote was not designated an intoxicant under federal law.
Instead, he was taken to Grand Junction, forced to plead guilty before a
state judge, and served thirty days for possession of peyote.[3]

This may have been a victory for the forces of virtue, but prohibitionists
on both sides of the state line knew that Cactus Pete only faced charges
because he was arrested beyond the boundaries of the reservation. Their
efforts would not be complete until the federal government, which had
sole jurisdiction on the reservations, passed a comprehensive peyote ban.
This seemed increasingly likely when, in early 1918, Congressman John

Tillman of Arkansas convened a hearing of the House Subcommittee on Indian Affairs with the express purpose of amending the Indian Act to include a peyote prohibition. Tillman was alarmed that the spread of peyotism was retarding the "progress and development" of at least nineteen Indian tribes, and proposed punishments that would include a maximum of one year in jail and a $500 fine.[4]

Working closely with several members of the Board of Indian Commissioners and the Indian Rights Association, Tillman invited a variety of interested parties to testify, creating a vivid account of the contemporary debates surrounding peyote. Setting the tone early on, Samuel Martin Brosius spoke on behalf of the Indian Rights Association, whose prime purpose was "the protection of the Indians and their development into the citizenship of the country."[5] These goals were at risk, Brosius insisted, because of "secret agents" who were spreading peyote across reservations throughout the West, and who were richly rewarded for their efforts. He told of one postmaster who reported that $800 had been sent to peyote promoters among the Uintah and Ouray, where half the population was now addicted. "The baneful effects upon the followers are soon apparent. The successful farmer neglects his fields and home; his health is often affected, and interest is lost in the things which tend to better living." He said several deaths were directly traceable to peyote and that parents were also taking their children out of school.[6]

Claiming to have witnessed the "evil effects" of peyote at the Uintah and Ouray Agency at Fort Duchesne, Utah,[7] Brosius submitted a series of testimonials based on that experience. One was a letter from the physician at the agency, who claimed peyote "has done more harm to them in more different ways than whisky, gambling, or any other influence. Its physical effect is appalling. Its harmful effects are most noticeable on those who are already weak and depressed from disease or age, and upon both mother and babe."[8] The doctor continued:

> Thus, the work of years in teaching the Indian to use the white man's methods of combatting disease is undone.. . . . The effect of peyote on the morals of these Indians is beginning to be decidedly noticeable. Especially is this true with regard to sexual matters. Several recent separations of husband and wife who had lived contentedly together for years may be traced to the use of this drug. . . . . A number of young girls, some of whom had been attending school, have gone to the bad under the influence of peyote. . . . The pretense of religious rite connected with its use is a travesty.[9]

Brosius was particularly incensed by the claim that peyotism was a religion, calling it "subterfuge,"[10] the work of a sinister group of lobbyists and drug addicts. A claim to it being a constitutionally protected right would open the door to "any vicious practice or use of drugs which undermines the morals and health" as long it did so in in a manner that connected it to "so-called religious ceremonies."[11]

Like others, his language was panicked. He saw disturbance, dangerous excitement, intoxication, physical degeneration, sexual predation, and addiction, and connected to these phenomena to similar effects caused by opium, cannabis, and cocaine. It was "an evil and nothing but an evil," "playing havoc within the ranks of our Indian population already so weakened by disease," "a habit-forming drug, stealing upon the victim like a thief in the night, it will clutch him in its deadly grip."[12] This language resonated in Washington, where just months earlier the US Senate had passed the Eighteenth Amendment (setting the stage for Prohibition two years later). Several at the hearing, including representatives of the Women's Christian Temperance Union, explicitly linked peyote to drunkenness. It is "a species of drunkenness. There can be no question about that. The lasting effect of it is the deteriorating effect upon the human system."[13]

In his written testimony, the Reverend Walter C. Roe, who had long been an outspoken proponent of a ban, left no doubt that peyotism was a "drug habit" lurking under the cover of the peyotist's claim to be practicing an "Indian form of Christianity," which thus held a particular appeal to the "racial instinct" of the Indians. It had caused many deaths, mostly from the slow, inexorably enervating effects of the drug. He was also "convinced that the offspring of confirmed users of peyote show marked nervous and brain disturbances, resulting often in early death, while the custom of administering the drug to young children must be deleterious." It was "an absurd cult, incompatible with Christianity."[14]

Scientific testimony in favor of the ban zeroed in on the terrified body. Peyote produced visions that could not be controlled, unbridled sexuality, and an experience that had lasting effects. Suggesting that the nausea one felt when first ingesting peyote was a sure sign that it was poisonous to the body, Robert D. Hall recounted his own disturbing experience with the drug.

> It was especially noticeable during my writing all the evening that I could not control my hand so as to write smoothly and evenly. In one instance I had to address an envelope four times before it looked right to me. Another peculiar thing was that I seemed to have lapses of memory and had to stop in the middle of a sentence, having forgotten what I had intended to say.[15]

Proponents of the ban also made their case through Indian voices, arguing repeatedly that they spoke on behalf of indigenous communities that supported the ban.[16] Typical was an exchange between Tillman and Chester Arthur, an Indian from the Fort Peck Indian Reservation:

Tillman: "You stated that while under the influence of this drug men and women are guilty of sexual excesses, or improper sexual relations, and I want to know whether or not you give that statement of your own personal knowledge or observation, or whether you give it upon some rumor?

Arthur: "I do not wish to state to you anything that was rumor or hearsay, but only those things that I know. My wife could have given you valuable testimony, but unfortunately she is sick to-day, and could not come. Now, I want to go on and tell you what I know. They had been eating this peyote and a young man came to me and invited me to go to this place with him. He was a man in the church also. He said, "Let us go there and pray for them." We went there and they had a circular place where they were sitting around, men and women together. They were singing songs, and they were passing peyote around. Two young men who were busy had their faces painted blue, and they had a bunch of their hair tied up with a red cloth or flannel. There was one who was the chief of them all sitting there, and he had this peyote. I do not know how many peyote buttons they had eaten before I came there, but as I came in they were passing it around again. Then as I came in two young men walked out. They disappeared, and they did not reenter the tent. My friend and I tried to pray for them then and there, and we talked about this peyote. Then they began to leave; some of them left before the women did, and some of them carried the women out. The women were under the influence of peyote. One man who became turned against peyote came to listen to what we tried to say, and they confessed it all to me, and told me of their sexual excesses at those times when they took those women out. We have never been able to attend a peyote meeting at that same place anymore, because they call their meetings at different places. Some other Indians may tell you good things about this, but, as for me and my people, we have seen the evils of it; we have seen it make our people act like dogs, and we hate it and we are opposed to it. That is all I have to say."[17]

Gertrude Bonnin, a Sioux Indian from South Dakota and another opponent of peyote acted as Arthur's translator at the hearing. She and her husband, Raymond T. Bonnin, had lived among the Ute on the Uintah and Ouray Reservation for fourteen years and compared peyote's impact to that of opium, morphine, and cocaine. It "creates false notions in the minds of the users, preventing sound logic and rational thought with which to meet the problems of their daily lives." Peyotists were slothful, neglectful of their responsibilities. They rejected the Church, the knowledge they could gain from book-learning, and the advice of doctors. And it was approaching epidemic proportions. Half of the population of the reservation was afflicted, and peyote had been directly responsible for twenty-five deaths.[18]

Mrs. Bonnin, who was also secretary of the Society of American Indians, offered a deeply personal testimony. "During the last two years, I saw my friends victimized, and that hurt my heart." To back this claim up, she presented a thumb-marked statement by Sam Atchee (Ute) and two witnesses, who claimed that peyote had caused thirty deaths among the Utes. The statement also recounted the story of the death of a community member named Weecheget in the spring of 1916. Having taken an "overdose," he "became wild; tearing his clothing off he jumped into a deep mudhole." This was a tragic example of the "baser passions" inflamed by peyote, which, when combined with the fact that peyote agents were growing rich at the expense of their fellow Indians, convinced Mrs. Bonnin that "peyote causes race suicide."[19]

. . .

Bonnin's words, like several other indigenous actors who spoke out at the hearings, painted an inescapably stark picture of peyote use. Here and elsewhere former "addicts" lamented the damage this drug had done to their lives, the madness, the sloth, the ruin inflicted on mind and body, the time spent in jail because of peyote drunkenness.[20] As such, they provided a powerful counterweight to those who had been publicly defending peyotism against the claims of the missionaries. James Mooney faced a very difficult task in answering these claims at the hearings.

Indeed, Mooney received a particularly hostile reception. Having begun his testimony at the hearings with a lengthy defense of the peyote both as medicine (an antidote to the illnesses Plains Indians suffered as a result of living in a damp eastern climate, and a substance that "destroys the appetite for liquor") and as the basis of a profound religious belief,[21] he was immediately attacked by the committee members, whose skepticism for his claims bordered on disdain.[22] General Pratt of the Carlisle Indian Industrial School went even further, seeking to dismiss the work of the Bureau of American Ethnology (The Bureau of Ethnology, which employed Mooney, was renamed the BAE in 1897) in its entirety. Pratt told a story about a particularly grizzly form of ritual mutilation performed by Indians solely for the benefit BAE ethnologists (here playing on the rift between the BIA and the BAE). Mooney insisted the story was an outright fabrication, but Pratt doubled down, condemning the entire BAE in the process.

It is a matter that can be easily proven, and I will furnish proof. These are the places and ceremonies you ethnologists egg on, frequent, illustrate, and exaggerate at the public expense, and so give the Indian race and their civilization a black eye in the public esteem. It was well established at the time of the ghost-dance craze among the Indians that white men were its promoters if not its originators. That this peyote craze is under the same impulse is evident from what appears in this evidence.[23]

Mooney vigorously defended the ethnologists, but Pratt's words were just what the committee needed to dismiss Mooney as a shill, working for drug dealers, whose agenda would maintain Indians in their heathen, uncivilized ways. This condemnation cleared the way for an uncomplicated view on the evils of peyote that easily justified a ban. Indians were ignorant, and their white allies corrupt.

. . .

Much to the delight of the Indian Rights Association and others who had been pushing for years to get a federal ban passed, this rendering of peyote was just what they needed to see the bill passed in the House of Representatives. It was not enough, however, to win over the Senate, where peyotists aggressively lobbied Oklahoma Senator Robert Latham Owen (Owen claimed Cherokee ancestry and had been a teacher and Indian Agent among the Cherokee earlier in his career), arguing that the ban represented a violation of their First Amendment rights. Owen managed to quash the bill in the Senate.[24]

Members of the Senate needed to look no further than the 1918 hearings themselves to find evidence that suggested a ban may have been both unwarranted and a violation of the First Amendment. Though Tillman, Knox, and others did their best to marginalize indigenous voices speaking in favor of peyote,[25] several healthy, intelligent, and politically savvy peyotists made a compelling case against the ban at the hearings. Against allegations of weakened bodies, sloth, and deaths, the peyotists who claimed a right to speak at the hearings offered their own bodies as living proof of the ways in which peyote could restore the sick and save the Indian ravaged by alcoholism—that indeed, peyotists were the healthiest individuals on their reservations.[26]

It was one thing for James Mooney to argue that peyote was medicine, but these subjects were the living embodiment of this claim. They were Christians, devout, and read the Bible as a part of their peyote worship. They used the cactus to "good advantage" and never to excess. Several also indicated that peyote was a powerful "medicine" that cured stomach and respiratory problems and had saved the lives of many young men who had contracted illnesses at the Indian boarding schools.[27] Cured of his "bad habits," the devout peyotist was not only a spiritually disciplined individual capable of being a good citizen, he was also sufficiently physically fit to undertake the hard labor of the yeoman farmer.[28]

Consider the exchange between Tillman and Fred Lookout, chief of the Osage tribe, Pawhuska, Oklahoma.

> *Lookout:* We are praying to God when we use this medicine that is known as peyote, and the Osage people, my people, use it to a certain extent. They use it in the right way. There is no harm in it. I like it and I am in favor of it.
>
> *Tillman:* Do you think this drug should be used generally among the Indians when it makes them lazy and when it creates in them an appetite for the drug, so that they feel that they are compelled to use it all the time, and that those who habitually use it in some places abandon work and become very dissipated on account of the use of it, and finally go back to using whisky with it?
>
> *Lookout:* I am a member of the peyote; I eat this peyote; I do not get lazy; I am on a farm; several of the men have visited my farm; the Commissioner of Indian Affairs has been to my home. I am farming there, and have several stock, and I am doing what I can to make money; I do not get lazy; I do not think the other Indians get lazy either, among the members.[29]

Arthur Bonnicastle, an Osage spokesman, Carlisle graduate, and self-professed Christian who had become quite sick while at Carlisle and believed he was cured of his stomach ailments by peyote, made similarly powerful claims. The Osages, who used peyote strictly for religious purposes and as medicine, had been using peyote for thirteen to fourteen years. Defending Osage peyotism on constitutional religious grounds, Bonnicastle insisted that "stopping the use of peyote among them would be an injustice, because they don't use it to excess and use it to good advantage—use it in religion and their prayers and in times of sickness, and they don't use it between times of religious meetings. It is a sacred plant to them."[30] Asked by Frank Knox of the Board of Indian Commissioners about its effects, Bonnicastle insisted that "It trains the mind to higher ideas in worshipping God" and leads the Indians who take it toward a "better life in worshipping the Almighty."[31]

The particular way that Bonnicastle positioned peyote as indigenous was critical to his claim to a right to use the cactus. It was a form of medicine and healing that belonged within a non-European tradition. It was owned by the Indians, rooted in a distinct history, even if it was not a history specific to any given tribe. In adopting peyotism, one could assert their desire to be Indian against the assimilationist claims of the missionaries and Indian Agents. Furthermore, this practice did not entail a complete rejection of modern life. Bonnicastle's language privileged healthy, productive bodies, even bodies disciplined by the Christian ethos (this, given the fact that Christian iconography played some role in most peyote churches), while also asserting a desire to be indigenous, celebrating the value of being Indian in the face of the injustices and marginalization they faced in the white man's world.

Francis La Flesche, who worked for the BAE and was an Omaha Indian, echoed Bonnicastle. La Flesche testified that, having heard some spectacular stories about the immorality and promiscuity of the people at peyote meetings, he decided to investigate the practice among his own people (the Poncas and the Osages). He expected to "see the people get gloriously drunk and behave as drunken people do," but he found the opposite. Describing one meeting with an Osage group, which he attended with Bonnicastle, he said that all he witnessed was some singing while attendees passed peyote around the fire. When he asked the man next to him what he expected to see, the man said, "We expect to see the face of Jesus and the face of our dead relatives. We are worshiping God and Jesus, the same God that the white people worship." That said, the great majority of attendees saw nothing, and the meeting was as orderly as any religious meeting he had ever attended.

La Flesche's investment in peyotism was rooted in the fact that his own people had been devastated by bootleggers and whisky, a problem that he believed had abated with the adoption of the peyote religion. "Practically all of those of my people who have adopted the peyote religion do not drink. . . . I have a respect for the peyote religion, because it has saved my people from the degradation which was produced by the use of the fiery drinks white people manufacture." Moreover, these people were earnestly worshipping God, healing their lives. If the government interferes, "the consequences will be grave."

La Flesche here offered a language of recovery, of bodies ravaged by the evils of whisky restored to health through the peyote cults. This was of course incomprehensible to the prohibitionists, who insisted that proper Christians disciplined their bodies through sacrifice and self-abnegation, though it made sense to James Mooney, whose experience among the Kiowa suggested that the claim was in fact true. More than this, peyotists insisted that the metaphor of drunkenness was misplaced. Some argued quite forcefully that the peyote had no effect on them, that they did not hallucinate, and that its only effect was to help them to stay up through the nightlong ceremonies. Thomas Sloan (a member of the Omaha tribe and an attorney-at-law) went further, linking peyote to abstinence. "The effect of the use of peyote among the Omahas has been to make a large number of drunkards decent, sober, honest men. The same is true of the Winnebagoes." Sloan had attended three meetings and used peyote in the meetings, one time eating fourteen pieces. The following day he was able to drive his car through the hills and on the rough roads along the Missouri River with no effects (what a modern, disciplined thing to do!). From these experiences he concluded that peyote was no different from "strong tea." There was no immorality in the ceremonies; the people who claimed this were simply mistaken.

Pressing him on the matter, Commissioner Knox asked Sloan if he experienced any hallucinations after eating fourteen pieces. Sloan replied: "None. Peyote produces strictly a mental attitude." Sloan then elaborated, insisting that reports of immorality connected to the ceremony were untrue and often spread by old-time medicine men who opposed peyote because it threatened their power. Other opponents were "those who have grown rich out of the whisky trade."[32]

Sloan also repeated another mantra of the peyotists, insisting that people who take peyote become "orderly."[33] Aside from acting as a direct repudiation of the stories about drunkenness and debauchery, the claim reminds us of the extent to which peyote churches sought to align themselves with a vision of the disciplined body that in turn aligned with the civilizing ethos. If peyote indeed counteracted the drunken body and substituted it with ordered (if racialized) bodies, the central lamentations of the peyote-phobes were without merit.

Perhaps more interesting here is the way that the ordered body of the peyotist acted as a means for making the healed and newly Christian body of the Indian legible to the state. Sloan, La Flesche, and others insisted that peyote was integral to phenomena in which they comported themselves well, where the slothful and drunken Indian became sober and hardworking, a devout, modern citizen. Sloan held up Arthur Bonnicastle as an exemplar of the orderly body and loyal citizen, as had been demonstrated by his willingness to volunteer for exceedingly dangerous duty as a soldier in the US Army during the Boxer Rebellion. "He was the American soldier who volunteered, with other soldiers of other nations, to make a breach in the wall around the city for the relief of the Christians who were in danger of massacre. He was the American who upheld the honor of the United States Army . . . the first of those brave volunteers to go over the wall in that dangerous task."

Sloan's claims were almost certainly a strategic effort to supplant the image of drunken bodies with that of the patriot defending his country (this, a remarkable recasting of indigeneity). The missionaries relied on drunkenness because it made these Indians legible in a certain kind of way, when the alternative—that is, a body that was beyond control instead of a body that was out of control—was unthinkable. But this is precisely what the peyotists were claiming. In carving out a space that they wholly owned and controlled, in which the spirit world might enter in ways that transformed or even marginalized Christian traditions, and in insisting that this cactus was nurturing and healing indigenous bodies that had been made infirm by colonialism, the peyotists openly confronted the nature of their insertion into the North American system. And they did so by deploying the very language of modernity— of healthy, disciplined bodies (even if those disciplined bodies rejected subordination to the missionaries and the state).

Along this vein, La Flesche also testified that peyote had done him much good personally. He recalled that the Omaha had suffered an epidemic of murders and sexual assaults after the introduction of whisky, reducing their community to a constant state of fear and dissolution. "Poor little children became afraid of their mothers because they drank. They became afraid of their fathers, and when they heard them coming home from town they ran into the ravines, into the bushes, so as to avoid getting hurt." It was only the introduction of peyote that had curtailed this epidemic.

> This peyote, they said, helped them not only to stop drinking, but it also helped them to think intelligently of God and of their relations to Him. At meetings of this new religion is taught the avoidance of stealing, lying, drunkenness, adultery, assaults, the making of false and evil reports against neighbors. People are taught to be kind and loving to one another and particularly to the little ones. . . . The persons who are opposed to the use of peyote by the Indians in their religion say that its makes them immoral. That has not been my observation. The Indians who have taken the new religion strive to live upright, moral lives, and I think their morality can be favorably compared with that of any community of a like number in this country.[34]

Under pointed questioning from Commissioner Knox, La Flesche insisted that he knew numerous "drunkards" who had stopped drinking because of peyote.[35] Sloan backed him up, saying that, among Omaha, Winnebago, and Yankton Sioux the effect "has been to make a large number of drunkards decent, sober, honest men."

. . .

It was in some ways an odd inversion of the narrative of white authority. Mooney could be dismissed, attacked as self-interested, while indigenous actors, in part because the robustness and physical health of their bodies undermined the claims by those who decried the evils of peyote, provided evidence that won the day in the Senate. Peyotists understood the power that this pressure had and would keep consistent pressure on Senator Owen and his successor in the Senate, Elmer Thomas. Thomas received a regular stream of visits by delegations of Indian "citizens" who insisted that Congress had no authority to ban peyote and that their religious practices were protected by the First Amendment. As Caddo Chief Enoch Haig put it in a 1924 petition to Thomas:

> You white people have no doubt different churches and different forms of religion. Well, all these different churches like their religion, and there is no reason why we should not be allowed to retain our religion. We have no objection to you white people having different churches and different religions, and I do not think it would be right now for Congress to pass a law to prohibit us Indians from having our Church and our religion. We are all under one Creator.[36]

No further efforts at passing a federal ban on peyote would reach the floor of the Senate until 1937, when a coalition of missionaries, incensed by the Indian Reorganization Act[37] (which, among other things, called for a diminished role for the churches, indigenous religious self-determination, and enhanced tribal government), once again managed to position peyote as a national threat. In the meantime, proponents of a peyote ban would need to satisfy themselves by working at the state level and within the administrative state (particularly the BIA) to impede the expansion of the peyote cults.

CHAPTER FIVE

1918

The Native American Church

It was given exclusively to the Indians, and God never
intended that white men should understand it.

—Albert Hensley, Winnebago, Nebraska, October 9, 1908[1]

With several state bans in place and a national prohibition narrowly avoided, in October 1918 the leading Oklahoma peyotists gathered to plot strategy in El Reno, Oklahoma. There was little chance that they were going to change the narrative of peyote as narcotic, as despite a steady stream of testimonials that countered this claim, the missionaries and Indian agents had an immense upper hand. Prohibitionists could represent the voice of the peyotist both as Indian (and therefore racially suspect) and as drug addled (equally suspect). Given their success in the Senate, however, peyotists had the slimmest of opportunities to represent theirs as a genuine religious practice, entitled to the same protection under the First Amendment that the Catholic Church enjoyed for sacramental wine.

Their battle could be won only if peyotists demonstrated that theirs was a well-organized religion, a codified set of practices that could be legible to outsiders by virtue of its institutions, organizations, and rituals. This claim would of course be enhanced if peyotists could demonstrate the ancient heritage of their religion and create a basis for claiming that peyotism, even if new, was somehow very old. This would allow them to insist that they were engaged in the recovery of something that had been lost, something that was essential to the indigenous experience and therefore ultimately inaccessible to whites. Moreover, if it was an ancient practice, it might be somehow safe for the Indian, who was rooted in a racial heritage that made them immune to the dangers of a drug that was otherwise dangerous.

What the peyotists who gathered in El Reno needed was a church, so on October 18 they elected to found the Native American Church of Oklahoma (NAC). The very name of the church emphasized both the Christian and indigenous roots of the church, as well as its pan-indigenous nature.[2] Its name also signaled larger aspirations. While its first goal was simply to obtain a charter from the state of Oklahoma that would then entitle members of the church to use of peyote as a First Amendment right, it was also designed to be a model for peyote churches in other states.

As the region with the greatest concentration of peyotists in the country, Oklahoma served as an ideal testing ground for claiming a First Amendment right to peyote. Oklahoma peyotists could point to practices that had long histories in their communities (claims varied from four decades to millennia), organized around one of two distinct traditions. The older and more common tradition in Oklahoma was based on the teachings of Quanah Parker and was called the Half Moon Way (it was popular among the Delaware, Caddo, Cheyenne, Arapaho, Ponca, Oto, Pawnee, Osage, and others). Parker, who was legendary in the Southwest as the half-Comanche trader who had been able to negotiate his way through the settler-dominated regions of Texas in order to gain access to the peyote gardens, traced his own peyotism to a serious illness he suffered in 1884, which he believed had been alleviated by a Mexican curer who gave him peyote. Parker then spread word of the miraculous power of peyote throughout the Indian Territories and taught his followers a tradition that drew mostly from the indigenous traditions of northern Mexico. Parker's ceremony took place in a tipi around a crescent-shaped alter, and though it had Christian references, these were marginal to the ceremony itself, which instead evoked mother earth and Indian spirits (the Bible was not used).

The other significant peyote ritual practiced in the West around this time was more explicitly Christian and was developed by John Wilson, who was of Caddo, Delaware, and French ancestry. Wilson was a well-known Ghost Dancer who learned about peyote from a Comanche teacher, ultimately becoming a peyote roadman (the title given to the individual who oversees the peyote ceremony) in 1880. He used Bibles and crucifixes in his rituals and regularly invoked Jesus. Called the Big Moon/Cross-Fire tradition, the Cross-Fire was more common among the Sioux of South Dakota and Winnebago in Nebraska and Wisconsin.

Despite these differences, both practices had numerous elements that made them recognizable as part of a single tradition. Various artifacts marked the ceremonies as consistent, one to the next. Officiants in both traditions often utilized an eagle feather fan, a carved staff, a whistle, a gourd rattle, and drums. Both were evangelical and regularly welcomed new members into ceremonies overseen by a cast of experts. In some instances non-Indians were excluded from ceremonies, though more commonly outsiders were welcome to participate. Indians from other tribes were almost always welcome. It also seems that some African Americans, especially from the community of southern blacks who had been allotted in Oklahoma, also participated.

Both ceremonies began at sunset on Saturday evenings, in a hogan or tipi, when participants would gather around a fire that illuminated an altar shaped like a crescent moon (to Father Peyote). In both cases the ceremony lasted all night and was followed by a communal meal. The cast of officiants was also relatively stable, a roadman, a cedar chief, the fire chief, the drum chief, and the water woman. Decorum and sobriety were considered essential in both. There were also taboos. Older men were forbidden from eating salt the day before and after a meeting and were not allowed to bathe for several days following.

More generally, both traditions were led by men, with women playing scripted subordinate roles (the actual roles of women varied widely). Women could attend the meetings, pray, and consume peyote, but were generally proscribed from drumming and singing. At the beginning of the ceremony worshippers were arrayed in a circle with the presiding roadman facing east. The ceremony generally began when a large peyote button, called "Father Peyote," was placed on a cross or rosette of sage leaves on the altar in the tipi. Once the peyote was on the altar, all talking would cease. Tobacco was then passed around the room for everyone to roll cigarettes while the roadman opened with a prayer. He would then bless the bag of buttons, take out a few, and pass it along. During several rounds the participants would take varying amounts—as few as three, as many as several dozen. As this process took place, the sensory charge was enhanced by the cedarman, who would throw cedar on the fire to produce a cleansing smoke.

During these rounds participants would sing and chant. They would typically take a brief break around midnight and then resume the ceremony, drumming, chanting, passing the peyote around again. During these hours there would also sometimes be healing ceremonies. At dawn the roadman would sing a special song to welcome the day, and at that point the water woman would bring in drinking water and a simple breakfast. Following a homily and songs from the roadman, the objects would be put away, the ceremony ended, and participants would gather for a feast outside the hogan or tipi.[3]

Collectively these practices made peyotism legible to the state as an ancient pan-Indian practice, seamlessly connected to a series of other icons—the tipi, the drum, the cedar fire, the eagle feather. None of these objects or practices was so specific, so local, as to be alien to a broadly conceived version of indigeneity. As the formal structure of the NAC spread, and new chapters were founded in states beyond Oklahoma, converts could identify with things they already believed to be signifiers of indigeneity in order to enter into the church.

More than this, various elements in these practices served as enormous draws for the church, which would count over ten thousand members within a few years. Both traditions of peyotism actively cultivated the belief that peyote was medicine—a sacred medicine that could not really be shared with whites. Both practiced rituals that focused on healing, sobriety (at least during the ceremony), and discipline. Just as importantly, both celebrated bodies freed of the vicissitudes of colonial subjugation, bodies that had reclaimed an autonomous space for indigeneity in which the mysticism of the Indian became a foil to white efforts to control their lives. It did not matter that this might be a novel practice, or one that in some ways reinscribed long-standing orientalist views of the mystical Indian. Indeed, in part because of white tendencies to view indigenous peoples as otherworldly, this was the form of indigeneity available to the members of the NAC, a space in which they might be legible to the state and subsequently make claims for certain forms of social being outside of a system that otherwise degraded them.

The oppositional nature of peyotism was clearly part of its appeal. Many of the young men who joined the peyote cults were drawn to the claim that this was an Indian thing, if not hidden from whites at the very least not understood by them. Bodies healed by peyote recovered a kind of truth, the truth of their indigeneity. Peyote was a means of expressing that truth because it allowed them to claim a space beyond the colonizers' gaze, in which their bodies gained a degree of distance from the marginalization and exploitation they faced in everyday life. With its Christian overtones, they could selectively engage the colonizer, articulating themselves to enough aspects of the colonizers' world to be legible and claim a certain level of legitimacy (especially if peyote was in fact producing disciplined bodies), and yet they could simultaneously claim a space that was clearly indigenous.

This ethos calls to mind a letter that Albert Hensley, of Winnebago, Nebraska, wrote to the commissioner of Indian Affairs in 1908. Hensley, who was the head of the Mescal Winnebagos, as well as a graduate of Carlisle, insisted that his people believed peyote to be both medicine and the body of Christ.

> We feel we are entitled to exercise one of those first and fundamental principles established in this country—the right to worship God in freedom and according to the dictates of our own consciences. . . . To us, this "medicine" is a portion of the body of Christ. . . . . We read in the Bible where Christ spoke of a Comforter, who was to come. Long ago this Comforter came to the whites, but it never came to the Indians until it was sent by God in the form of this holy medicine. . . . We have tasted God, and our eyes have been opened. It is utter folly for scientists to try and analyze God's body. No white man can understand it. It came from God. It is part of God's body. God's Holy Spirit is enveloped in it. It was given exclusively to the Indians, and God never intended that white men should understand it.[4]

Peyote was, then, an Indian thing, beyond the comprehension of the white man, something that could form the basis of a religion that was both a source of healing and exclusive to indigenous peoples.

In the long run this would be a winning strategy. In aligning peyotism strictly to the indigenous sphere, and shrouding it in claims to timelessness, members of the NAC began to elaborate a set of cultural and religious claims that aligned neatly to the racialized politics of indigeneity in the US. Absolute difference, expressed through the spatial organization of the reservations and the politics of blood quotients, placed peyotism beyond the legitimate reach of a state that assumed the unassimilatibility of the racial other. True, Indians might become more like whites, but they could never be white and would always remain a degraded copy of whiteness, even if they adopted the values and beliefs associated with the ideal of the yeoman farmer (as envisioned in the Dawes Act). Given the racial politics of the US, they would always be inescapably Indian. What the NAC gave them was a structure, based in the First Amendment, that mobilized marginalization as a means for healing and creating an empowered version of indigeneity.

. . .

In the short run, however, members of the NAC would still need to contend with a BIA that remained fully committed to suppressing the peyote cults, beginning with an effort to crush James Mooney. Long a thorn in the side of the BIA, he was banned from the Kiowa Reservation in late 1918, and shortly thereafter his career began to unravel. By 1921 Mooney was broke and ill. His salary at the BAE had been slashed for "non-production." He was reduced to relying on friends in the NAC to pay mounting medical bills.[5] In a letter to his colleague Joseph Thoburn just before he left the service that September, Mooney lamented that the government was looking for opportunities to "impede and suppress" his peyote investigations "altogether, to leave the way clear for hostile legislation." "It is high time the Indians realize the danger."[6]

With Mooney effectively neutralized, prohibitionists in the BIA went on the offensive, using all means at their disposal to destroy the new church. At the local level they lobbied state legislatures for further prohibitions, harassed peyote churches, and tried to disrupt the flow of peyote from the border regions northward. Nationally they tried to bring an end to the debates over peyote's virtues once and for all, publishing a pamphlet in 1922 that claimed to set the record straight on peyote. In this official publication of the BIA readers learn that peyote is "a narcotic drug," but that for reasons that seem absurd it is not banned by the Harrison Narcotic Act or Prohibition. It was "harmful" to users, habit forming, the cause of "imbecility, insanity, and suicide."[7] Yet it was

> more than another 'dope' problem to be disposed of by legislating it into the class of drugs covered by the national narcotic law. It is, as one writer stated, 'a system of pagan worship, inimical to Christianity, which has its roots deep into the historic past of the red race, and because of this it makes the strongest kind of an appeal to the Indians.' To the missionary the use of peyote is paganism arrayed against Christianity—the power of a drug against the elevating influence of the Cross.[8]

Said to be a product of the Indian's unfortunate "craving for stimulants,"[9] the pamphlet explained the peyote cult as a dual product of ancient indigenous practices and the social dissolution brought on by conquest.

> Something in his nature—it might have been the coming into consciousness of knowledge long hidden in his subconscious mind, or it might have been the prompting of cell cravings—told him that there was a better intoxicant than whisky, an herb known to his ancestors, and he sought that herb and found it in peyote, and he believes that his people now have an intoxicant that satisfies and yet leaves consciousness to witness the strange orgies that are taking place in the underworld of their mentality.[10]

It "stimulates and entrances far beyond the powers of alcohol and yet permits the retention of consciousness, thus leaving the mind free to witness, although in helplessness, a panoramic scene of color visions that transport the soul into a paradise where it is lost in wonder, love, and praise, or into an inferno on the wall of which in fiery characters are written the sins of the observer."[11]

Claims about its positive effects on health were summarily dismissed. "There are others who may eat peyote believing that it is a cure for drunkenness, not knowing that when the drug takes away the desire for whisky it is only because the subject is saturated with a drug which is much worse than whisky in its ultimate effects on the body and mind."[12] "Even when it is administered for the ostensible purpose of relieving pain, the dose to be effective must be sufficient to obtund the sensibilities of the nerves by its narcotic effect—that is, by its intoxicant properties."[13] Moreover, it was dangerous to children. The pamphlet notes with alarm that the Indians pour it into the ears of newborn babies as a sacrament of baptism.[14]

As for the NAC:

In Oklahoma, the Peyote Church has been chartered under the name of the Native American Church. It is probable that other States will grant charters to the cult, but in doing so will they be preserving the right of religious freedom, or will they be giving charters to organized bodies to use a habit-forming harmful drug? In the opinion of many, to give recognition to the Peyote Christian Church is as incongruous as it would be to recognize the Opium Christian Church, or the Cocaine Society of Christians.[15]

The NAC was thus dismissed as a cover for illicit drug use.

. . .

The 1922 peyote pamphlet was not enough to prompt a full peyote ban, though it did prompt Congress to classify peyote as an intoxicant in the Indian Appropriation for 1923. This allowed the BIA to set aside $25,000 to combat its use on the reservations. It also gave legal cover to BIA agents who confiscated peyote shipments they found in the mail (even if they could not arrest the recipients of those shipments). During the following decade eight more Western states would ban peyote in what federal officials and missionaries hoped was a slow but inexorable process leading to a total eradication of peyote on the reservations.[16] And yet, as had been the case in the previous decades, the matter was not entirely settled. During the 1920s a new generation of social scientists and budding bureaucrats followed the development of the NAC with great interest and began to find themselves in vicious battles with the missionaries that recalled James Mooney's earlier struggles. Among those who found themselves in this position was a young social scientist named John Collier, who in the early 1920s had the opportunity to witness in person the rapid growth of the peyote religion on the Navajo Reservation. His experiences in the field made him a fierce critic of the assimilationist policies of the BIA (and the Dawes Act) and pulled him into a public and direct confrontation with both the BIA and the missionaries. Collier founded the American Indian Defense Association in 1923 and was a principal author of the Meriam Report in 1928, which called for a complete transformation of Indian administration in the US. He would have the opportunity to implement his proposals, which included a staunch defense of the legal right of peyotists to practice their religion, when he was appointed commissioner of the BIA in 1933.[17]

CHAPTER SIX

1937

The Goshute Letter

The use of peyote by the Indians was learned from the Mexicans.
—"Peyote," Office of Indian Affairs, 1929[1]

On the first of November 1937, Chief Annie's Tommy and nine members of the Goshute Tribe in Ibapah, Utah wrote a desperate appeal to John Collier, the US commissioner of Indian Affairs. Tommy and the other signatories told Collier that something needed to be done to stop the use of peyote in the tribe, because "the Indians that are using this peyote are not using it right." Peyote was flooding the reservation (a community where there was no tradition of peyotism), brought by sinister outsiders who were growing rich from the devastation of the tribe. Their neighbors were falling victim in large numbers, their bodies and souls destroyed. Several people in the community had even reportedly died from its use. And yet for reasons they could not fathom, Collier insisted on using his power as commissioner to defend the peyotists, effectively making it impossible to fight this plague. Why, if he cared about indigenous peoples, would Collier not enact and enforce a ban on this dangerous drug?[2]

Their pleas fell on deaf ears. Tommy's request was initially rejected by E. A. Farrow, superintendent of the Paiute Agency, who reminded him that there was no federal law against peyote and that Utah law was not enforceable on the reservation.[3] Collier in turn responded to the whole affair with suspicion, suggesting that the letter was the work of either missionaries or his enemies in the bureau. When Farrow assured him that it was a genuine letter sent by tribal authorities, he still dismissed Tommy's concerns, insisting that the claims about the increase in deaths on the Goshute Reservation had to be incorrect, a claim he pointedly repeated to the Utah attorney general, Joseph Chez (who voiced his support for Tommy). "I should be entirely surprised to learn that it had killed anybody," Collier wrote to Chez, adding, "possession and use of peyote is not an offense under Federal law."[4]

It is possible that someone was ventriloquizing through Tommy and his council. This kind of manipulation has long characterized encounters between indigenous peoples and the state and would have been particularly powerful at a moment in time when the BIA was explicitly committed to Indian self-rule.[5] Collier had innumerable critics in the BIA, who made a litany of claims about peyote even as Collier refused to intervene. Like Tommy, these missionaries, doctors, nurses, and superintendents claimed that peyote was a poison, a narcotic, and a cause of physical degeneration, sexual profligacy, and death.[6]

On the other hand, Collier's suspicions may have spoken to his reluctance to confront the possibility that peyote was not simply a source of disgust to outsiders—that his decision to support the religious self-determination of peyotists had opened something of a Pandora's box on the reservations, where many viewed peyote as an alien threat to their religious traditions. When Collier asked officials in the area who might have been behind the letter, they all replied that it was genuine. There were no missionaries in the area agitating against peyote. It seemed that Tommy and whoever supported the letter were genuinely dismayed by what they saw around them—forms of social change and disruption that may not have been caused by peyote but that seemed somehow connected to the spread of this new religion.

Peyote lent itself to those conflicts in part because it was often used as a medicine for people who were in the final stages of terminal illnesses. Though Tommy does not detail the precise circumstances of the deaths, peyote was used with some frequency in the treatment of tuberculosis on western reservations, where its effect as a cough suppressant may have given the impression of a cure. Some medicine men (of the new variety, not the old) would give peyote to patients suffering from tuberculosis on their deathbed. Missionaries were quick to then attribute the death to peyote, while most doctors cautioned that there was no clear connection. Nonetheless, claims that the peyote killed the ailing patient would have found some purchase in a community in mourning.

These anxieties offer an important reminder that the lines between enchantment and disgust over the peyote effect did not invariably map onto the lines of difference between indigeneity and whiteness. Most accounts of the history of peyotism in the US posit an indigenous actor defending an indigenous tradition against the white oppressor.[7] Indians and whites in these accounts become fairly uniform categories. Such does not seem at all to have been the case here. Peyotism was new, recently introduced among the Goshute, and threatened the old guard. Here as elsewhere community leaders complained that the teachings of the peyotists "departed from those of their ancestors" or that the Christian-influenced practices of the peyotists seemed to be an imitation of white religion.[8] In extreme cases, as in the epigraph that began this chapter, opponents insisted that peyote was foreign not just to specific tribes but to the country as a whole. In letters written to federal officials over many decades, former peyotists spoke of the dangers of the drug (described as a habit), its alien nature in their communities, and its rapid growth. Children were said to be peyote's worst victims, either suffering from neglect because of their parents' habits (especially their increasing tendency to marital infidelity) or "becoming dull and irresponsive in their schoolwork."[9]

. . .

These lamentations make it all the more interesting that one of the most powerful proponents of peyotism in the US during the 1930s was none other than the commissioner of Indian Affairs. Until 1933 the BIA was allied with the antipeyotist factions, which worked throughout the 1920s to secure the suppression of peyote on the reservations. From 1923 to 1934 the federal appropriations bill included language defining peyote as an injurious drug, allowing liquor-control money to be spent enforcing a ban.[10] In 1935, however, Collier turned the old logics on their head when he requested that the language linking peyote to other drugs be removed from the appropriations bill (and in so doing no doubt prompted Annie's Tommy's consternation).[11]

His reasoning? Collier testified before Congress that he had compiled 150 monographs and studies of peyote and found no evidence that it was habit forming. While he would make no case for its medicinal qualities, he insisted that there was no scientific evidence to link it to degeneracy or any injurious effect on the body.[12] Nor was it a sexual stimulant. Peyote was simply an "innocent drug" that caused nausea and vomiting, followed by visual hallucinations, most of which comprised brilliant and beautiful colors.[13]

In remarks before Congress Collier also noted that peyote had never been classed with dangerous drugs under the Harrison Act and was labeled an intoxicant only because of pressures from within his own agency. When

Commissioner Burke put language in the appropriations bill in 1923 describing peyote as an intoxicant, "it was never done," insisted Collier, "on the basis of any showing that peyote was a deleterious drug." More importantly, the NAC, which by the mid-1930s was organized on fourteen reservations and had well over ten thousand members,[14] was a Christian church, and used peyote exclusively for religious purposes. This, of course, was the issue that most incensed peyote's most ardent critics, who tended to see the peyote churches as both blasphemous and a threat to their own missionary work. For Collier, though, who loathed the missionaries, it represented a further reason for the state to stay out of the conflict. If the battle over peyote was a battle between churches, the government had a constitutional obligation to refrain from intervening.[15]

Collier faced swift condemnation for lifting the ban,[16] both from within and outside of the BIA. In one typical example, H. Bruce of the Potawatomi Agency wrote Collier in June 1935 to complain about peyote, insisting that there was a clear difference between the Kansas tribes where peyote was used and those where it was not. In prosperous tribes there was virtually no use, while those where it was used

> seem to have more than an average percentage of degeneracy. We have an unusually large number of Indians in asylums and institutions and there is a large class at home who appear to be sub-normal and to lack mental capacity for progress. Many of this sub-normal class are pointed out by the other Indians as peyote "addicts."[17]

When Collier ignored these entreaties, his enemies recruited indigenous allies to travel to Washington to lobby Congress for a peyote ban. These efforts culminated in February 1937, when Senator Dennis Chávez of New Mexico introduced bill 1399, which would make it illegal to bring peyote into a state that had statutes prohibiting the cactus (peyote was then illegal in ten states)[18]. Those caught transporting anhalonium (as peyote was identified in the bill) across state lines or selling it would face fines of up to $200 and ninety days in jail.[19]

Backed by the very strong support of Harold Ickes, the secretary of the interior, Collier orchestrated an impressive attack on the bill in the Senate, disputing everything from the classificatory language in the bill to the claims about harm.[20] As in 1918, indigenous peyotists played a significant role in the struggle (notably Chief Fred Lookout of the Osage), but in a sign of just how much the intellectual tenor of the BIA had shifted under the New Deal, Collier also amassed a wealth of expert opinion, ranging from social scientists to botanists. Collier's experts included Franz Boas

(Columbia), A. L. Kroeber (UC Berkley), Ales Hrdlicka[21] (Smithsonian Institution), John P. Harrington (Bureau of American Ethnology at the Smithsonian and curator of the Southwest Museum), M. R. Harrington, Weston La Barre (a recent PhD from Yale), Vincenzo Petrullo (then with the Works Progress Administration [WPA]), Richard Evans Schultes (Harvard Botanical Museum), and Elina Smith (WPA).[22] Collectively, they argued that there was no credible evidence that peyote was associated with degeneration, slothfulness, physical dependence, or illness of any kind, and that, moreover, it was clearly associated with a series of practices that were leading to a positive resurgence of individual and communal well-being in the communities where it flourished (especially given peyote's role in combatting alcoholism). As such, they offered a powerful and overwhelming rebuttal to the claims of the missionaries.

More than this, the defense of peyotism here was strongly aligned with Collier's insistence that decades of assimilationist policies had been a disaster for Native Americans, and that respecting this religious right was part and parcel of a reimagined relationship between the US government and its indigenous wards. Though it was a shift that raised the ire of conservatives (traditionalists who remained committed to a unilinear version of cultural evolution that saw the erosion of indigenous lifeways as a mark of progress), it aligned well with the values of a growing number of social scientists, especially anthropologists trained in the traditions of Franz Boas, Bronislaw Malinowski, and A. R. Radcliffe-Brown, whose work rejected simple models of social change in favor of theories that sought to understand cultures as systems unto themselves (sometimes under the guise of cultural relativism, and at other times functionalism).

. . .

The range of scientific testimony offered in defense of peyote gave the 1937 hearings a very different tenor than those that took place in 1918. Though attacked, these scientists were not so easily dismissed as their predecessors, in part because after decades of research the evidence of the relative harmlessness of peyote was overwhelming. But beyond the Senate hearings, these arguments had almost no impact. The missionaries, public health officials, and superintendents who had long sounded alarms about the dangers of peyote saw in their defeat the sinister hand of Collier, whom they had long suspected of moral and ideological turpitude—of happily maintaining Indians in their heathen state, of mismanaging the bureau, and perhaps of even being a Communist—and they would continue the fight any way they could. Dr. Charles Tranter, a vocal foe, described the entire expert testimony in the Senate hearings as the product of "the misguided tenderness of certain eminent gentlemen towards the ancient habits of a group of semi-Christian Indians."[23] In the decidedly right-wing (according to Collier, Nazi-sympathizing) *Scribner's Commentator,* Malcolm Easterlin blasted Collier and his ilk for spreading moral degeneracy (again, sexual infidelity being a critical claim), Communism, and paganism on the reservations.[24] Scientific authority carried no weight with the critics, whose visceral disgust with peyote countenanced no dissent.

In a stark rebuke to Collier and his allies, on 16 December 1938 the surgeon general of the US Health Service identified peyote as an addictive drug. Addiction here signaled several ominous things for peyotists. Rooted both in the ascendance of Alcoholics Anonymous (which relied on disease theory to describe alcoholism) and a growing consensus within the psychiatric community (addiction would be included as a mental disorder in the first *Diagnostic and Statistical Manual of Mental Disorders* [*DSM-I*], published in 1952), the designation suggested both that peyote produced bodies that were physically dependent on a continuing diet of peyote in order to avoid the negative side effects associated with withdrawal, and that, even if bodies were not physically dependent on peyote, they could also suffer from psychic dependence; that individuals could come to depend on peyote for psychological reasons that were troubling enough to be designated a "mental disorder." Idiocy, lunacy, insanity, and other "mental diseases" resulted from these forms of addiction. The seriousness of the charge left little room for claims to a religious right.[25]

More significantly, Collier also faced a significant backlash on the reservations. Collier's commitment to tribal self-government could work two ways, both paving the way for a robust defense of peyotism and empowering factions that could use tribal law to outlaw peyote, which is exactly what happened on the Navajo Reservation, where peyote churches were growing more rapidly than anywhere else in the country in the 1930s. Peyotists managed to win power in the early 1930s in Taos but were defeated by the "whisky faction" in the June 1934 elections. The new authorities then set about to harass the peyotists, banning peyote from the reservation and disrupting their meetings.[26] The peyotists in turn attempted to enlist John Collier in their cause, claiming that members of the NAC were being denied their religious rights. The NAC in Oklahoma also pleaded for Collier to intervene, claiming that Navajo peyote meetings "have been disturbed by drunks. The governing body has fined and jailed the religious participants rather than the disturbers."[27]

According to one contemporary account, peyote was then quite new to Navajoland, having spread from the Ute country, where many Navajo migrated for work during the 1930s. Peyote was first introduced to the region as an herbal medicine, but by the mid-1930s had become quite popular both as medicine and as a religious sacrament, used in ceremonies where peyote priests would openly decry the evils of whisky. At times their condemnations of whisky inspired violence against local bootleggers, a few of whom were killed in conflicts with peyotists. As one might expect, this raised the ire of the Navajo bootleggers who dominated Bluff City and the area around Four Corners. By 1936 the bootleggers and peyotists were openly warring with one another, a conflict that saw bootlegging wiped out on the north bank of the San Juan River by 1939. Peyotism then began to expand on the south bank of the river, setting off renewed conflicts between peyotists, Navajo elders, and medicine men.[28]

Convinced that the very survival of Navajo tradition was at stake, in 1940 the whisky faction proposed a vote for a formal ban on the entire reservation. In the lead-up to the vote, antipeyote forces circulated stories about young girls dying after peyote meetings, of sexual debauchery, and of the larger moral degeneracy of peyotists.[29] Senior members of the Navajo Tribal Council issued public condemnations of the influence of peyote, highlighting both the moral decay caused by the drug and the supposedly sinister role that "secret agents" played in promoting drug use for their own personal profit. Members of the NAC in Oklahoma were accused of growing rich as money flowed from Navajoland to them.[30]

Leading up to the vote, Howard Gorman, vice-chairman of the Tribal Council, was particularly critical of "the indecent conduct of Navajos while under the influence of peyote." Lamenting that the drug was increasingly popular among students in both residential and day schools, he claimed that peyote enlarged and stimulated the "prostrate [sic] glands" and "makes a man or a woman crave sexual intercourse," leading to a great deal of immorality at the meetings. He claimed the meetings were sites of unrestrained adultery, where young men propositioned other men's wives, and that the peyote tea "makes the young girls and young men lose all self-respect or respect for the opposite sex."

> The young men who have been holding peyote meetings prey on young women of the tribe. After they become drunk with peyote they shout at the top of their voice, "bring on your women, your beautiful daughters and we shall take them unto ourselves as wives." On several occasions or meetings girls have thrown their dresses off and men took their pants off and throw themselves down on the hogan floor and layed around half-naked, in a degenerated state...[31]

Others confirmed Gorman's claims about the evils of peyote.[32] Medicine Man John Harvey emphatically insisted that peyote was not part of the Navajo religion. Roy Kinsel declared his wife's use of peyote had ruined their marriage and left them destitute. Members of the cult had even kidnapped his wife, taking her away for several days. "The young men performing the peyote ceremonies prey on our young wives and are tearing down the morals of our proud Navajo people . . . breaking up families." Mattie Benet Dole (aged seventeen) recalled a meeting in November 1939 where two young men followed her to the toilet and attempted to have sex with her.[33]

Clarence Chischilly (aged thirty), who had been witnessing meetings for the previous two years at a hogan in Naschitti, lamented the loss of decorum he saw in these meetings. He recalled with particular horror an incident on 4 May 1940, when a woman

> came riding on horseback. Her hair was floating in the air; she was half dressed; she was screaming and giving the whip to the horse even though it was rocky. It appeared that she was out of her head. This woman rode past Drolet's Store; she was not recognized by bystanders, because her face was in an unrecognizable condition.[34]

Released in the run-up to the 1940 tribal elections, these testimonies paved the way for a clean sweep by the whisky faction. The new Tribal Council banned peyote on the reservation by a vote of fifty-two to one on the third of June. Among the elements of the resolution was the statement that "it is not connected with any Navajo religious practice and is in contradiction to the traditional ceremonies of the Navajo people" and that it is "harmful and foreign to our traditional way of life."[35] The first arrests under the ordinance were made in early December, when two Cheyennes, one Kiowa, two Utes, and one Navajo were arrested and placed in the Fort Defiance jail by Navajo policemen, charged with possessing a large amount of peyote.[36]

. . .

Collier was disappointed, even angry, with the results of the vote in Navajoland. He continued to argue with members of the council and his critics in the BIA that there simply was no evidence that their claims were accurate.[37] Nonetheless, he found himself in a bind. He supported the religious rights of the peyotists. He also believed that tribal self-government mandated that if a law against peyote was passed on the reservation, the federal government was required to respect that law. He thus recommended that Secretary Ickes approve the ordinance. In correspondence with Ickes he also conceded that peyote was a recent introduction, "not in keeping with their traditional ceremonial rites," that many in the tribe found proselytizing by the peyotists disruptive, and that the Tribal Council possessed the authority to pass the ordinance. Ickes approved the ban on 18 December 1940.[38]

At this point all Collier could do was order that Indian Service employees play no role in enforcement.[39] He had lost the battle on the Navajo Reservation, was facing considerable criticism on other reservations for similar reasons,[40] and was losing a larger war for public opinion. By 1940 the mainstream press had picked up on a story that had until then been the preserve of scholarly journals and missionary magazines, drawn in by haunting images of a peyote epidemic that had rendered half the Indians in the country "incapable of working steadily for a living" (*New York News*) and was rumored to be the cause of a growing incidence of syphilis in Indian country.[41]

Given the weight of the scientific evidence presented at the 1937 hearings, and the BIA's commitment to defending peyotism (a posture that remained in place even after Collier left the agency in 1945), it is noteworthy that this was the version of peyote that became the mainstream narrative. Most likely the explanation for this lies at least in part in the fact that the images of degeneration, the hysteria of a society in danger, made better press than the reasoned arguments of tweedy academics, especially when the academics were effectively arguing that there was no story here. Yet it was not just the sensationalism that sold papers, but the ways in which the particular effects of peyote—hallucinations, delirium, bodies chanting and seemingly unwilling to follow the moral order—had the capacity to cause alarm. In a society where the body under the influence is understood as a threat to the social order, Indians weakened and disoriented by peyote made more sense than the more carefully reasoned renderings of the anthropologists, chemists, and other scientists ever could. Indeed, in June 1951 an article in *Time* magazine complained that the BIA was undermining efforts by the Tribal Council to keep peyote off the reservation, where there were now sixty-one thousand addicts. *Time* reported significant side effects from peyote use, including "impairment of the heart and kidneys." Users were also said to suffer stupendous hangovers, and "there have been many reports of sex crimes against children, committed under the influence of peyote." The article quoted one medical missionary who reported two cases of infanticide and one of fatal child neglect. In the face of this evidence, the

BIA comes across as clueless at best, heartless at worst. "The bureau is committed to the view that peyote is harmless. The men on the spot in the desert think they know better."[42]

Weston La Barre, who by 1951 had long since published his doctoral dissertation as *The Peyote Cult,* grew enraged as he read the *Time* article and immediately sent off a series of angry replies to the magazine. He also wrote to several colleagues in an effort to spark a broad condemnation of the piece,[43] which ultimately resulted in a statement defending peyotism that was signed by La Barre, David P. McAllester, J. S. Slotkin, Omer C. Stewart, and Sol Tax, which was published in *Science* in November 1953.[44] Unmoved by these declarations, however, the editors at *Time* refused to retract the story. In their response to La Barre they insisted that "while anthropologists in general agree with your statements, we have found other equally responsible citizens who take a different view. Our sources denied, or at least questioned, the statement in your letter that peyotism is a bona fide religious movement."[45]

And that was all it took to give La Barre the brushoff. As peyotism continued to grow in Navajoland and elsewhere, the basic nature of a continuing conflict over its impact on indigenous bodies remained relatively unchanged since the days when Pussyfoot Johnson tried to corner the market in Laredo. Indian bodies beyond the control of missionaries or the state represented something glorious to the likes of Collier and his friends among the anthropologists and scientists, who saw in these bodies recovery from the tragedy of colonial rule, self-determination, and at times an antidote to the grinding alienation of life in the West. To the missionaries, the agents of assimilation, and certain traditional authorities in Indian communities, where peyote threatened to disrupt not just the project of assimilation but also the authority of medicine men, bootleggers, and old-timers, bodies under the influence were bodies drunken, intoxicated, enfeebled, degenerated, destroyed. As Willis de Jaques wrote in 1952, peyote was "America's Newest Dope Horror."

> The most vicious dope menace in the United States today is a twisted, dirty cactus plant called peyote. . . . [It has] inspired weird, sex mad cults and religions and has destroyed civilizations in the Western Hemisphere since the 16th century when the Spaniards discovered its use among the Aztec tribes in South America. Some scholars have attributed the rapid fall of that great Indian culture to the widespread use of Peyotl. Today the drug is stretching its filthy tentacles into our school systems and enticing teen-agers into its grip.[46]

It was only a matter of time before innocent white children fell under its spell.

CHAPTER SEVEN

1957

The Holy Thursday Experiment

These drugs have produced better citizens.
—Senator Alejandro Aislic, 1974[1]

In the early hours of Holy Thursday 1957, a thirty-six-year-old doctor named Salvador Roquet arrived at the Sanatorio Psiquiatrico Santiago Ramírez Moreno in Mexico City for an experiment in the therapeutic use of mescaline. Roquet was already an accomplished man, having previously overseen antimalarial campaigns in southern Mexico for the Ministry of Health, but he was at a crossroads in what had become an unsatisfying career within the federal health bureaucracy. Troubled by the social dislocation and familial discord he witnessed in his work, two years earlier he had decided to train to become a psychiatrist. His plan was to work with families, and particularly children, to produce healthy and happy homes.[2]

The product of a conservative education, Roquet knew next to nothing about the drug he was about to take. And he was not alone. After early twentieth-century experiments with mescaline and peyote had yielded no obvious or easily marketable medical uses for these substances, mescaline had been relegated to the sidelines of research, sometimes described as a psychotomimetic because of its capacity to produce hallucinations (read as temporary psychosis). It was not until researchers in Canada proposed that mescaline could be used in the treatment of alcoholism that the psychiatric community would take more than a passing interest in the drug.[3]

If the claim that mescaline could treat alcoholism was eerily reminiscent of the assertions made by early members of the NAC that peyote was an antidote to whisky, the connection was largely lost on these researchers, including Roquet.[4] His first foray into psychedelics could not have been further removed from its indigenous origins. Synthetic mescaline, first produced by Ernst Späth in 1919, was the drug of choice, and the setting was the relatively sterile environment of a psychiatric hospital, where Roquet would be surrounded by men in white lab coats. It was a scene that in many ways directly mimicked experiments that were taking place twenty-five hundred miles to the north, under the direction of Humphrey Osmond.

Osmond plays an important role in this story. In 1951 the Health Ministry in the Canadian province of Saskatchewan recruited him to take up residence at the province's primary mental health hospital, which was in the sleepy prairie town of Weyburn, a couple of hours north of the US border. Osmond and his colleague John Smythies jumped at the opportunity to move to Weyburn, where they would have unparalleled opportunities to work with psychedelic drugs (Osmond in fact coined the term), starting with mescaline. Osmond was particularly struck by the potential therapeutic uses of mescaline, to which he attributed a variety of effects. Under the influence of the drug patients experienced a loss of a sense of time, intense mental focus, feelings of euphoria, and a capacity for reflexivity—all of which made therapeutic breakthroughs possible. As he later argued for LSD, he came to believe that a single intense experience with a psychedelic could help patients resolve their problems; a practice that if successful promised to upend both psychiatry and the pharmaceutical industry.[5]

Effectively divorced from its origins in peyote, synthetic mescaline had all the properties of a wondrous new drug. And that distance from its origins not only transformed the cactus, with its inconsistent effects, multiple alkaloids, and varying degrees of potency, into a purified pharmaceutical drug, it also resituated mescaline from the world of indigenous ritual (and attendant anxieties over degeneration and backwardness) into the world of the modern clinic. This was a world where whiteness, the controlled setting of the clinic, and scientific expertise obviated any concern about the potential for sloth and degenerate behavior. It was a world where Humphrey Osmond could administer synthetic mescaline to Christopher Mayhew (the British MP) and film Mayhew's session for the BBC.[6]

Though Mayhew's session was not broadcast (BBC censors were uncomfortable with Mayhew's mystical experience), the ease with which psychiatrists adopted mescaline-based therapies spoke very much to the ways that class and race had long characterized mainstream attitudes toward peyote. New York socialites and famous artists and writers had long been free to experiment with mescaline. Nowhere—not in the US, Mexico, or Europe—was mescaline prohibited, and while the avant-garde might take criticism from social conservatives for their experiments with hallucinogens, at no point did that concern turn into an orchestrated effort to ban mescaline, as had repeatedly been the case with peyote. Moreover, the concerns that conservatives raised about the likes of Havelock Ellis, Antonin Artaud, and later Aldous Huxley (who Osmond injected with mescaline in 1953, an experience that inspired him to write *The Doors of Perception*) were that they had not undertaken the sacrifice required of true mystical experiences, and that they might encourage lesser people (workers, children, racially suspect members of the underclass) to abuse these drugs. Class here was expressed through the fear that while the elite might escape the prison of drug addiction, lesser people would be drawn into the drug's vice. Moreover, the indigenous origins of peyote were so distant in these settings that it could either be ignored completely or refashioned into a pastiche that drew more extensively from Hindu mysticism than anything that approximated Native American or Mexican indigenous practices.[7]

. . .

By the mid-1950s psychiatrists across the West were undertaking their own mescaline studies, seeking to replicate the results observed by Osmond and Smythies, and imagining a host of potential new uses for the drug. It was this wave of experimentation that sparked the interest of Dr. José Rodríguez in Mexico City, who in turn recruited Roquet to participate in his study. Rodríguez had a rather simple plan, which replicated experiments Osmond had done with several patients. He would inject Roquet with mescaline and observe while Roquet experienced the effects of the drug. Imagining that he might get a little work done during the experiment, Roquet brought along a copy of Erich Fromm's *Ethics and Psychoanalysis* as reading material.

The session did not go as planned. Roquet panicked shortly after receiving his injection. He felt simultaneously deeply connected to and disconnected from the world. He was confronted by his many distinct personalities and selves. When asked by the doctor to stand, he found that he could not, as he was paralyzed by fear. According to an interview he gave in 1971, he felt he was dying. "I could not breathe, suffered a terrible inner fire, extreme palpitations. I was scared . . . I felt like a caged lion." He tried to calm down by reading but found that he could not make sense of the book. The doctor then tried to soothe him with food and games, to no avail.

As the session went on, Roquet could not overcome his feelings of horror and anxiety, which he carried long afterward.[8] He felt shattered, so much so that Dr. Rodríguez decided to halt his mescaline studies. He also put Roquet on a regimen of tranquilizers that lasted over a year. Some months later Roquet had a dissociative breakdown while on a trip to Germany and had to be helped onto an airplane bound for Mexico by a local psychiatrist. Rodríguez met his disconsolate test subject at the Mexico City airport and took him under his care.[9]

In all, the experience entailed transforming a relatively minor affect—curiosity, or mere interest—into a major affective response to the drug. Roquet had panicked as his body literally escaped from his control and revealed his deepest fears, and the experience stayed with him for years. But unlike some others, who translated that panic into a sort of disdain, a feeling that peyote was dangerous, even disgusting, Roquet never quite managed to turn his experience into a cautionary tale about a dangerous drug. To the contrary, over time he came to believe that mescaline had revealed something critically important, truths he had concealed from himself for many years. Even with all the horror, it had ultimately "allowed a deepened understanding of the soul."[10]

Of course, it took Roquet several years to reach this conclusion. In the meantime, he went to work as a psychiatrist at the Instituto de Seguridad y Servicios Sociales de los Trabajadores del Estado (Social Security Institute for State Workers, or ISSSTE).[11] By 1965 he was chief of mental hygiene at the agency, where he was tasked with dealing with what he perceived to be growing epidemics of alcoholism, drug addiction, autism, depression, and anxiety in Mexico.[12]

The experience at the ISSSTE convinced him that humankind was suffering from some sort of sickness—a sickness he had gained some small insight into while he was under the influence of mescaline. Though the experience had been horrifying, mescaline had somehow revealed his deeply hidden sources of inner pain. The drug had cleared away the detritus of lies and obfuscations required by modern life and forced him to confront the truths it revealed, offering a glimpse of a powerful means of exposing his inner wounds and beginning the healing process. For him personally this would mean jettisoning the unhappiness that had followed him around in life. For others it could act as an antidote for mental illness, addiction, and other manifestations of human crisis.[13]

The idea of turning to indigenous hallucinogens crystallized while he was on a trip to Paris in 1962. Roquet bought a copy of Roger Heim's *Les Champignons allucinogenes mexicaines* in a Saint–Germain-des-Prés bookstore, intrigued by what these strange mushrooms that grew in the Sierra Mazateca might reveal. Back in Mexico, and unsure even of the location of Huautla de Jiménez (the center of the then burgeoning magic mushroom craze), he turned to Heim, who put him in contact with Alfonso Caso, director of the Instituto Nacional Indigenista (INI), who then introduced him to Carlos Incháustegui, the anthropologist who ran the Centro Indigenista in Huautla. Incháustegui and Caso opened doors in the Sierra Mazateca, paving the way for Roquet to undertake a project in the region that would combine public health work, school construction, and a series of intellectual exchanges with local healers. Starting in 1967, Roquet worked with Incháustegui, Ricardo Bogrand of the Instituto Mexicano del Seguro Social (IMSS), and several others on an integrated study of the ethnobotanical properties of the region, in which he catalogued cultural practices and studied local medical, philosophical, theological, and chemical knowledge.[14] While in the sierra he opened medical clinics, distributed vaccines and medicine, and offered rudimentary advice on health issues. In exchange for these services, Roquet asked local curers to teach him lessons in the use of their medicinal plants.[15]

It was here that he would also begin to build a long-standing relationship with María Sabina, the shaman made famous in a 1957 *Life* article by the New York banking executive and amateur ethnomycologist Gordon Wasson.[16] Sabina had long had a reputation as a powerful curer locally, and it had been for that reason that the local political boss had sent Wasson her way in 1955. Sabina also fit into a long tradition of shamanism, in which the authority of the curers was tied at least in part to their capacity to act as interlocutors, to cure for outsiders, translating local knowledge in the process. Shamans are probably best understood in these terms, as experts who believe in the universality of their knowledge, who often authorize their knowledge in part through their relationships with outsiders, and who generally expect certain forms of compensation for sharing it. They might alter their ceremonies to meet the needs of outsiders, but since no two ceremonies were exactly alike, this merely reinforced their expertise.[17]

Sabina did this to great effect during the 1960s, meeting with famous international pop stars (members of the Beatles among them) as well as an assortment of North American, European, and Mexican seekers of mystical knowledge. By the time Roquet arrived, however, the flood of outsiders had begun to wear on the community, as the foreigners often ate mushrooms indiscriminately and behaved in public in ways that offended local tastes and sensibilities. Roquet was thus part of the last wave of outsiders, but unlike most, he was able to create lasting friendships in the community and with Maria Sabina, visiting her regularly over the next decade and a half, taking part in numerous *veladas* (the mushroom ceremonies), and acting as a patron to members of her family.[18]

Roquet translated the Mazatec customs he observed into his own conceptual language with little difficulty, often drawing parallels between western and indigenous healing traditions. In one instance, he observed the use of a seed that cut short the psychosis caused by hallucinogens, and proposed that it be used to treat schizophrenia.[19] In another, he interpreted a story about a young indigenous man whose "fallen" spirits had lifted after being prescribed salvia by a local curer (the man had been the victim of a violent assault) as a story about depression its alleviation.[20]

In these and other instances, it seems entirely possible that Roquet misconstrued or misunderstood the nature of the healing, mistaking a social cure that linked the individual to a world of communal belonging and responsibility for an individual cure. In this he shared something with Weston La Barre, Dorothea Leighton, and others, who described peyotism in the US in similar terms. Like Mazatec shamanism, peyotism in the US had long had a link to "doctoring" and other remedies (especially to whisky drinking), a phenomenon that experts often mistranslated as something like therapy, mistaking a culturally specific ritual and catharsis for something that was a universal expression of individual healing.[21]

Were Roquet's descriptions of a three-thousand-year-old tradition of "indigenous psychotherapy" gross misreadings of a local cultural practice?[22] At some points this seems to have been the case. Roquet clearly relied on a series of western diagnostic tools to make local ailments legible. And yet what mattered most to Roquet was that he was witnessing some sort of cure, and that much of the cure revolved around the relationship of the individual to his world and his cognitive experiences.[23] Roquet also tried to avoid mapping his views onto those of his interlocutors, insisting that he did not really understand the inner lives of the indigenous peoples he studied. He did not in fact think that psychiatric traditions that privileged individual subjectivity had much value in this setting, preferring to believe that the curers of the sierra understood what ailed their patients far better than he could.

Indeed, it was not the mentally ill in the sierra he felt he could help. Rather, he saw in ceremonies like the velada elements that had the capacity to transform other curing processes, in part because they addressed universal conditions—depression, anxiety, fear of death, and various forms of trauma. He was impressed by the well-known capacity of indigenous psychedelics to loosen tongues, revealing the darkest of secrets, but he was impressed with the form as well as the content. He was quite taken by the cleansing rituals that were woven into the psychedelic ceremonies, the careful manipulation of set and setting, and in the capacity of the *curandero* to "become god."[24] He saw in these rituals how the disruptive bodily experiences of psychedelic drugs combined with language, music, light, and dark to produce a profoundly cathartic sensory/curing effect. Roquet thus became convinced that the therapeutic value of the drug was rooted not just in the physiological action but in the sensory charge produced by certain settings, and the set of expectations created by the cultural context of consumption—what might otherwise be considered a constructivist approach to drug intoxication.[25] If he could capture the essence of this process, he would be able to "assimilate and integrate ancient indigenous practices to the science of modern psychiatry with the respect they both deserve." The result would draw from both traditions to produce "integrated men," subjects who were of both the West and the East.[26]

After accidentally taking some datura (*toloache*) and having a terrifying experience during one of his trips to the sierra, Roquet settled on the term "sensitivity" to describe the essence of this integrated subject. Datura, he discovered, was unlike LSD, with slow, profound effects. As he recounted to Alberto Villoldo, under its influence "we saw monumental changes in the personality occurring. . . . The personality of the individual lost it rigidity, and change and syntheses rather than analysis became a possibility."[27] The madness he experienced during the trip took him back to his origins, to where he "found what I had lost: sensitivity."

Modern man had lost his sensitivity and was in the midst of a "century of anguish," where despite constant striving, progress, and technological change, one saw escalating rates of suicide, war, and alcoholism. Modern humans lived a soulless antilife, suffering from fear and "the inability to love," which in turn resulted in an inert life of pain, violence, the absence of contact with the essential energy of life: love. "Lovesickness" lay at the root of widespread neurosis and psychosis.[28] With the reanimation of sensitivity came the reanimation of love.

Indigenous psychedelics, with their capacity to "produce a state of greater clarity, vision, and energy in the person who ingests them,"[29] were ideally suited to helping his patients recover their sensitivity. Those who took these drugs in the proper settings would be taught to embrace fundamental universal values, experience love and God, see themselves as part of the universe's energy, lose their fear of death. They would recover their "innate capacity for love." This in turn could produce men of peace instead of war, people who lived in a more natural fashion, whose sensibilities owed as much to the Mazatec shaman as they did to the Mexico City doctor.[30]

. . .

We might understand Roquet's musings through the concept of appropriation. The Mexico City doctor went into the mountains and literally took not just the thing (first mushrooms, later peyote) but also the ritual surrounding the thing, and then used both in his Mexico City practice, growing famous while failing to adequately compensate the true owners of this knowledge.[31] On some level, this claim is impossible to dismiss. Roquet clearly sought out indigenous knowledge of psychedelic plants, and did so with the goal of applying that knowledge in a nonindigenous context. If we are to consider that knowledge proprietary, only not recognized as such because of a long history in which elite Mexicans failed to respect indigenous rights, at the very least his practice relied on longstanding forms of privilege to claim for himself something that belonged to someone else.

Appealing though it may be, this positioning only takes us so far. Roquet could not have imagined himself as appropriating indigenous learning. He claimed to be a student of learned teachers, doctors in their own right. His time in the sierra represented for him an extension of his training, in which he compensated his teachers materially (offering his own expertise and bringing social and health services needed in the community) and through his words and deeds, invariably crediting them with what they taught him and positioning himself not as expert but as apprentice. For the most part he and his informants seem to have framed their relationship as an exchange, which while asymmetrical (he was a Mexico City doctor, after all, and they indigenous curers) was nonetheless voluntary. It was an exchange rooted at least in part in mutual respect. Roquet sought to take the lessons he learned in these settings and recast them so that they might apply to a clinical urban setting, and to do so in a way that honored his teachers.[32]

Roquet differed in rather significant ways from most of the other psychiatrists who found themselves attracted to psychedelics. Unlike those who maintained a strict distinction between the indigenous origins of the drug and the pharmaceutical form (though, to be fair, Osmond did attend an NAC ceremony in 1956 and was deeply interested in the nature of these rituals[33]), Roquet thought that knowledge that existed outside a clinical setting was critical to unleashing the power of these drugs. Still, he was not interested in abandoning the clinic in its entirety and had little interest in following the path set by Timothy Leary (Leary was trained as a psychologist), whose enchantment with psychedelics was such that after being fired from Harvard, he abandoned scientific pretense altogether and wholeheartedly embraced an immersive drug experience.[34]

Though called a modern-day shaman by some, Roquet explicitly rejected this label. While it is true that Roquet's attraction to vibrations, his allusions to universal energy, the boundaryless body, and devotion to that which was unseen veered perilously close to shamanism, Roquet always thought of himself as a psychiatrist, a doctor committed to careful experimentation and evidence-based medicine. He did not seek to become a shaman and scoffed at those who labeled him with the term. He gathered data about his subjects and sought to classify and understand the drugs he encountered in shamanistic settings according to their precise effects and proper doses and to produce an empirically defensible mental health practice. More than this, he never imagined that he could possess the skills that people like Sabina had in managing a velada, and he repeatedly expressed amazement about her ability manage these rites with such ability even after consuming many mushrooms. Unlike some in the mental health community (including R. D. Laing and later Andrew Feldmar), he would not consume the substances he administered with his patients, but would instead adopt a more traditional role of doctor administering a cure. This is not to say that he explained the differences between himself and Sabina as one of the modern doctor (the possessor of knowledge) and the primitive shaman (possessed by knowledge). He clearly saw her and the other shamans as expert curers.

One particular exchange between Roquet and Sabina is telling. Describing the velada, she told the Roquet that

> the veladas are not done to find God; We do them with great respect and with the sole purpose of curing the diseases from which our people suffer. Whoever does it to simply feel the effects, can go crazy and stay so temporarily. Our

ancestors always took holy children in a velada presided over by a wise one. The mushrooms are the blood of Christ, they are the flesh of God.[35]

Roquet responded:

Yes, Dona Maria, this is exactly my interest. Look: I am a doctor and I believe that the problems of the mind and soul, . . . sadness and madness, can be cured with this sacred food. . . . I come to learn from you. . . . And my companions come with the idea of healing.

She replied: "Jesus Christ! Doctor? So you are a wise one too, like me?"They both laughed, and Sabina then said:

In order to heal I must go through the demons of death. I dive in and walk down below. I can look into the shadows and the silence. That is how I arrive to where the illnesses are crouching, where I can watch how the words fall; They come from above, like little luminous objects coming from the sky. The words fall on the sacred table and heal.[36]

Playful, full of delight, these exchanges highlight Roquet's enchantment not just with the powerful drugs he had encountered but with the sacred forms of knowledge to which he had been exposed. The contrast with the attitudes toward indigenous cultures manifested earlier in the century could not be starker, and neither did this align with arguments that North Americans had used to negotiate a legal space for indigenous peyotism in the US. Roquet was not simply respectful of cultural difference and willing to defend an indigenous religious right. He believed that these teachers could revolutionize the way he and his compatriots lived.[37]

Roquet and Sabina did not endeavor to erase difference. Rather, they did not locate themselves within difference in ways that would have impeded the common understandings that underpinned their transactions. And for his part, Roquet did the thing that we often imagine subaltern subjects doing; he revealed the instability of his own whiteness by crossing over, while at the same time never losing a sense of his origins.[38] He was a scientist, a doctor who understood that the power of these substances was intimately connected to the setting in which they were consumed, and he sought to build a professional practice that could adapt some of the curing techniques he saw in the sierra to a modern urban clinic.

. . .

Roquet opened the Clínica de Psicosíntesis in the Condesa neighborhood of Mexico City in October 1967. It proved immediately popular.

Over eight years he held 764 sessions in the clinic, in which 813 patients were treated with psychedelic drugs. According to his records, the vast majority of patients were neurotics (83.4 percent), followed by drug addicts (6.7 percent), patients with "problems of a sexual nature," primarily homosexuality (3.75 percent), psychotics (3.1 percent), and alcoholics (2.4 percent). His patients were overwhelmingly middle class, with 40 percent lower middle, 45.3 percent higher middle, and 11 percent upper class. Only 4.1 percent came from lower class backgrounds. Most were well educated and had some sort of professional occupation, and a majority were male.[39]

The clinic practiced what was by all accounts a unique method of psychotherapy. In the diagnostic phase Roquet met with patients, discussed their personal issues, and administered the Hartmann test (an axiological scale that allowed him to measure the progress of his patients through their capacity for love). The intake session was designed to prepare the patients for their session, and Roquet insisted that they be absolutely truthful, so that their treatment would be appropriate (this also being a form of purification, common both to the Mazatec velada and Huichol peyote ceremonies). Some days after the initial intake, groups of between fifteen and thirty patients, selected for age, sex, and other factors, would gather with several assistant therapists at the clinic for a session that began at nine p.m.

The all-night session was designed to move patients through five distinct psychedelic phases. The first and most superficial included an expectant and anxious stage, in which patients became nauseous, confused, and experienced perceptual alterations and euphoria. The second stage, characterized by visual hallucination, was pleasant, Dionysian. Patients became lost in fantasy, escaped from reality, and experienced false mystical and religious visions. This was a hedonistic, pleasant, childlike state, where individuals could imagine God as a projection of themselves but experienced no real insight (Roquet and Sabina both saw this as the phase sought by those icons of the 1960s, the hippies). In the next stage, darkness set in. The patients achieved a naked, pitiless vision of reality, a clear vision of what was meaningful in their lives. They became both observer and observed and experienced a cleansing catharsis as the unconscious became an observer of itself. This tended to be both painful and dramatic to a degree that depended on their level of neurosis and repression. The patient might gain insights about themselves, but they often panicked as they were engulfed by death, feelings of falling, drowning, and various other forms of anxiety. This was followed by the fourth stage, madness, which entailed the complete loss of ego. Drawn directly from the *locura* Mazatec shamans produced in their veladas, madness was the phase in which all traces of personality and boundary disintegrated. This was the maximum point of regression, the nothing point, the psychotic stage. Only then, with the help of the therapist, could the patient reconstruct their personality, reintegrating the forms of sensitivity that had been fragmented by their life traumas.[40] The patient could then recover their capacity to live in the world, not as the repressed and disassociated subject, but as an integrated individual, aware both of the source of their traumas and their connection to the universe in ways that offered a new beginning. It returned the unfeeling person to the place where humans "lost our soul," and made "communion with the divine" possible.[41]

This was accomplished by dividing the session into a series of distinct phases. At the very start, patients would take part in a brief, free-flowing conversation, followed by a shift to yoga and meditation, undertaken to quiet the conscious mind. The group session ended between eleven p.m. and midnight, when patients would leave their shoes, watches, and cigarettes with an assistant and enter the session room, which was a six-by-eight-meter space with large foam pads on the floor. Mimicking the aural and visual effects of the velada, the session room was also equipped with record players, tape machines, movie projectors, psychedelic art, and various forms of colored and modulated lighting.[42]

Flashing lights greeted the patients as they entered the room. Record players offered three different types of music, and projectors displayed images designed to produce a "sensory charge." These included photographs of money, bearded yogis, skulls, smiling families, crying women, sunsets, naked men and women, cemeteries, corpses, vultures, starving people, demons, and saints. To this Roquet added images and sounds from his patients' own lives (in one case he played a speech by Díaz Ordaz for a former guerilla),[43]—all designed to elicit powerful responses and cognitive overload.[44]

At the end of the stimulation phase each patient received a prescribed psychedelic (Roquet called them psychodysleptics). Of the drugs administered, LSD (34.1 percent) was the most common, followed by Ketalar (a commercial name for ketamine) (15.4 percent), rivea corymbosa (14 percent), psilocybin (13.7 percent), datura (10.3 percent), ipomena violácea (7.4 percent)[45], peyote (2.3 percent), and mescaline (0.6 percent). Each drug was carefully chosen for its specific effect and administered at set points in what was typically a four-session cycle that took place over four months. LSD, peyote, and psilocybin and ololiuqui were given in the first session because of their capacity to produce a variety of psychotomimetic effects. Datura was administered only in the final two sessions of a cycle—used to dissolve the ego's final defenses and allow the disintegration of the personality, forcing patients to regress to childhood, "to the primitive, the very roots of being,"[46] where change, reintegration, creativity, and inspiration would occur. Ketamine was similarly administered late in the cycle and later in the session and was used to break down resistance to the effects of the other drugs. It was especially useful for patients with prior experience with LSD, who had learned to manipulate the drug to avoid painful experiences. Whenever possible, Roquet used pure forms of the drugs provided by indigenous interlocutors, as he believed that this allowed the closest approximation to an indigenous cure.

This practice signaled the special role that peyote and other indigenous plant medicines played in Roquet's practice, as it distinguished his method rather starkly from that of many of his contemporaries in the US and Europe. He was not searching for the purified form of the drug, the mescaline as opposed to peyote or the psilocybin as opposed to mushrooms. No, it was the complex makeup of the plant medicine (the many alkaloids in peyote, the different effects depending on when it had been harvested) and the ritual practices within which that medicine had been traditionally embedded that Roquet thought were essential to the effective use of these particular plants. What mattered was not merely the bodily effect of the psychedelic drug but a series of practices rooted in specific indigenous contexts. This was, Roquet believed, what made his work a nationalist endeavor—an effort that would elevate a local Mexican drug and practice to international prominence.

After receiving their doses, the patients returned to the floor to watch more images. Some were then blindfolded and listened to music on headphones. By five in the morning most would be peaking (those given datura would not peak for another eight to ten hours), at which point they were shown the final film, which depicted a child being born. Visuals then ceased, the music changed, and the room was shrouded in total darkness. Soft religious music would be interposed with sounds of an airplane diving and crashing, machine guns, car horns, followed by flashing strobe lights. This period lasted three hours, and during it patients felt a great deal of anguish, particularly the pain of death and rebirth. Roquet believed that at the very least these moments allowed patients to experience a profound catharsis, but believed that it also offered the possibility of something greater: a transcendental mystical experience that would allow the possibility for something beyond analysis. He called this *synthesis*.

To facilitate synthesis, the room was made pleasant, colored lights were illuminated, and the patients were encouraged to interact. Roquet would then talk with them, bring out their files and allow them to look at old photos, letters, and journals. Those who were prescribed ketamine would then get their injections and experience a short period of psychedelic involvement—one to one-and-a-half hours—before they too moved on to synthesis. Between ten and eleven a.m. they would take a three-hour break, during which the patients practiced yoga, meditated, and breathed deeply. They would then take a short nap while the drugs fully metabolized.

In the next part of the session, patients were free of the drug effect but still psychologically impacted by the experience. Their defenses were low, and their sense of self fragile, giving the therapists an opportunity to work on the reintegration of their personalities. They were awakened by music, read from their journals, looked at family pictures, and interacted with the therapist for six to eight hours. Music was again used, but this time as a catalyst of integration. Only one stereo played, and the music was typically classical. Some would practice psychodrama. Some would meet with family members and friends or reach them by phone. The patients would then return home late in the evening, with the expectation that they would return eight days later for an eight-hour group session unassisted by drugs.

. . .

Roquet's reconstituted subject was something quite different from the individuated and analyzed subject of modern psychiatry. In part this was because psychedelic involvement undermined the forms of subjectivity that patients brought into their sessions. Their bodies became newly visible through a powerful refocusing of the senses—in chills, nausea, vomiting, sweating, heat, visual hallucination, shaking, screaming, and tactile changes. Beyond simple affective responses, the treatment released embodied memories, undermined sequential thinking, revealed things long forgotten, provoked bizarre ideas, free associations, and "alterations in reality with or without depersonalization." Bodies "released" traumas that had long been stored, causing the "rupture of repression and the release of unconscious material."[47] Agnostic as to whether these traumas lay entirely in the mind, Roquet's focus on the terrified body, his effort to promote the bodily release of these traumas, and his general embrace of the physical experience within psychosynthesis uneasily skirted the line between the Cartesian body of the rational West and the holistic body of Mexican shamanism. Under the influence, the boundaries between mind and body, and the self and other, seemed to melt away.[48] This is where transcendence lay.

Through his experiences with psychedelics Roquet came to believe that humans possessed a vital energy. They did not create this energy, which was in any event timeless. They simply transformed it into their life-force. He believed that patients experienced a profound love by accessing that energy, which in turn led them to God (God goes undefined), and the realization of their own immortality. This was particularly important for those patients who had developed a fear of feeling, a fear of suffering because they had not experienced the right kinds of love as children, and had in turn devoted their lives to the search for bodily pleasure through substitutes—alcohol, sex, and drugs.[49]

That vital energy recognized neither the mind-body separation nor the boundaries between the self and other. Humans were connected to one another on an atomic level through that energy. Those with sensitivity could feel these connections, and patients regaining theirs developed "a certain ability to vibrate in unison with other human vibratings; the ability to feel (to sense) without the senses." Quoting a patient, he wrote, "I felt that even though I wasn't a definite entity, and that I was changing each instant, I was part of an energy and a plan that had been forged somewhere in the universe, and that energy was working within me."[50]

Again quoting a patient:

I felt that my arms were stiff, that I couldn't use them as I would like to. They were paralyzed for a moment. After a while, they began to soften; I felt some sort of electric energy moving my arms very softly, following the concert's beat. Energy began to have a consistency; it became like a ball that I had in my hands in the moment that I discovered with the most immense surprise of my life that all of me was love. You asked me what was the matter. I stood up, a force reaching me from above similar to the force I had in my hands only much stronger, started to pull me. The only thing I saw was light, and the only thing I felt was an irresistible attraction. God was calling me. He called me. . . . The force became more intense and I could not resist. I went; I went with him and he enveloped me. I cannot describe what I felt. The words that might approach this are happiness, totality, eternity, and I don't know what any of them mean. I only felt them at that moment.[51]

These descriptions remind us of the powerful role the actant plays in this story. Descriptions of vibrations, flights, the melting of boundaries, and a feeling of connection to the universe appear in any number of cultural contexts where individuals seek language to make sense of the bodily experience of psychedelics. While we should not go too far in attempting to suggest a universal experience (some, for instance, may have referred to flight literally, while others might have meant it metaphorically),[52] the common language deployed at these moments is noteworthy, especially given the fact that, in order to hold sessions that hewed more closely to the indigenous origins of his practice, Roquet regularly took patients to visit Sabina and other shamans (at first Mazatec and later Huichol) during these and later years.[53] The cure, like the bodies undergoing the cure, could transcend cultural boundaries.

. . .

These were radical gestures, in some ways aligned to the aspirations of what was then a growing counterculture in the US and Mexico, but Salvador Roquet was no hippie. Like other more conservative Mexicans, he viewed the burgeoning hippie movement, with its tendency toward hedonism, widespread drug use, and the flouting of social norms, as a significant threat to society, and the hippies themselves as stunted individuals.[54] However radical his therapy was, Roquet invariably sought to cure a very specific series of ailments: addiction, schizophrenia, homosexuality, and the like. His embrace of shamanism was practical, intended as form of intellectual and cultural exchange in which the shaman's specific expertise could be made legible to a medical profession that viewed these substances in more mundane ways, as drugs with a specific effect on a medicalized body.

Roquet carefully recorded the doses he offered his patients, adjusting them to maximize the effect, and recorded the results of his work in detail, all with an eye toward producing scientific knowledge, that is, knowledge based on careful experimentation, documentation, predictable effects, and repeatable results. And the results seemed extraordinary. If his data was correct, 85 percent of his patients showed improvements in their relationships with family, work, and others, and healthier attitudes toward life and love, which compared exceptionally favorably with other forms of therapy.[55] Moreover, in contrast to the four years patients typically spent in psychotherapy, patients in psychosynthesis could complete their treatment in twelve months, significantly reducing the cost of therapy and bringing it within the reach of ordinary people.[56]

Patient testimonies confirmed his claims. In an extraordinary session held in the Salon Verde of the Mexican Congress in 1974, organized by his daughter and several patients in order to defend his methods (as will be discussed in chapter 10, many of the drugs used in the clinic, including peyote, were outlawed in 1971, and Roquet was arrested in November 1974), several spoke of the transformative effect of his therapies. According a patient named Rosa María, Roquet's clinic was a godsend.[57] She had been a juvenile delinquent, a hippie, a pot smoker, and sexually promiscuous. Suffering from depression, she turned to cocaine, amphetamines, and psychedelics to escape her problems. It was only Roquet's treatment that saved her from the abyss. After the first treatment (which took place two and a half years earlier) she quit cocaine entirely. It took a year to get off amphetamines, in part because her depression had been so acute that she could not get out of bed without them, but in the end Roquet was instrumental in alleviating both her addiction to amphetamines and the underlying depression.

Rosa María's rescue narrative reinforced one defining aspect of Roquet's practice. His practice was said to be abundant with ex-hippies, "all of whom have become followers of Dr. Roquet and practitioners of his theories on sensitivity and love."[58] In their willingness to enter Roquet's care, they in turn adopted a narrative about the counterculture that was strikingly similar in its tenor to that of the antidrug establishment,[59] and even in some sense echoed María Sabina's views (she despised the hippies). Hippies were immature, the product of failed families, were searching for something that did not exist. They longed for love and God, but their beliefs were "distortions," "mirages." Their version of God was in fact "the devil, the fantasy, the denial of love."[60] Their indiscriminate use of psychedelic drugs had led to "depression, panic, psychosis and suicides." It was only under the good doctor's care that his patients had found a way out of these afflictions.[61]

In the hearing in the Salon Verde, Senator Alejandro Aislic insisted that the use of "Mexican psychodysleptic drugs" helped Roquet's patients become more integrated and capable of resolving their problems, producing "better citizens." According to the senator, who had been a patient of Roquet's, they "are people you could encounter on the streets, just like any of you, and like everyone, they have all had to face some serious emotional problems." It would be a tragedy if that treatment was put in jeopardy because "unfortunately the use of psychodysleptic drugs has fallen into the hands of the famous hippies, who are fleeing from life, who are fleeing from reality, who do not want to integrate and contribute to their country."

More about the hippies, later.

CHAPTER EIGHT

1958

Alfonso Fabila Visits the Sierra Huichola

The Plan Huicot will be impregnated with a true respect for indigenous cultural values, and will seek all means possible to elevate their standard of living

—Plan Huicot, *27 February 1971*[1]

Around the same time that Salvador Roquet agreed to take part in the Holy Thursday experiment, officials at Mexico's Instituto Nacional Indigenista (INI) were preparing for one of their own. After decades of neglecting the mountainous regions north and west of Guadalajara—a four-thousand-square-mile region that was home to some of the most inaccessible communities in the country—they concluded it was time to act. With the aid of the recently completed Guadalajara-Nogales highway and a fleet of new aircraft capable of landing on small airstrips located deep in the mountains, they would bring the modern world to those otherworldly, peyote-worshipping mystics of the sierra: the Huichol Indians. It was going to be a big job, made even more challenging by the fact that the bureaucrats and experts working in Mexico City possessed only cursory knowledge about the Huichols.

This, then, is how Alfonso Fabila found himself venturing into the sierra in a fact-finding mission in 1958. Unable to enter the region by road, he was forced to hire a small plane to take him to an airstrip in Tuxpan, Jalisco, one of the key Huichol ceremonial centers (locals had earlier built an airstrip to assist in the transport of *artesanía*). Once in Tuxpan he recruited guides to ferry him to other Huichol communities, where he found little evidence of schools, a population that was almost wholly unable to speak Spanish, and few traces of the Mexican state.[2] On paper the region had seen several major land reforms in the mid-1950s (mostly at the behest of Huichols who had traveled to Mexico City to complain about the depredations of local mestizos), but there was no evidence that any of the reforms had been carried out.

Palpably disgusted by what he saw, Fabila was struck by "the centuries of backwardness that afflict the Huichols,"[3] by the absence of roads, post offices, telegraphs, and telephones. The Huichols lacked water, and what water they had was dirty. Their homes were "disorderly and dirty."[4] They had no idea what caused illness and death, and diarrhea and digestive ailments, along with tuberculosis, flu, measles, and complications at childbirth, were endemic. Modern medicines were unknown, and their "hygiene and public and private sanitation" dreadful. They were entirely unaware of government services.[5]

Like the region's geography, the Huichols were impassable, inscrutable, filthy. According to Fabila, the Huichol world was "impregnated with great pantheistic, animistic, fetishistic, Catholic and magical religious sensibilities, in which polytheistic ideas are intertwined in strange ways."[6] And like their pastureland, they were under threat from neighboring mestizos who lived on their margins and coveted their lands. Desperately poor, they were in dire need of both "aid" and "protection." Moreover, in some ways they were their own worst enemies, people who destroyed their own forests out of "need and ignorance."[7]

In the years that followed Fabila's visit, as government agents and the occasional journalist made their way into the sierra, dirt was a common theme in outsider's renderings of the Huichols. This, and the sense that the deficiencies seen in the region could only be fixed by a strong, cleansing hand. To be sure, their shock at the poverty they saw in the sierra was understandable. The infant mortality rates, malnutrition, endemic illnesses, illiteracy, and general human misery government officials witnessed here stood out in comparison with much of the rest of the country, where rapid industrialization was producing significant gains in health, education, and general well-being across a wide spectrum of classes. Indeed, what matters here is not so much that they saw poverty in the region. It is instead the interpretive lens through which they made sense of that poverty. Their renderings of the Huichols were nothing like those found in Lumholtz, sixty years earlier. They did not see a distinct, even pre-Columbian cultural tradition, rich in symbolism and unlike other communities in Mexico. They did not see people who were marginalized, victimized by racism, and often subject to violence in their transactions with outsiders. They saw dirt, primitives, and impediments to progress.

In this reading, Huichol mysticism, which may have produced fantastic art and a certain harmonious relationship with nature, presented a critical challenge to those who sought to improve the lives of these primitives. Desperately poor, exploited by mestizo ranchers, and beholden to curanderos, Huichols lived in a universe where modern scientific explanations for everyday phenomena—ranging from the reasons that birds could fly to the causes of illness—simply did not have any purchase. Ignorance, and not distrust, was the reason that pregnant women absolutely refused medical help, leading to high infant mortality (75–80 percent), and only strong adults lived beyond thirty. Worse still, government officials believed that the men refused to work, leaving their women to shoulder the labor of child rearing and fieldwork. They refused to educate their daughters because they thought it useless. They would not cooperate in development efforts, in the building and maintenance of schools, in tending school agricultural plots, or in any of the efforts the government deemed necessary for their improvement. Like children, they would need to be dragged, kicking and screaming, into the twentieth century. [8]

In some sense, then, the story of the post-revolutionary Mexican state's first substantial encounter with the country's most important peyotists was quite different from the story that unfolded north of the border during the preceding years. Whereas their northern neighbors responded with great passion to an evangelical peyote cult among the western tribes, battling in the press, the courts, and state and federal legislatures over the legality of peyotism, the Mexican officials who came into contact with the Huichols dismissed or ignored their religious and spiritual lives, focusing instead on the urgent need for transformation. Modernization in the sierra is a story about a peyotist people in which peyote itself was generally absent. The question is why?

. . .

In 1960 Mexico was in the midst of its high modern moment. Flush with cash from a program of Import Substitution Industrialization that had not yet run its course, the federal government created a series of great monuments to the mix of endogamous creativity and rational order that constituted Mexican modernism (consider the Museo de Antropología, opened in 1958, and the UNAM, which opened its new megacampus to the south of Mexico City in 1954). Oil refineries, factories, roads, dams, electrical grids, and airports promised a departure from generations of economic inequality and political instability. Mexico's working class would reap the benefits of an economic miracle, and an industrial powerhouse would replace a country long dependent on the rural export sector.

This version of modernity was an urban affair, planned from Mexico City, and did not require much attention to the conditions on the ground, which would in any event be erased by roads, dams, tractors, irrigation systems, electricity, and telecommunications, designed outside the sierra and imposed on an unruly landscape and people. This ethos informed the very creation of the INI's *Centro Coordinador Cora-Huichol* in July 1960. Eschewing a sierra that had almost no transportation or communications infrastructure and offered dreadful living and working conditions for agency employees, the INI chose Guadalajara as its base, a decision that would allow much coordination with other federal agencies and a comfortable place to live, but almost no opportunity to align government programs with local needs or sensibilities.[9] Two years later the CCI was moved a little closer to its erstwhile clients, to the mestizo community of Mezquitic, Jalisco. The move was temporary, however, because in short order INI officials deemed Mezquitic too inaccessible, and in 1966 it was moved to an office adjacent to the airport in Tepic, Nayarit, which allowed easy access to landing strips in the sierra as well as great ease in traveling to Mexico City. Officials could visit the sierra with some frequency but sleep in their own beds at night, leaving only a skeletal state presence across the region.[10]

The first major project, the Plan Lerma (named for the river system), began in June 1965. As a part of the project, Operación Huicot would target the Indians in the region, who had "remained at the margin of all human progress, and live at primitive levels," and whose lives were characterized by "marked backwardness and misery."[11] Operación Huicot was in part phrased as an intervention by a protectionist state in the conflict between hapless Indians and their cunning mestizo adversaries, who were exploiting the Indian's naïve ideas about land tenure to invade their lands.[12] But it was not enough to restore those lands, as they needed to be transformed, and worked with new techniques by people who had shed their antiquated (and often destructive) practices.[13] Land reform was thus accompanied by a host of educational and other social interventions, intended to produce literate, hygienic, healthy, and connected citizens, capable of making use of the variety of programs the Mexican government had to offer. They would vaccinate themselves and their cattle, use the judicial system to defend their property against mestizo invaders, take their artesanía to market on highways and in a fleet of aircraft, sow their fields with the latest techniques and the most profitable crops, learn how to use credit, manage their forests wisely, and send their children to school.[14]

Though transparently paternalistic, INI officials insisted that their efforts were also antiracist in nature, a true program of national incorporation. This, they believed, distinguished them from their colleagues north of the border, who had never really sought to include North American Indians in the national community. Mexicans did not measure blood quotients, or relegate Indians to reservations, but instead offered protocitizens the tools that would allow them to share the benefits of citizenship with their compatriots, many of whom were both indigenous in origin and fully Mexican in their sensibilities. In this context Huichol peyotism was simply not legible as a right in the way it was then being phrased by the NAC (religious, human, or otherwise), or something that might be experienced differentially within Mexico, acceptable for Indians but illicit for whites. Because Huichol mysticism was a form of difference that stood in the way of an urgently needed national project, one in which a backward Mexican peasantry would be transformed into modern workers, it was something best erased in the interests of progress.

Up to this time, when US officials and social scientists defended the legality of peyotism, their arguments invoked an Indian subject whose racial identity was absolute. The trenchant battles over harm or benefit focused on Indian bodies—subjects who because of their alterity posed almost no risk to white bodies, no risk of contamination. In part this was because of the hardened lines of racial distinction in the US, and in part because indigeneity and peyotism were spatially segregated from whiteness. Both phenomena played out on reservations, relegated to these spaces in part because state laws made it difficult to practice peyotism anywhere else, and federal law permitted peyotism in these spaces. Peyotism and indigenous mysticism in the US was an Indian thing, unmistakably.

In Mexico, by contrast, backwardness was a much larger problem, at least in the eyes of the modernizing elites who continued to hope that their country would one day escape its history of poverty, inequality, and political instability. Much of rural Mexico was primitive, poor, illiterate, uneducated, and dominated by the sorts of mystical thinking that urban elites disdained. Far from being limited phenomena tied to a group with no chance of ever being considered part of a white America, in Mexico peyotism spoke to the larger and endemic problem of rural backwardness. Revolutionary nationalism, which held that Mexico was a mestizo nation (that is, partly indigenous), and that all Mexicans could enjoy the benefits of citizenship if they simply adopted the habits of the modern, mestizo subject, was incompatible with a claim to immutable difference. It was thus inconceivable to these modernizers that peyotism be framed as a right. They had no interest in a long tradition in which peyote had been both everyday medicine and sacred (the two being indistinguishable), a core element of a millennia-old cosmology that Europeans had been attempting to eradicate without success since the sixteenth century.

Peyote was so obviously associated with mysticism—itself a threat to the project of modernity—that it merited scant attention. This was, after all, an authoritarian project of modernization, one in which access to the public sphere was limited to those who professed loyalty to the state and its commitment to progress. Indigenous Mexicans, inasmuch as they had any opportunity for voice, were forced to align themselves to developmentalist goals.[15] Moreover, it was not simply indigenous Mexicans who were expected to fall into line. Those curious outsiders who traipsed through the Sierra Huichola, studying and sometimes celebrating Huichol peyotism, were objects of great distrust, their fascination with indigenous customs seen as a curious indicator of just how foreign they were. When, like Juan Negrín, they decided to remain in the region and set up programs centered on economic development and the defense of indigenous customs outside the purview of the INI, they were treated as enemies of the Mexican state. Negrín and other "foreigners" faced constant surveillance and harassment from INI officials, who jealously guarded their own prerogatives in the sierra.[16]

. . .

Development would eradicate all aspects of the Huichol world that could not be aligned to modernity, leaving intact only those practices that gave Huichol ethnicity a feeling of nonthreatening, quaint rusticity (like artesanía).[17] Nurses and doctors working in Operación Huicot and later projects were instructed to supplant traditional medical practices with modern ones, with the tacit assumption that inasmuch as peyotism was linked to witchcraft and curanderos, it too would wither away as the Huichols discovered the power of modern medicines and shed their mysticism.[18] The thought that peyote might be an efficacious medicine in the treatment of some ailments (from rheumatism to illnesses of the soul) never crossed the minds of most of these missionaries of progress.

Their inability even to imagine peyote as medicine spoke to the cognitive failures that lay at the heart of the attempt to instill modern medicine in the sierra. Health officials misread peyote use as a simple primitive holdover, failed to win converts to their way to treating illness, and then blamed the victims. Framing their task as the challenge of introducing "modern medicine into the mentality of the Cora-Huichol population," they concluded that the Huichols were unable to trust people of a "different culture" and unwilling to seek out medical help because of "the profound mental maladjustments that the indigenous patient suffers when he is brought to a strange and unknown environment, as he is in a contemporary hospital." They lamented that they could not fight even relatively treatable illnesses like malaria because it was almost impossible convince sick people to take pills or injections, let alone go to the city for treatment. Children also suffered malnutrition, vitamin deficiencies, and other illnesses at elevated rates because the local population simply refused to cooperate. They would not send their children to the city for treatment. Because of this, "there are numerous groups of silent, unhappy, and malnourished children who live in the canyons, along the banks of rivers, and in the valleys and mountains."[19]

More generally, health officials lamented the existence of "a magic medicine that the indigenous population uses to explain the etiology of diseases and their cures." These forms of traditional medicine, while perhaps useful for certain "psychosomatic" illnesses (and here, once again, the Western body), were useless against even basic infections and needed to be "eradicated." The Indians needed to be incorporated into "our system of life," to abandon a "magical-religious nexus" that was impenetrable to outsiders.[20]

It is little wonder that Ministry of Health workers with scant experience in the sierra placed the blame for their failures on the Huichols. Aside from making good sense from a bureaucratic point of view, blaming the Indians allowed these representatives of the modernizing state—like the missionaries before them—to avoid looking too closely at their own mistakes. Their programs were important, their interventions in the lives of poor, backwards campesinos urgent, their frustration at how their work was received palpable. And that frustration would only grow worse after 1970, when the Plan Lerma then gave way to the Plan Huicot.

The early 1970s saw a major increase in government spending in Mexico, much of it designed to reestablish a social pact between the PRI and the rural poor that had been jeopardized by the economic, social, and political crises of the late 1960s. In the Sierra Huichola the infusion of resources came in the form of the Plan Huicot, which promised investments of over $201 million in the region from eleven federal agencies.[21] The initiative was focused on raising incomes and standards of living and building infrastructure (roads, electricity, clinics, schools, water). In its first five years, the plan built 170 kilometers of roads, thirty-two health centers, twenty-two residential schools, seventy classrooms, twenty-three airstrips, eight cooperative stores, and sixteen CONASUPO stores. Federal agencies also extended telephone service to parts of the region, distributed radios, built irrigation networks and bridges, and electrified thirty villages.[22] BANRURAL (the Rural Bank) authorized agricultural credit for Huichol communities, but on condition that their parcels be subdivided and demarcated by barbed wire.[23]

All this spending did have some significant short-term results. The region seemed physically transformed, and health and education officials reported early and immediate increases in local participation in their programs.[24] Heady numbers in the schools (reported attendance that year approached two thousand students) so pleased the wife of President Echeverría that on the Day of the Child in 1971 she sent the students a half ton of sweets as a reward.[25] It was a fitting gift, oddly symbolic of the entire project of development in the sierra. Official statistics offered an impressive vision of a region forcibly transformed from the outside, and supporters insisted that this was the only way to improve a region so profoundly characterized by backwardness; but like the cavities invariably caused by a half ton of sweets, failure lurked everywhere just below the surface.

Hatched with the specific mandate that it avoid becoming an unwieldy bureaucracy,[26] the Plan Huicot rapidly became a bureaucratic nightmare, characterized by paternalism, theft, and limited community participation. Every time new projects were undertaken, earlier ones were left in states of disrepair. The situation grew increasingly dire once the Plan Huicot was shelved at the end of the Echeverría *sexenio*. By the end of the decade the sierra was littered with the detritus of failed development programs. Schools built by the government were largely abandoned. The diesel engines installed to generate electricity were generally out of service. The radios and other equipment were either in a state of disrepair or had been taken away. The few tractors remaining in the region were more than ten years old, in terrible condition, and unsuitable for agricultural use.[27] Had there been functioning radios, jeeps, pumps, and other equipment remaining in these communities, it would not have helped, because there was no fuel or electricity to run them. The radio network established to communicate among communities was for the most part off the air.[28] Roads built in the region were in disrepair or half-complete.[29] Federal programs in the region lacked the personnel to carry out basic tasks. The Ministry of Health clinics were abandoned.[30]

Worse still, even as most of the region remained incommunicado except by air, in the early 1980s the INI lost use of its airplane due to budget cuts.[31] INI officials watched helplessly as state officials in Nayarit facilitated mestizo invasions of Huichol land, and CONASUPO, Tabamex, and Imecafe pursued policies that made it virtually impossible for campesinos in the region to survive without taking on unpayable debts.[32] The rural banks in turn would not let small growers sell their harvest if they had not paid their debts, while offering little technical assistance to deal with irrigation problems, pestilence, and other challenges.[33]

By 1983 the CCI was again on the move, largely because it had little contact with actual Huichols. At this point the entire Mexican state was in a fiscal crisis. With no funds for hiring aircraft, anything moving into or out of the sierra had to go by ground, on often impassible roads. In what today seems like an almost tragic irony, the *nueva política Indigenista* (new Indigenist politics) embraced by the INI during these years called for agency staff to remain in indigenous communities to get to know community members at least in part because officials could no longer fly into and out of the sierra with relative ease. But the INI lacked the funds to build the necessary housing. For a good part of the rest of the decade, much of the sierra was virtually inaccessible.[34]

. . .

In retrospect, the INI's modernization project seems like a farce. As has often been the case in Mexico, the agencies that pursued a development agenda in the sierra from the 1960s through the 1980s did little more than serve the interests of their employees. This practice grew worse when INI budgets were flush during the 1970s and became catastrophic after the economic collapse in 1982. Even more grim is the fact that all along the erstwhile clients of the developmentalist state actively communicated their unease with the project and its personnel.[35]

In some sense these complaints spoke to the ways that the philosophies behind the development projects did not align well with the attitudes of residents of the sierra. Many Huichols seem to have been perfectly happy to engage in modern technologies, to fly in airplanes, and to use medicines and communications technologies, but they often insisted that these new technologies be adopted in ways that did not violate deeply held notions of the sacred. For instance, while federal officials tended to treat maize simply as a commodity, in the sierra it was sacred, the source of life, and needed to be treated as such by engaging in long-standing rituals around its planting, harvest, storage, and consumption. New machines needed to be purified and blessed before being used. And some were unwelcome in the sierra. Generators, for instance, were a constant source of noise, disturbing the soundscapes of the communities where they were installed, and sometimes of only marginal value, given the relatively few uses they had in the region.[36]

That said, federal and state officials often failed at even more mundane tasks. Parents complained about teachers who lacked a vocation, who could not even fill out their own paperwork, who lacked a "sense of responsibility."[37] They criticized teachers for repeated, sometimes chronic absences from their schools,[38] or for allowing their buildings to fall into dangerous states of disrepair, their patios filled with rubbish, their classrooms unfit for students. Teachers were likewise faulted for providing inadequate nutrition to their students, in some cases forcing students in hostel schools (*albergues*) to return home in order to eat.[39] Those same schools were often filled with mestizo students, much to the alleged detriment of Huichol children.[40]

Teachers, doctors, nurses, and other personnel were faulted for treating their erstwhile clients in a deeply disrespectful manner, for violating local norms, and engaging in egregious conduct. Well into the 1980s personnel evaluations at the INI centros in the region often found employees who lacked both an understanding of the programs they were meant to implement and an interest in doing the work. Meanwhile, community leaders often accused government agents of self-dealing, appropriating Huichol lands, forests, and other resources and doling them out to their friends, often at great environmental cost.[41]

This profound disconnect between government officials and their erstwhile clients in the sierra was shockingly evident in November 1983, when Raymundo Maldonado Plato, a zoologist at the CCI-Huichol, caused an uproar in Tuxpan. Maldonado Plato, who already had a reputation for treating community members poorly, began to openly pursue an affair with a teacher named Lorenza Hernández Sánchez. On several occasions, he arrived at the *escuela albergue* in Tuxpan in the middle of the night, drunk, in a car belonging to the CCI, and demanded to know where he could find Hernández Sánchez, who did not reciprocate his ardor. When rebuffed, he tried to force his way into the building. Residents of the town were furious, prompting the director of the school, Jesús Carillo Hernández, to plead with the director of the

CCI-Huichol, Maximo Gonzalez Salvador, to remove Maldonado from his post. "We don't want to contribute to a tragedy," Carrillo wrote.[42]

Maldonado may simply have been a bad actor, but his particularly odious behavior in the community—his rudeness, drunkenness, and his open and violent pursuit of a sexual relationship with the teacher despite her refusals—was more likely to be tolerated in Tuxpan than it would have been in Guadalajara or Mexico City. Life in Tuxpan was life on the margins, where the rules of social comportment need not apply. Not only were there few actual threats of accountability here—Maldonado was removed, but misappropriation of funds and authoritarian, disrespectful behavior was commonplace—these were Indians, people who did not count. They were backward, primitive. They disgusted people like Maldonado, who played out his revulsion by treating his time in the community as a "state of exception."[43] At the same time, the ways that other INI officials responded to this crisis (their disdain of his behavior and their fear that he was going to wind up dead) spoke to two other issues: the first being their awareness that his conduct threatened their work in the sierra, and the second being a fear that the people they were dealing with were predisposed to resolve their problems with violence. This leaves us with two images of the Huichol. In the former the Huichol is invisible to the modernizing state. In the latter the Huichol becomes visible through violence (a third image, rooted in the embrace of cultural pluralism, is discussed in chapter 11).

The invisible Huichol was ultimately a passive subject, incapable of helping him/herself and given to dependence on government largesse.[44] Federal officials working in the Plan Huicot continually complained that community members let government officials do all the work in the program, rarely lending a hand in programs that existed for their benefit (except, one supposes, the manual labor, which was exclusively done by Huichols).[45] Even equipment breakdowns were blamed on the Huichols, who supposedly lacked the capacity to care for the tractors, radios, motors, and other materials donated to their communities. Rather than learning how to care for these things, they simply expected this work would be done by the state.[46]

Faulting the program for creating "a mentality of dependence,"[47] a 1979 report by Arturo Toriz y Álvarez noted, among other things, that the good work of the Plan Huicot was undone by paternalism, which limited the participation of the community and in turn could be blamed for the lack of support for its projects once it ended.[48] Paternalism here could be read as an authoritarian project, planned with little consideration of the actual desires and needs of its erstwhile beneficiaries, but in Toriz y Álvarez's rendering, the problem was not that projects were poorly planned and coordinated, but that they did not engender a can-do attitude among the Huichols. Similar things could be said of those who sought to attribute the failure of the modernization in the sierra to the profound cultural difference between the Huichols and their bene-factors.[49] Whatever the reason, it spoke to a recalcitrant Indian who had failed to embrace the opportunities offered by the Mexican state.

. . .

The tensions in these explanations (do we blame a lack of fuel or Huichol alterity for development's failures?) indicate something of the Kafkaesque quality of the dilemmas faced by the Huichols living under the Plans Lerma and Huicot. Government officials knew early on about the problems—about poor behavior, corruption, bureaucratism, and poor planning. Yet somehow it was still the fault of the Huichols that they had failed. All the potential explanations—that they were resistant, that they could not comprehend those who were trying to help them, that they were given to violence, and that they were passively depend-ent—evoked long-standing tropes of indigeneity in Mexico—tropes that remind us that most of these federal officials saw the people they were working with, first and foremost, as Indians. As Indians they could never really be counted upon to be participants in their own salvation.

For most of these officials, Huichol peyotism simply reinforced their views of the Huichols as subjects living outside time. The language they used to describe Huichol rites was in some sense not that different from the language deployed by turn-of-the-century researchers at the IMN, or even Inquisitional judges centuries before. Peyotism was vice, intoxi-cation, a sign that these people remained trapped by forms of mystical thinking that impeded their ability to embrace what was good for them. Dug up out of the ground, covered in dirt and unclean, the peyote itself was a symbol of what had to be left behind if the Huichols were to share in the benefits of the modern world. There was no need to study it, no need to understand how it fit into their medical and religious lives. It was, like them, disgusting.

There were those in the INI who pushed back against this view. As we will see in chapter 11, in the early 1970s a growing chorus of INI anthropologists began to reconsider peyote's place in the lives of the Huichols and increasingly came to favor the idea that the Huichols deserved a right to cultural self-determination, but the ascendance of that faction of intellectuals was both slow and uneven. To this day an urgent focus on economic development, a tendency toward bureaucratism and rampant self-interest, and a deeply paternalistic attitude toward marginalized peoples remain the hallmarks of the Mexican government's policies toward poor and marginalized peoples. Raymundo Maldonado Plato was not the first federal official to think that he could act out his fantasies with impunity in an indigenous community, and he would be far from the last.

CHAPTER NINE

1964

Bona Fide

There is no particular variation in the effect of the drug on Indians and white people. If peyote is good for the Indians, it is good for the white people: if it is bad for the Indians, it is bad for the whites. It is a drug with definite physiological action, which, under similar conditions, is no respecter of persons or races.

—Peyote: An Abridged Compilation, 1922[1]

On 24 August 1964 the California Supreme Court handed down two landmark rulings on peyote. In the more famous case, *People v. Woody*,[2] the court ruled six to one in favor of Jack Woody, Leon Anderson, and Dan Dee Nez, three Navajos who had been arrested on 28 April 1962 while taking part in a peyote ceremony in the desert near Needles, California. Woody and his companions faced arrest if they conducted their ceremonies on the Navajo Reservation, but peyote was also prohibited under California's Health and Safety Code.[3] At the time the cactus was illegal in more than a dozen states, leaving the 225,000 members of the Native American Church (NAC) at risk of arrest for practicing their religion.[4]

Woody may in fact have been hoping for a confrontation that would allow him to challenge California's peyote ban in court. When the police entered the hogan where he and his compatriots were holding their ceremony, Woody immediately presented the arresting officers with a "gold-colored portrait frame containing a photostatic copy of the articles of incorporation of the Native American Church of the State of California," signaling that he was a part of a movement within the NAC that sought to challenge state laws prohibiting peyote (n.b., the

California church was affiliated with Native American Church of North America, which served as an umbrella organization for state level churches. In the following pages, NAC refers to the umbrella organization and its affiliates). By the late 1950s peyotists and their allies across the US West were increasingly willing to risk arrest in the hope that these prohibitions would be ruled unconstitutional, and up to this point they had already seen some significant victories. In 1954 state prosecutors in Texas declined to prosecute Claudio Cardenas, who had been charged with shipping peyote out of state to church members.[5] Rulings in Montana (1957) and New Mexico (1959) had eased the restrictions faced by peyotists in those states. In July 1960 a state judge in Arizona ruled that the state law outlawing peyote use by Indians off the reservation was unconstitutional (peyote remained illegal on the Navajo Reservation itself until 1966).[6]

The latter was a major victory for Navajo peyotists, who had been fighting the Arizona ban in court for years, but it was also part of a judicial process that would increasingly codify licit peyote use as exclusively belonging to the indigenous realm. While the NAC had for a long time been a rather fluid association, with a certain amount of diversity in both its practices and the criteria used by different chapters for membership (into the 1960s some refused admission to non-Indians, whereas others were openly "all-race"),[7] the legal victories won by members of the NAC tended to produce a judicial understanding of peyotism that flattened out this diversity. Typical of these cases, Judge Yale McFate's ruling in Arizona rehearsed a series of claims about peyote that would over time come to be accepted as truths within the US courts. One of those claims, which cropped up in this and other cases challenging the Navajo ban, was that "from time immemorial, the church and its predecessors have used the vegetable substance, in connection with and as a part of its religious ceremonies."[8] McFate accepted this claim and ruled in defendant Mary Attakai's favor because this was an ancient, bona fide religious practice, and "there is no significant use of peyote by persons other than Indians who practice peyotism in connection with their religion."[9] The logic was obvious: Peyotism was an Indian religion, and as such, the critical measure of its authenticity was that the practitioner was Indian.

These dubious claims were very much on display in *People v. Woody*. The judges in Woody did not strike down the law prohibiting peyote. What they did instead was conclude that based on evidence provided by the defense, the ways that peyote was used within the NAC did not constitute a threat to public health. Dismissing the claims by prosecutors that it was dangerous because it was used by small children and as a substitute for real medicine, and that there was a "possible correlation between the use of this drug and the possible propensity to use some other more harmful drug," the judges concluded that in the case of NAC members, there was no evidence that peyote was addictive or had caused any harm. Indeed, they concluded both that "the moral standards of members of the Native American Church [are] higher than those of Indians outside the church," and that "to forbid the use of peyote is to remove the theological heart of peyotism." Collectively these conclusions opened a very limited space for peyotism to be exempt from state laws banning narcotics. Peyote, an otherwise dangerous substance, could be licit if it met two conditions: It had to be used in ways that did not cause harm, and It had to be central to the religious beliefs of a community.

In some sense this logic represented a victory for those scientific authorities who had for decades been arguing that much of the hysteria surrounding peyote was misguided, but it was a very limited victory. Though they took evidence about the use of peyote in a specific setting into account, the judges in *Woody* did not dismiss the state's claim that peyote was a dangerous narcotic. They merely found that the way members of the NAC used the drug did not pose enough risk to create a "compelling state interest" that could justify laws that violated their right to the free exercise of their religion. As such they left open the possibility that this exemption might not apply to non-Indians, an opening that would prove critical at a time when the use of peyote and other psychedelics by non-Indians was rapidly expanding.

We could read this as the judicial branch adopting a constructivist approach to understanding drug intoxication. In looking closely at set and setting, history, and the specific rituals around peyote consumption, the court, based on the scientific evidence, concluded that the dangers posed by peyote were nullified by the context in which the drug was consumed, and by the bona fide worship of peyote as a sacrament. It was left, then, for the courts to determine whether claims could be made in other cases, and what the criteria for measuring the bona fide worship of peyote use might be.

The logics the California court used in determining the bona fide nature of Woody's belief mirrored Judge McFate's reasoning from four years earlier. Woody's was a bona fide practice because it was undertaken within an organized and legally chartered church with specific traditions,[10] and because this was an ancient religion, said to date to the sixteenth century. Though he indicated that religious freedom was central to the ruling, Justice Tobriner wrote that he was also clearly influenced by the fact that it was an "ancient tradition" and that these were "Indians who honestly practiced an old religion in using peyote."

Moreover, in a specific rebuke to the police, the court also distinguished Woody, whose arrest took place in full view of his certificate of membership, in a hogan, and amid the paraphernalia of an NAC ceremony, from defendants whose use of peyote was not a part of a religious ceremony. "Law officers and courts should have no trouble distinguishing between church members who use peyote in good faith and those who take it just for the sensations it produces."[11]

. . .

This distinction was critical to the other case in which the court released a ruling on August 24. Twenty-eight-year-old Arthur Charles Grady, a self-professed peyote priest was arrested on 24 May 1962 in Palm Springs and charged with possession of peyote. A couple of weeks before the arrest, Palm Springs police officers discovered a "drug victim unconscious in the desert" and determined that the origin of the drugs was a house located in an isolated area on East Ramon Road belonging to Gerald Kelly. They set up surveillance of the house between 18 and 24 May, during which time they noticed a large number of parties. There were a number of cars and substantial activity around the house. On three occasions the officers observed someone go to a spot seventy feet from the house and dig in the sand. This was enough to obtain a search warrant on 24 May. When police entered the house, they confiscated a quantity of peyote in gelatin capsules, arrested six people, and remanded a sixteen-year-old girl who was sleeping in one of the bedrooms to juvenile services. They also found a sack buried in the yard that contained a substantial quantity of peyote buttons.[12]

The local papers had a field day with the story. On 28 May 1962, the *Desert Sun* splashed the case across its front page with the headline, "Rare Indian Drug Nabbed in Spa 'Party-House' Raid." Below the headline in big bold type was the hook, "Peyote Believed Cause of Orgy; Seven Jailed." In the article we learn that peyote is "an exotic Indian drug which Police Chief August G. Kettmann said was believed responsible for a series of sex orgies conducted in the home," a claim that seemed all the more sinister because it reported the presence of the sixteen-year-old girl as well as the fact that two of those arrested had recently been arrested for marijuana possession.[13]

All the adults in the house were convicted of possession of illegal narcotics, but Grady appealed his conviction based on the claim that he was a "peyote preacher" and "way shower." According to his claims before the court, "although petitioner did not share in the living expenses of the group, he selected their food, taught them deep-breathing exercises, how to pray, and in general how to love the Christian Life." He also provided and prepared the peyote they used, which he insisted "is a very spiritual plant because it gives you direct contact with God." As a peyote priest and leader of a spiritual group, he claimed that he deserved the same First Amendment rights as the Native American Church.

Though the court did not find that this was a bona fide claim, they did conclude that it had not been fully examined in the trial, and returned the case to the Superior Court of Riverside County for a finding of fact. The case was reopened in February 1965, after which the trail goes cold.[14] It is remotely possible that the court in Riverside found in Grady's favor, but given what happened in a series of other cases decided during the 1960s, in which courts in California and elsewhere ruled that drug-based religions did not generally enjoy the protection of the First Amendment, it seems likely that Grady's conviction was upheld.

Woody succeeded because of the institutionalized nature of the Native American Church and the integral role that peyote played in their rituals, which outweighed the state's right to pass antidrug legislation. Grady lacked the credentials he needed to make an equal claim. As his critics later noted, he was a self-styled preacher who had "devised his own religion, which includes deep breathing, prayer, peyote, and 'planes of consciousness.'" His group had no charter and no formal name, tradition, or structure. The presence of the teenage girl sleeping in a bedroom further undermined his claim, suggesting that his religion lacked "safeguards against the misuse of peyote" that the court assumed to be in place in the formal setting described in Woody.[15]

More than this, Grady committed the cardinal sin of mixing peyote use with the consumption of other drugs, most notably marijuana (though no marijuana was confiscated in the raid, the recent arrests of two members of the household on marijuana charges had a clear impact on the case). From the scant record that we have, Grady seems to speak to a pattern of peyote use that was more closely tied to a burgeoning drug culture than to the sorts of religious rites that Jack Woody had been participating in when he was arrested in Needles. Peyote circulated freely among a bohemian crowd during the 1960s, often purchased by mail from suppliers in south Texas and sold in coffee houses and on street corners in New York City, San Francisco, and elsewhere. Accounts of the wondrous effects of peyote could be found in settings as varied as the poetry of Alan Ginsberg and the work of Alice Marriot in the *New Yorker*.[16] These were the types of settings that the California Supreme Court invoked when it made a distinction between bona fide use and those who merely seek new "sensations." They were also spaces that bore little resemblance to NAC ceremonies both because of their location (urban, generally), and the absence of or marginal role played by actual indigenous people in the rituals.

. . .

Peyote began cropping up in the accounts of bohemian and avant-garde circles even in the 1910s, consumed in Greenwich Village and Parisian apartments and celebrated in the memoirs of writers as diverse as Antonin Artaud and Mabel Dodge Luhan,[17] but it was the growing use of psychedelics more generally that prompted a surge in peyote's popularity in the late 1950s and early 1960s.[18] Like LSD, psilocybin, and synthetic mescaline, peyote was largely unregulated, a product that could be bought perfectly legally in many states, and was so thoroughly associated with indigeneity that officials in those states where it was illegal were much more concerned with its impact on the reservations and largely oblivious to its spread among white, middle-class youths.

Spurred by the cactus's link to indigeneity, urban college students and beatniks took to peyote with great enthusiasm in the early 1960s. It was natural, from the earth, associated with a variety of symbols of indigeneity (the tipi, eagle feathers, rattles, drums), and provided these early warriors of the counterculture with both an interesting high and the opportunity to embrace an alternative form of spirituality. The new enthusiasts might not be members of the Native American Church, but they could claim certain self-actualized forms of spirituality, even that they had formed a new religion. During these years one could find an array of peyote and other drug-oriented "churches" in New York City, San Francisco, and elsewhere, offering a generation of generally well off but disaffected North Americans an alternative to the grinding alienation of middle-class life in Cold War America. Adding to its appeal, peyote was one of a handful of hallucinogens associated with sexual pleasure, advocated by Tim Leary as a source of sexual ecstasy that was otherwise unattainable and even explored in the pages of *Playboy* in 1967.[19]

Social conservatives took a dim view of these mostly young, largely white drug enthusiasts, and dismissed these phenomena as "the new

Bohemian life ... odorous saloons ... [filled with] misfit artists and writers who never write."[20] These were addicts, abusers, lives lost in drug-fueled hazes. Moreover, among the critics of the drug culture, abuse did not simply mean the consumption of a drug to the point of causing physical harm. It could also, argued Arnold Ludwig in an article in the *Journal of the American Medical Association* published in 1965, refer to "the self-administration of these substances by individuals who have procured or obtained them through illicit channels and/or taken them in medically unsupervised or socially unsanctioned settings."[21]

Ludwig's essay encapsulated the fundamental challenge faced by those who sought to create licit spaces for psychedelic use outside of the indigenous realm, whether for religious or medical purposes. Beyond their own challenges in demonstrating the efficacy of these drugs, advocates for their strict contextual use were hamstrung by the drugs' growing popularity as mechanisms for altering consciousness. Ludwig lamented that peyote was widely available for purchase on the streets of nearly every major US city and easily purchased through the mail from suppliers in Texas.[22] He described patterns of drug use where hallucinogens were mixed with other, more powerful drugs like heroin or morphine, to which users were addicted. Other users he described as "professional potheads." "'Creative' and 'arty' people, such as struggling actors, musicians, artists, writers, as well as the Greenwich Village type of 'beatnik,' tend to fall in this category."

Ludwig wrote scathingly about the parties held by psychedelic enthusiasts. "Overt sexual activities were carried out. Folk singing was also common." That said, he did concede that psychedelics were not sexual stimulants (aphrodisiacs) in the clinical sense, but instead substances that in most cases made "pleasures associated with the sexual act ... much more intense." Ludwig also conceded that users did not develop physical addictions to peyote. They did not, for instance, suffer withdrawal when they stopped taking the drug. Nonetheless, he suggested that hallucinogens might be "psychologically addicting." He also feared that these drugs caused individuals to act out "homosexual impulses" and to become withdrawn, paranoid, or depressed while under the influence. One patient described attempting to stab himself. Another believed he was invincible under the influence. Another tried to jump off a bridge (this on mescaline). Two patients reported near accidents while driving under the influence of hallucinogens.[23]

Published under the imprimatur of the American Medical Association, these allegations provided added ammunition to those who sought to limit the meaning of bona fide peyote use as articulated in the *Woody* decision. Though at the time there was no federal law restricting peyote, in states where prohibitions had been passed this would mean that legal use had to meet three thresholds: that it be part of a well organized religion with a clear institutional structure and history, that it include the worship of peyote as a god, and that it involve the exclusive use of peyote as a sacrament. The presence of other drugs, even in a NAC ceremony, invalidated any claim to bona fide belief.

Timothy Leary's December 1965 arrest at the US border with Mexico for smuggling marijuana into the US became an early and much-discussed test of these principles. Citing *Woody,* his lawyers claimed a religious exemption based on a bona fide belief (Leary claimed he "derived spiritual benefit" and achieved a "third level of consciousness" from marijuana and that he smoked it as a follower of the Hindu religion), but his appeal was denied.[24]

William Robert Bullard, a student at the University of North Carolina, suffered a similar fate.[25] Bullard, who was then twenty-five, was arrested in August 1964 in his Chapel Hill apartment in possession of 1.7 grams of marijuana and a dozen peyote buttons. At some point after his arrest he joined a group called the Neo-American Church, and in appealing his conviction he insisted that the use of peyote was necessary to the practice of his religion. Buttressed by his claim of church membership, the appeal identified Bullard as a "Peyotist with Buddhist leanings," and indicated that "peyote is most necessary and marijuana is most advisable in the practice of my church's beliefs." According to Bullard's brief, church meetings were marked by the sacramental use of peyote, which was the cornerstone of the religion. After taking it "the members pray, sing, and make ritual use of drum, fan, eagle bone, whistle, rattle, and prayer cigarette, the symbolic emblems of their faith. The central event, of course, consists of the use of peyote in quantities sufficient to produce a hallucinatory state. [P]eyote constitutes in itself an object of worship."

The court was unmoved. Bullard had made no claim to a religious exemption at the time of his arrest, so the presiding judge concluded that he had simply "invented" these claims to mount a defense.[26] Aside from this, the court found that

> even if he were sincere, the first amendment could not protect him. . . . The defendant may believe what he will as to peyote and marijuana and he may conceive that one is necessary and the other is advisable in connection with his religion. But it is not a violation of his constitutional rights to forbid him, in the guise of his religion, to possess a drug which will produce hallucinatory symp-

toms similar to those produced in cases of schizophrenia, dementia praecox, or paranoia, and his position cannot be sustained here in law nor in morals.[27]

The judge saw no contradiction of *Woody* in making this ruling. Based on court testimony, he concluded that, whereas the NAC worshipped peyote as a god, the Neo-American Church saw it as a means to an end (in this case, getting stoned).

. . .

In the time between Bullard's arrest and the denial of his appeal, peyote was outlawed by the US Congress. In 1965 a peyote prohibition was added to the Drug Abuse Control Amendments (the prohibition came into force in March 1966).[28] Four years later both peyote and mescaline were included as Schedule I drugs in the Controlled Substances Act (CSA), classifying them as drugs that had no legitimate therapeutic use and a high potential for abuse. Possession of either substance was now a federal crime and could result in a fifteen-year prison sentence and fines of up to $25,000.[29]

It almost goes without saying that the first federal bans owe a great deal more to a moral panic over peyote use by the likes of Timothy Leary, William Bullard, and Arthur Charles Grady than to concerns about the continued growth of the NAC.[30] The role of race in these prohibitions is nowhere better demonstrated than in the explicit decision of both Congress and later the DEA to exclude indigenous peyotists from the ban. Though the 1965 amendments did not specifically mention this exemption, advocates of the bill agreed to a regulatory exemption adopted by the department of Health, Education, and Welfare that would protect the religious use of peyote by the NAC.

During the subsequent decade only the NAC would prevail in court challenges over the peyote prohibition. Some petitioners failed because the courts found that their religious practices did not truly entail worshipping peyote as god (it was an instrument, not an end in and of itself). Some failed because their ceremonies used other drugs (typically marijuana) or a combination of drugs. Others that simply used peyote were denied because as non-Indians, the practitioners could not demonstrate that theirs was an indigenous tradition.[31] Federal officials often drew a stark line, insisting that if they countenanced any non-native use of peyote as a religious sacrament, they would open the floodgates to myriad spurious and drug-addled claims to religious exemptions.[32] This anxiety lay at the heart of what became the DEA's special exemption for peyote, which permitted "the nondrug use of peyote in bona fide religious ceremonies of the Native American Church, and [by] members of the Native American Church."[33] When used in the NAC, peyote was not a drug.

In hearings over the 1970 ban, Michael Sonnenreich, deputy chief counsel of the Bureau of Narcotics and Dangerous Drugs, made it clear that the agency viewed this exemption very narrowly. In his testimony he indicated that while he would grant permissions to the NAC, he would deny it to other churches. He reasoned that the NAC was "sui generis. The history and tradition of the church is such that there is no question but that they regard peyote as a deity as it were, and we will continue the exemption." No other body could reasonably claim traditions that merited the exemption. Moreover, in keeping with the approach the state of Texas had taken on this issue, the bureau also asserted that it would deny the exemption to members of the NAC who were less than 25 percent Indian by blood.[34]

In subsequent decades these provisions were repeatedly reaffirmed in federal laws, including the American Indian Religious Freedom Act (passed in 1978 and amended in 1994), and the Religious Freedom Restoration Act of 1993, both of which were intended to further protect the rights of indigenous peyotists (the latter in direct response to the US Supreme Court ruling in *Employment Division, Department Of Human Resources of Oregon v. Smith,* in which the court found that the state was entitled to deny unemployment benefits to two drug counselors who had been fired over participating in a NAC ceremony).[35] In due course Arizona, Colorado, Idaho, Iowa, Kansas, Minnesota, Nevada, New Mexico, Oklahoma, Oregon, South Dakota, Texas, Wisconsin, and Wyoming recognized limited exceptions to their drug laws for "bona fide religious use" of peyote. In Arizona, Colorado, Minnesota, Nevada, New Mexico, Oregon, and Utah, this generally applied to any bona fide religious organization, whereas in Idaho, Iowa, Kansas, Oklahoma, South Dakota, and Wisconsin, use of peyote was only protected within Native American Church ceremonies. In Kansas, Texas, and Wyoming one was also required to be a member of the NAC to enjoy the exemption, and in Idaho and Texas the requirement included a certain amount of Native American ancestry.

. . .

Peyote's new status as a Schedule I drug had immediate implications for the more ecumenical traditions within the NAC, decisively shifting the balance of power within the church away from those who favored a racially inclusive approach to peyotism. The small number of "all race" chapters were immediately shunned by the national organization and ultimately disbanded. Non-Indian members of the remaining chapters likewise found themselves in an untenable position and were either forced out or shifted to a more informal position. Non-Indians increasingly faced greater hostility in some settings, even non-Indians who had married into Indian communities.[36]

For the most part this practice was affirmed by federal and state court rulings in which peyote use by non-Indians was found be in violation of the law even when practiced under circumstances that mirrored practices within the NAC.[37] And yet the extrication of whiteness from the NAC was neither clean nor easy, as was demonstrated in the prosecution of Janice and Greg Whittingham in 1969 after a peyote ceremony in Coconino County, Arizona (it was held to celebrate their wedding).[38] Undercover agents from the Arizona Department of Public Safety raided the ceremony, and the Whittinghams and all those present were charged with violating Arizona's peyote ban. The Whittinghams claimed that this was a ceremony of the Native American Church and thus perfectly legal. According to the trial record, the Whittinghams were part of a group of over forty people, some Indian and some not. "Although neither Mr. nor Mrs. Whittingham appeared to be of Indian descent, Mrs. Whittingham testified, without rebuttal, that her grandfather was a full-blooded Blackfoot Indian."

Though initially convicted at trial, during the appeal the Whittinghams were able to challenge a number of the assumptions that had led to their conviction. First, though the prosecution had based the charges on the claim that because the Whittinghams were not Indian, they could not legitimately be members of the NAC, the appellate court rejected this assertion. The court instead found both that the ceremony met the standards of a typical NAC ceremony and that even though the NAC had "always been primarily an 'Indian religion,'" "membership to persons who are not members of Indian Tribes or do not have Indian heritage, is usually not refused." The judges further found that "defendants Whittingham were serious and sincere participants in what they considered to be a ceremony having religious significance."

Dismissing the prosecution's claims that peyote was a dangerous drug (the evidence introduced by the prosecution did not convince the judges), the appellate judges found both that the Whittingham's belief was bona fide and that "a substantial threat in the sacramental use of peyote has not been proven." "Most of the members who testified at trial, e.g., were active participants in the Native American Church and had been for years, in fact, in many instances, for decades." The ruling thus validated the claim that there was a long and continuing history of white participation in the NAC, a form of participation that was much more clearly framed as actual membership than observation or intervention by outsiders.[39]

Two decades later, Robert Lawrence Boyll adopted a similar defense strategy in a federal case. As a non-Indian member of the Native American Church, between 1981 and 1989 he had participated in peyote ceremonies every two to three weeks in Mill Valley, California, often sponsoring the meetings. He had been a drummer, a cedarman, and a fireman in the ceremonies, and had even been "explicitly recognized" as a member of the church by Rutherford Loneman, former vice-chairman of the Oklahoma branch of the NAC.

Boyll was arrested for possession with the intent to distribute on 10 May 1990 after mailing peyote from Mexico to his home in San Cristobal, New Mexico (he did this, he claimed, because he was concerned about the ecological decline of the peyote gardens of south Texas). Federal prosecutors claimed that Boyll, who was white, could not be a member of the Native American Church because "membership is limited to persons who [sic] ethnic descent is at least twenty-five percent derived from American Indian stock, and to the spouses of such persons." His actions had therefore been in clear violation of the CSA.

The judge in the case, Juan Guerrero Burciaga, dismissed this claim, agreeing with the defense that the government's position that only members of the NAC who were American Indians were entitled to an exemption from the Controlled Substances Act was "racially restrictive" and violated both the free exercise and equal protection clauses of the US Constitution.[40] He was particularly troubled by the question of whether or not the peyote exemption could apply to non-Indian members of the NAC, concluding that this rule in particular placed a "racial restriction on membership in the Native American Church." This was particularly odious given that "the history of the Native American Church attests to the fact that non-Indian worshipers have always been, and continue to be, active and sincere members of the Native American Church." He concluded the government's position represented a "fundamental misunderstanding of the history and present structure of the Native American Church."

. . .

The injustice of the case seemed obvious to Judge Guerrero, but not to others. As Robert Boyll was winning in New Mexico, the Peyote Way

Church of God was nearing the end of a long and ultimately losing legal battle across the Texas state line. No single entity fought more persistently in the years after the peyote ban to establish a legal basis for the bona fide use of peyote for non-Indians than the Peyote Way. A stand-alone peyotist church located on an old 160-acre homestead in the Aravaipa Valley in eastern Arizona, the church was the brainchild of Immanuel Trujillo, a former NAC member, beatnik, and friend to any number of the stars of the 1960s counterculture.[41] Trujillo's life history had an epic quality. Born in 1928 to a Mexican-born Apache veteran of World War I and a Jewish woman from New Jersey, he was adopted as a baby into an Irish family in Phillipsburg, New Jersey, and renamed Jimmy Coyle. He enlisted as a teenager in the Royal Marines to fight in the Second World War and returned home at the end of the conflict with a traumatic brain injury and PTSD. While searching for a way to ease his pain, he was introduced to peyotism by a medicine man named Apache Bill.

Trujillo joined the NAC in 1948 and became a roadman in 1962 but was never entirely comfortable within the NAC, where church leaders regularly discriminated against non-natives. Facing pressure to exclude whites after the passage of the peyote ban, Trujillo opted instead to quit the church in 1966 to set up his own all-race church at the Aravaipa homestead. Originally called the Church of the Holy Light, the church was a rather modest affair until the arrival of Anne Zapf and Matthew Kent in 1976. Matt and Anne, who came from the Philadelphia area, arrived at the ranch serendipitously and never left, having found in the "medicine" a powerful antidote to their own suffering.[42]

Over time Kent, Zapf, and Trujillo developed a doctrine for the Peyote Way.[43] They opted for a life of voluntary simplicity, in which they abstained from meat, alcohol, tobacco, junk food, and television. They embraced a form of environmentalist minimalism, eschewing most consumer goods. The church survived on donations and material gifts from their supporters (the greenhouse where they have been attempting to cultivate peyote for decades was donated by a wealthy financier), along with a mail-order pottery business.

The Peyote Way's religious doctrines draw from a variety of inspirations, including the Native American Church, Mormonism, and Christianity. In contrast to the NAC, in which a five-man team controls set and setting and guides participants through the experience, the Peyote Way embraces the individual experience (they argue that the power of the roadmen and others in the NAC is easily abused). Church members (a loose grouping that over time has included people from as far away as Russia and at least one NBA legend) visit for short periods to take part in their spirit walks (a practice Trujillo learned from Apache Bill), a ceremony that begins with a twenty-four-hour fast, which is followed by the consumption of a tea prepared by Anne. The spirit walk itself is a solitary all-night ritual in one of several specially prepared sites around the property, where participants will find a fire, a lawn chair in which to sit, a lean-to, and little else. Ideally, the quiet isolation of the night-time ceremony allows participants to more fully feel their connection to the planet and to all living things.

Trujillo, Kent, and Zapf have never had an easy time with the law. Trujillo was first arrested for peyote possession in Denver in 1966, but acquitted at trial (being one-half Indian and a member of the NAC, he had a clear-cut defense). He was next arrested in Globe, Arizona (the nearest town to the ranch), in 1987. In this incident Trujillo was pulled over driving forty-five miles per hour in a thirty-five-miles-per-hour zone. After noting that his driver's license gave his address as "Peyote Way Church of God," the arresting officer asked if he had any peyote in his possession. Trujillo thought he did not, but then remembered he had a little in the medicine pouch around his neck. He took it out, ate it, and was arrested on the spot, only to be acquitted at trial. Though in this case he could no longer make a defense based on his membership in the NAC, the jury nonetheless concluded that his peyotism was bona fide.

In 1980 Zapf, Kent, and Trujillo elected to take the battle over their religious rights to Texas, which remained their principal source for the peyote consumed at the church. By the 1980s the legal status of peyote there had settled into a somewhat uneasy arrangement in which a small number of licensed dealers provisioned members of the Native American Church under a Texas law that exempted NAC members (as long as they had 25 percent Indian ancestry) from the Texas laws outlawing peyote possession, distribution, and consumption.[44] On the ground, the peyote traders followed Texas regulations only loosely, and Texas officials intermittently detained or harassed nonnative peyotists.

In November 1980 Anne, Matt, and a companion traveled to Texas in a truck with large signs advertising the church, effectively challenging police to arrest them—which they did, in Richardson, Texas, on 11 November.[45] In their search of the vehicle, police found twelve peyote buttons and arrested Zapf and Kent. The case was ultimately thrown out because of police misconduct, but having failed to get a verdict that established their right to consume peyote, and having been denied an exemption by the DEA on 4 March 1982, the church (with Kent and Trujillo as plaintiffs) sued the US Attorney General and the Texas Attorney General for the right to possess peyote.[46] Peyote Way's challenge claimed that although they were not the NAC, they worshipped peyote as a deity in the same way that the NAC did, and that because the peyote they consumed grew only in Texas, that state's laws made it impossible for them to practice their bona fide religious belief. Their belief, which entailed an active commitment to healing alcoholics and drug addicts, was supported by a doctrine, a formal organizational structure, and, as of 1979, a charter as a church.[47] Moreover, they claimed that laws that allowed American Indians a right because of their racial ancestry but denied members of the Peyote Way that right violated the principle of equal protection before the law as well as their due process rights.[48]

In their responses, both the US and Texas attorneys dropped any claims that the Peyote Way was a cover for drug dealing (this was made in earlier briefs) and that that their belief was not bona fide. Instead, they relied on a very narrow reading of the history of US–American Indian relations to argue that the exemption for the NAC and Texas's 25 percent requirement did not amount to racial discrimination. They further argued that the state had a clear and compelling reason to include peyote as a Schedule I drug.[49]

The latter claim was often taken at face value in court rulings that concluded that since peyote was dangerous to the health, the government had a compelling interest in restricting its use.[50] As for the former, several different federal courts concluded that this was a political restriction, not a racial one, based on three factors. First, it applied only to members of federally recognized tribes. Second, those tribes had an ancient tradition of worshipping peyote (this fallacy, first asserted in *Woody,* was repeated in subsequent rulings).[51] Third, the traditional role that the state played as guardians of the Indian tribes (they were, literally, wards of the state, who would one day be liberated, at which time they would hopefully stop taking peyote) justified making a special exemption in these cases.[52]

Reading the NAC's own practices quite selectively, the courts concluded that only members of federally recognized tribes who were 25 percent Indian by blood (along with their wives, whether Indian or not) could be members of the NAC. To Trujillo's own claim that he had been a member of the NAC without ever being a member of a federally recognized tribe, the courts tweaked their logic without changing their position. Trujillo may have been a member, but that was before 1966. Now he could not be.[53] According the final 1991 ruling in the matter, "Trujillo's testimony does not establish that the NAC has admitted members who are not tribal Native Americans since the federal government outlawed peyote possession and promulgated the NAC exemption."[54] This particular ruling directly asserts the role the state was playing in making race through these laws, cleaving those peyotists who did not belong to federally recognized tribes off from the NAC, and ensuring that they did not enjoy legal protection for their religion.

The result was a legal morass. By the turn of the century appellate courts in Arizona, New Mexico, and Utah had established a protection for bona fide non-Indian peyotists while condemning racial restrictions,[55] while the federal government and the state of Texas pressed for ever-tighter racial restrictions. Federal courts also reached contradictory findings on the matter of membership, finding in *Boyll* that "the vast majority of Native American Church congregations ... maintain an 'open door' policy and does not exclude persons on the basis of their race,"[56] but finding in Peyote Way that "the record conclusively demonstrates that NAC membership is limited to Native American members of federally recognized tribes who have at least 25 percent Native American ancestry."[57] Testimony from leading members of the NAC, such as national chairman Emerson Jackson, muddied the waters further. Despite continued disagreement among chapters as to who could and could not belong, Jackson, who sought to discredit both the Peyote Way and other non-native peyotists, told federal officials that all official NAC chapters required their members to be at least 25 percent Indian blood.[58] Jackson and other high officials in the national-level NAC (the NAC-NA), such as Douglas Long, have argued that peyote is an Indian religion and whites should not be allowed to join or partake in the cactus.[59]

Rewriting their own histories, NAC petitions to the Supreme Court during the 2000s emphasized the exclusively indigenous nature of the church. Deploying a claim of insider versus outsider knowledge, several have argued that while whites might claim membership in the NAC, none had ever actually been insiders, authentic members of the church.[60] Though belied by a long history in which J. S. Slotkin, George Morgan, and others were broadly and openly accepted as members of the church (Slotkin was even elected an officer of the church in 1954), it plays well at a time when the politics of indigeneity call for rigorously policed boundaries between indigenous peoples and outsiders. It is also an argument that plays particularly well in an era of environmental crisis, when many fear that the peyote gardens of south Texas are increasingly under threat from climate change and overharvesting. If the gardens need protection, so the logic goes, peyote must be reserved exclusively for Indians.[61]

It goes without saying that the basic premise of the NAC claim about the vulnerability of the peyote gardens is uncontestable. Between active efforts to convert the desert soils in the region to other forms of agriculture and periodic overharvesting, the amount of peyote growing in south Texas (and the size of the peyote cacti collected) has diminished steadily in recent years. South of the border, Mexican peyotists similarly fear that their peyote ecosystems are under threat, in part from over-harvesting, but more immediately from proposed silver mines in the region known as Wirikuta (this will be discussed in chapter 11). The solution to these problems is not obvious. For the Peyote Way, it entails attempts to cultivate peyote in a complex of greenhouses, though they have found it extraordinarily difficult to create the optimal conditions for growing the cactus, which in any event takes more than twenty years to mature. Too much light and the cactus pencils—a process in which it grows vertically and does not develop the proper alkaloidal structure. Too much moisture and it rots. Matt and Annie have yet to find a way to address all of these challenges.[62]

Even this solution does not please everyone. Though some in the NAC are untroubled by the idea of cultivating peyote,[63] others claim that efforts to transplant and grow peyote in an artificial setting (the Peyote Way's greenhouses, for example) violate the sacredness of the cactus. This, indeed, was one of the bases upon which Victor Clyde of the NAC of Navajoland disavowed Leo Mercado, the Arizona peyotist who was arrested for peyote possession on several occasions in the late 1990s. Mercado was attempting to grow peyote (he had a collection of 11,300 plants), which Clyde insisted was too holy to be cultivated.[64]

Ultimately, then, those in the NAC who object to the cultivation of peyote must also insist that it is not simply the peyote but the peyote gardens as well that represent their sacred heritage. As a scarce and endangered resource, these gardens must then be protected, especially from those who cannot claim an ancient and ultimately racial connection to the cactus. Their insistence that non-Indians and nonmembers of the NAC be banned from the gardens and prohibited from consuming peyote does, on the one hand, represent what seems like a reasonable claim aimed at the preservation of an endangered sacred tradition. On the other hand, it has certain deeply troubling implications. Aside from denying the long history of nonnative enchantment with the cactus and asserting an ancient, pan-indigenous practice that is neither ancient nor pan-indigenous, it relies on a practice of marking space as racially exclusive in ways that resonate with the practices of those reactionaries who seek to demarcate and defend spaces associated with white supremacy. Even as we acknowledge the deep asymmetries between a NAC claim for an exclusive place for indigenous peyotism and conservative claims for safe spaces for white, wealthy men (privileged men who have mobilized with remarkable success the language of victimization and vulnerability), the symmetries in the language of a defensive form of racial exclusivity are troubling.

. . .

There is some irony in the fact that the NAC has increasingly taken over from the state in policing racial difference, even if now they do it in the interest of defending a scarce resource. More ironic perhaps is the fact that it is now the Peyote Way that occupies the liminal space, continuing to pursue what its members believe is a religious right in spite of laws that say otherwise. But the law has proven malleable for the Peyote Way. Though their lawsuits against the state of Texas and US government were dismissed, prosecutions against them have also failed. After two trials in which they were acquitted by juries, state prosecutors in Texas have left them alone. Every year they send reports to the US attorney general listing their inventory of peyote plants (Kemp claims they have somewhere between eight thousand and ten thousand), taunting federal officials with their flagrant violation of the law. They have not received a response in decades.

Currently Peyote Way enjoys an exemption for bona fide peyote use under state law in Arizona, Colorado, New Mexico, and Oregon.[65] Their land is exempted from local property taxes, and they have 501(c)(3) tax-exempt status. Still, they walk a fine line. Their church is sanctioned neither by Native peyotists nor by a state that continues to consider peyote a dangerous drug subject to a compelling state interest.

CHAPTER TEN

1971

Peyote Outlawed in Mexico

Its effects are destructive and terrible. It destroys the body
and soul with a crushing evil that leads the mind to darkness
and chaos.

—Dr. Antonio Prado Vértiz, 1971[1]

The police burst into Salvador Roquet's Clínica de Psicosíntesis just
before midnight on 21 November 1974. Twenty-three patients, along
with the doctors and staff, were arrested. Roquet, Pierre Louis Favreau,
and Rubén Ocaña Soler, who were not at the clinic that night, were
detained by police the following morning. Over the next several days,
while Roquet and his colleagues sat in jail, government experts were
called in to identify the drugs seized in the raid. They found peyote,
mushrooms, and ololiuqui, which they took to be clear evidence that
Roquet was administering dangerous drugs that possibly caused cerebral lesions. Worse still, they found records that proved that Roquet
was charging fees for these drugs (estimating that he had collected on
average five hundred pesos from over one thousand patients), which
made him a drug trafficker. If this were not enough, the raid yielded
several "pornographic" films, suggesting that Roquet was also guilty of
the crime of moral turpitude. According to the Procuraduría General de
la República's (PGR) press release announcing the arrest, he was a
"charlatan" and would face trafficking and morals charges.[2]

Roquet was in an difficult position. While the drugs used in his clinic
had been technically illegal since 1971 (designated as "without therapeutic value" in the sanitary code that year),[3] until that fateful night he
had been able to carry on his work with relatively little interference
from the authorities. In part this was because he had long cultivated

close ties with government officials.[4] More than this, he had won public acclaim for a therapeutic method that seemed to be unusually effective in treating a variety of afflictions. In his mind, the suggestion that he was somehow peddling dangerous drugs was ludicrous, defamatory.

Eight years earlier, when Roquet opened the clinic, the psychedelic drugs he used seemed miraculously powerful, potential antidotes to a wide array of illnesses. And Roquet had not gone the way of Timothy Leary or Richard Alpert. Remaining the committed doctor to the end, he had not embraced a larger consciousness-altering project. He instead administered these drugs in closely controlled clinical settings, generating a wealth of data to support his research. But his methods invited controversy. Informed by his own experience, Roquet was devoted to the terrified body, the body that had shed all its engrained defenses until it was capable of revealing its deeply buried truths. The experience was jarring, difficult, painful, and entailed a total loss of control. This, more than anything, was the problem, as was starkly revealed in an article published four days after his arrest in the magazine *Tiempo*.[5]

The address of the clinic, "Av. México, 199", was splayed in bright letters across the front page, and the cover pictured two hunched figures, a young man and a young blond woman, a huge syringe, an array of pills scattered around a desolate-looking room, which was splashed with blotches of red, black, and yellow.[6] In the article Ignacio Ramírez Belmont described his experience in a psychosynthesis session in lurid detail. He claimed he was enticed to visit the clinic by a girl he met in a bar, who told him that whatever his problems, the clinic would cure them. After paying two hundred pesos for a consultation and agreeing to pay a further seven hundred for therapy, he was told by Roquet that he had a variety of problems and would likely require eight to nine sessions. He was then asked for an autobiography, photos of family members and other mementos, and was told that he was not to drink alcohol for eight hours before his session.

His compatriots in the session included a lesbian who feared the damage she was doing to her child, a man who was searching for himself (as he had been doing during two years of sessions), a woman who had left her spouse, a man who was angry at his father, and a soldier. Some had been in treatment for as long as six years, and several told Ramírez it was helping them with their problems. One said it had helped him quit marijuana.

The session went according to script, except that Ramírez was so overwhelmed by the experience he panicked. He was shocked by the images—color transparencies of sexual acts, many of which appeared to depict adolescent boys and girls. There were also images of war, funerals, and student rebellions, but apparently 80 percent comprised naked men and women, followed by what he described as a fifteen-minute pornographic movie. He was then given his medication, which was identified as peyote. He tried to palm the pills but was forced to ingest them. He grew nauseous, then felt chills and sweaty palms. Things got worse when he was exposed to other stimuli, including flashing lights. He found himself screaming in terror and driven crazy by the syncopated music. He locked himself in the bathroom and tried to escape but was blocked by the bars on the window. "There are no words to transcribe what Bélamonth [his alter ego] felt in those moments; he suffered dizziness and syncopated sounds of music hammered inside his head. He could not stand it." By the time the session ended at 11 p.m. the next day, his distress over the experience was unshakable.

Ramírez's experience mystified Roquet, who told him that over eight years he had treated two thousand patients at the clinic and had never had one who acted this way. Of course, had he known the real purpose of Ramírez's visit at this point, he might have concluded that his terror was rooted in the surreptitious nature of his task. Ramírez falsified his biography during his intake and attempted to play a fictionalized role in the session. It seems likely that his panic was at least in part tied to the fact that he was unaware of peyote's power as a disinhibitor. Efforts to dissemble under these circumstances could easily have produced a terror that one's body would no longer participate in the conscious mind's efforts to conceal. This is one of the reasons psychosynthesis was preceded by cleansing rituals—the need to purify the body of alcohol, but also to confess one's sins before partaking. Absent these moments in which the participant surrendered to the truth, madness could follow.

. . .

Ramírez's account of his terror in the clinic offers an important reminder that Mexico's war on drugs was not simply a stage-managed affair prompted by US pressure on a society where drugs were produced but not consumed to any significant degree.[7] The growing incidence of drug use in Mexico during the late 1960s and early 1970s prompted a furious response from social conservatives and members of the health care community. References to Roquet's supposed use of pornography were enough to offend, but the claim that he was in fact peddling dangerous drugs transformed Roquet from visionary psychiatrist into pariah.

In the eight years that this transformation required, Mexico went through some very tumultuous times. Foreign hippies flooded the country in the late 1960s, drawing Mexican youths into the counterculture by the thousands.[8] Social conservatives responded to the *Jipitecas*[9] with disgust, viewing their *desmadre* as an existential threat to the modern, industrial, orderly postrevolutionary state and society their parents had worked so hard to create. And while the drug-taking, libertine youths who embraced the counterculture were nothing like the disciplined student activists who planned revolution during these years, older Mexicans often collapsed these different strains of youth protest into a single category: the out-of-control child.[10]

Drug use epitomized the problem. Even though a relatively small number of Mexicans were consuming illicit drugs during these years,[11] the headlines in national newspapers suggested that the country was beset by a crisis brought on by a "new plague" of drugs.[12] Typical of the genre, in April 1970 *El Universal* called parents to attention with the news that drug use had jumped 1300 percent between 1967 and 1969. If left unchecked, drugs would soon be consumed by 80 percent of students in the preparatory and secondary schools in the federal district.[13] A few months later *Novedades* reported that that for every 100 patients seen at the Hospital Siquiátrico Nacional, 1.3 "suffer severe brain damage" due to drug use.[14]

These fears lent particular urgency to the projects advocated by the early pioneers of the drug-counseling profession, who in their effort to garner support for new institutions to study and treat drug addiction made sweeping claims about how they were "safeguarding the moral and material interests of our society, as well as the preservation of our own species."[15] Between 1969 and 1971 the new addiction specialists (*toxicomania* became *farmacodependencia*) continually reminded Mexican parents that the drugs their children were taking could "modify the structure or function of a living organism"[16] or cause "changes in the genetic structures."[17] Mexicans were told that even if the youthful user escaped the genetic threat, they were still likely to become more neurotic while young and suffer from depression and schizophrenia as adults.[18] It was a terrifying prospect, the most intimate worlds of the Mexican family undone by these new threats. And drugs were not simply a physiological threat. They also deformed the values of their victims. Images of unruly young women in jeans and sandals and unscrupulous foreigners[19] spoke to the enormous threat of "moral contamination" and "corruption" that drugs posed for Mexican youths.[20]

Typical was Dr. Alfonso Quiroz Cuarón's 1969 description of one of his drug-addled patients.[21] The patient was eighteen years old but suffered deficiencies in memory and imagination and had the mental capacity of a thirteen-year-old. The young man had used drugs daily for three years, including peyote and mushrooms (he had made fifteen trips to Huautla).

> He loathes work. Rejects both money and thrift. He despises his father. Since childhood he has been afraid of the dark. He remembers with great pleasure the times his father would go on trips and he could sleep with his mother.[22]

Quiroz Cuarón viewed his (clearly oedipal) patient and thousands of others like him as the products of fractured families, of war, of automation. "Their drug use is both self-injury and a lateral aggression against those who marginalize them in the family, criticizing their hair, clothes, and language."[23] And while the parents were clearly to blame (divorce, neglect, poor morals, and their own substance abuse), youthful experimentation with drugs was a problem in and of itself. Early experiments with marijuana, peyote, and psilocybin mushrooms later turned into serious problems with LSD, cocaine, and other drugs. Middle-class youths felt "purified" by their drug use but were becoming stunted individuals.[24]

. . .

Peyote was the object of much of this anxiety. Much like the Indian, peyote was both "exotic" and "repugnant."[25] The very fact that some Mexican youths sought out its effect was a source of significant concern. Writing in *El Universal* in March 1969, the teacher and chemist Antonio Lara Barragan commented that "the statement that young drug addicts recently made before the Public Ministry, that they are looking for God through drugs, seems to me to be blasphemy." Going on, he wrote: "Drugs imprison the individuals who have experimented with them through a process of regression to the most basic and primitive stage of man." Drug users had embraced animism, witchcraft, and magic, the very phenomena that "populate the intimate universe of the savage." Their myths, demons, and gods, rooted in the "ignorance of the primitive," were what the hippies laughably imagined as "new horizons of the spirit." In reality, these youths were simply regressing to a demonic world—a primitive state. They were "beings degraded by the use and abuse of peyote . . . this cactus whose destructive properties on the brain have been known since the earliest times."[26]

Lara Barragan was of course wrong in claiming peyote "abuse," but that was not the point. The abuse claim situated peyote squarely within contemporary drug discourse (all drugs are dangerous because they are all abused) while also reminding readers of the threatening specter of indigeneity. Mexican youths were reverting to animal instincts and practicing an exalted sexuality (Huichols were falsely reputed to have orgies while under the influence of peyote) because they were unable to cope with their economic power. The return to indigeneity was "a protest against the abundance that prevents parents from sharing their lives; partaking of their joys, their sufferings and problems." Peyote, like other Indian drugs, was promoting "perversity, vice, and degeneration."[27] And even if it was transmitted through the hippies, the Indian was ultimately contaminating Mexican youths with these perverse forms of mysticism, causing "terrible spiritual damage."[28]

These images mapped remarkably well onto Mexico's dominant narratives of indigeneity. Since at least the colonial period religious and civil officials have identified peyote (like psilocybin mushrooms and ololiuqui) with a series of threatening iterations of indigenous subjectivity—in the first instance a threat posed by the devil, and with the advent of racial science the threat posed by degenerate and backward peoples—the disordered and undisciplined bodies of Indians under the influence invariably revealing the thinness of colonial (and then modern) authority over those bodies. Indians who, because of the diabolic root's power, refused to submit to the state's authority invariably represented a significant source of anxiety in a society that was both held together by the forceful discipline of an authoritarian state and had repeatedly descended into chaos at the hands of a racialized multitude.[29]

This was a double mapping, because the hippies relied on a series of similar images of the Indian as vehicles for their desires and aspirations. Their Indian was also primitive, backward, primordial, though for them this represented the possibility of escape from the alienation of modern life. For the moment, however, the terror that the establishment felt at seeing bodies beyond their control trumped hippie enchantment with the Indian. The country's drug-crazed youths were stunted, degraded, and depraved, a "generation in degeneration."[30] The body of the hippie was structurally weakened by the chemical composition of the drugs and vulnerable to the depredations of various sexual perversions, especially homosexuality. Bodies under the influence were said to panic, grow confused, and experience flashbacks, anxiety, and depression. If those bodies were youths, they might find it hard to concentrate in school, drop out, lose interest in life, and turn to "pseudo mystical ideas, regressive tendencies, and a nomadic and naturalist life."[31]

In need of compassion and tutelage, the drug user was an "other" in ways that were analogous to the Indian.[32] Huichols too were degenerate and needed both aid and compassion, in part because of inequality and poverty, but also because of forms of drug use they embraced from childhood, which produced dimwitted and irredeemable subjects.[33] The danger now was that a whole new generation of non-Indian bodies was regressing to a degenerated state, morally retrograde, and unfit for civilization.[34]

Antonio Prado Vértiz's March 1971 *Novedades* essay about peyote made the connection to indigeneity inescapable, describing the long history of indigenous use and the resulting "paranoia" that it produced among indigenous users. Indians foolishly believed that under the influence of peyote, "they speak with God, as equals." He then commented on the impact he saw on modern youth:

> The drug is unleashed on youths who, eager for unknown pleasures, [are drawn to] the sophistry of Huxley, who said that mescaline lets you view all kinds of internal or external phenomena, in time and space, as something infinite and eternal. Disoriented youths in Europe and America, made ill from their inheritance of wars and hatreds, receive it as a call to poetry, art and rebellion. Mescaline, or those cursed cactus buttons, is consumed in huge quantities in the most exclusive literary circles and in the most distinguished salons. . . .

> The drug, like all of them, becomes tyrannical. It dominates users to the point that, as Jacques Lebel says " . . . this drug is now as indispensable to me as is my body's respiratory system . . . ", this clearly indicating their dependence, like a miserable slave, yoked to the drug. Its effects are destructive and terrible. It destroys the body and soul with a crushing evil that leads the mind to darkness and chaos.[35]

. . .

Given these anxieties, it should be no surprise that abstinence was the animating ethos of Mexico's two most prominent public initiatives in addiction treatment during these years: Mexico's Centros de Integración Juvenil (Youth Integration Centers) founded under the direction of Ernesto Lammoglia, and the Centro Mexicano de Estudios en Farmacodependencia (Mexican Center for the Study of Drug Dependence, or CEMEF), which was founded under the leadership of Guido Belsasso in 1972.[36]

Roquet blamed Belsasso personally for his troubles, intimating that the latter was jealous of the rapid progress patients made at Roquet's clinic.[37] It is more likely, however, that a drug-centered approach to addiction simply offended the sensibilities of Lammoglia, Belsasso, and Ramón de la Fuente (then the most powerful figure in Mexico psychiatry, and another enemy of Roquet). These establishment figures embraced an addiction language in which the drug itself was the source of danger, and they defined addiction in ways that specifically made room for the inclusion of peyote. In their view addiction could be one of two things. It could be a physiological phenomenon, rooted either in a body's need for the substance to function "normally," or a body's ability to develop tolerance, thus requiring an ever-growing quantity of the drug.[38] Addiction could also be psychological, or "psychic," a rather mushy definition that classified need as a desire for the drug in which the craving was not expressed through bodily discomfort. Psychedelics did not create physical dependence, but the new addictions experts insisted that they created "psychic dependence" due the addicts' need for the "distortions in perception" that they produced.[39]

The CEMEF was instrumental in raising the alarm over psychedelics.[40] Chronic use, researchers at the CEMEF believed, produced a need for the drug that when unfulfilled resulted in psychotic states. One could observe profound effects in the victims of these drugs, individuals who "have dramatically changed their value systems," shifting from being useful citizens to embracing "passivity, mysticism, and fantasies."[41]

These themes come up again and again in the CEMEF's proclamations about the dangers of psychedelics. Psychedelics were of no medical use. They caused a variety of negative physical and mental states (nausea, vomiting, mystical-religious states, dissociation). The erratic conduct caused by these drugs had "on more than a few occasions driven youths to murder or suicide."[42] Mescaline was specifically held to produce psychic dependency, tolerance, psychosis, panic, and extreme emotions. Psilocybin was said to have similar effects, but was not known to produce psychosis. LSD was the worst, linked to all three effects, the inability to work or study, possible genetic damage, cerebral lesions, or damage to the central nervous system.[43]

These alarming reports suggested that hallucinogens were an integral part of a drug problem that constituted the "crisis of our time."[44] Reports from the CIJ and CEMEF painted a picture of a surge in drug addiction so severe that the addled children of the Mexican working and middle classes had nowhere to go for treatment. One story in *El Universal* in April 1976 claimed that there were between five hundred thousand and eight hundred thousand minors in the federal district alone who needed treatment for glue, marijuana, and other drugs.[45] Untethered to their traditional values, these youths were turning to crime, living promiscuously (even experimenting with homosexuality), and having children out of wedlock.[46]

. . .

If indeed eight hundred thousand youths in Mexico City were drug addicts, Mexicans had real reason to be alarmed, but the numbers don't quite add up. While some drugs seem to have grown steadily in popularity during the 1970s (cocaine and paint thinner, among them), illicit drug use in Mexico remained low compared to the US and Western Europe.[47] As of 1970 less than 10 percent of Mexican youths had tried marijuana, and less than 2 percent had tried LSD. In subsequent years arrests, overdoses, hospitalizations, and even casual use of most illicit drugs declined.[48] The use of psychedelics, and peyote in particular, declined to statistically insignificant levels.[49] A 1975 survey on drug use in the federal district estimated that less than 0.31 percent of the population had used peyote or mushrooms and found no regular users of these drugs. Not a single person in the survey admitted to being a user of LSD. More importantly, the respondents who indicated that they had used mushrooms and peyote tended to be older and were likely indigenous migrants to the city. Others who had tried these substances at one point but did not regularly consume them tended to be upper class and university educated.[50]

A close reading of these figures reveals a fragmented landscape of illicit drug use. Among middle-class youths drug use probably declined somewhat and consolidated around marijuana and alcohol. More powerful psychedelics fell out of favor, while cocaine use began to climb among the well-heeled, and the use of thinner and industrial cement seems to have spiked among poor urban residents living in the slums. Some of these drugs did represent public health crises, most particularly the expansion of glue and thinner sniffing among the poor (this crisis itself was left largely unaddressed because public health officials found it impossible to regulate the circulation of these legal construction materials in the self-built, continually expanding slums), while others, especially psychedelic use, remained so marginal as to be insignificant.

For reasons small and large, however, the public hysteria around claims to a massive growth in drug use captured none of the nuance of actual experience. Drug addiction led to permanent bodily impairment, and if it was easier to see in marginalized urban youths addled by paint thinner than peyote users (easier to see, in part, because the former were present in public spaces, while the latter were not), the damage to the latter was no less real. Collectively these drugs were signs of "moral decadence," evasion, and a "lack of intrinsic values," as well as a cause of social "disintegration."[51] And here Roquet's own methods did him no favors. The crazed, terrified patient that he saw as the starting point for an integrated subject came across in the press as a horrifying version of desmadre, a return to a primitive state that most found repugnant.[52]

This, then, was the challenge that confronted Roquet as he worked to keep his clinic afloat. He had long done everything he could to secure his future, maintaining close ties with friends in the government, especially the Secretaría de Salud Pública and Dirección de Seguridad (the secret police, or DFS). He invited psychiatrists from the National University to witness his sessions and hosted a parade of foreign dignitaries in the clinic.[53] He kept assiduous records, measuring as concretely as he could the progress of his patients through their treatments and codifying as much of that treatment as he could in order to give it the imprimatur of science.

Still, as he lamented in increasingly bitter terms to his friends and colleagues in the months leading up to his arrest, he knew he was in danger of losing everything. Behind closed doors his colleagues in the psychiatric profession were spreading rumors about the clinic. The arrest itself was preceded by negative reports that Roquet believed had been planted in the press, preparing the public for a smear campaign that would destroy his reputation and put him in Lecumberri Prison, stewing about the "defamation, calumny, and intrigue" that a corrupt Mexican psychiatric community had used to silence him.[54]

Among the most galling elements of his plight was the fact that all of this was happening despite his long service to the state, which did not end with his resignation from the Secretaría de Salud Pública in the mid-1960s. As Roquet and his supporters reminded the government, he had willingly offered his services to the state in the aftermath of the 1968 Tlatelolco massacre (in which Mexican security forces opened fire on a group of student protesters, killing between three hundred and four hundred), working with political prisoners to address the causes of their deviant behavior. In the hearing held in the Salon Verde to defend Roquet, Senator Aislic addressed the issue directly. Seamlessly linking the problem of the misguided hippie with the misguided revolutionary, he reported that after 1968 Roquet had treated several young revolutionary students—who had intended to blow up electrical towers—with psychotherapy and psychodisleptics, and that his treatments had cured

them of their subversive and antisocial behavior. These former revolutionaries were now committed to working for the betterment of Mexico
and to paying their taxes like everyone else. Having cured some of the
most recalcitrant radicals, Roquet was anything but a threat to the
established order.[55]

Far from it. Aislic's testimony obliquely referenced the fact that
Roquet actively supported the state in its efforts to fight both the counterculture and student revolutionaries. Beyond simply treating former
addicts and revolutionaries, Roquet kept tabs on his patients for members of the secret police,[56] and even went so far as to cooperate with the
DFS to elicit information from at least one political prisoner.[57] Decades
later that prisoner, Federico Emery Ulloa, recounted his encounters with
Roquet at Lecumberri prison in legal proceedings against Luis Echeverría. He claimed that, among other things, Roquet forced him to take
pills he identified as peyote and then aggressively interrogated him.
According to Emery Ulloa, Roquet warned his unwilling patient that he
should not resist the power of the peyote, because "you can wind up
crazy or dead." Roquet then showed him "pornographic videos,"
played Wagner at high volume, and repeatedly peppered him with questions about the names and whereabouts of Emery Ulloa's associates in
the student movement and about his contacts in other countries. According to Emery Ulloa, the experience had a lasting impact on him. He
reported that "this psychological torture produced intense depressions,
especially in moments of economic difficulties," and occasional homi-
cidal rages. Asked in 1985 if he still suffered the effects of these experiences, he replied that it all made him tense, but not tense enough to seek
help. "I've never seen a psychiatrist—well, besides Roquet."[58]

. . .

His clinic and reputation destroyed by his time in prison, Roquet was
quietly released from jail in April 1975. A further arrest in the US a year
later for LSD possession served as a final blow to the doctor's aspirations as a revolutionary psychiatrist. He decided to shift his psychosynthesis sessions to the Sierra Mazateca and the Sierra Huichola, where he
collaborated with Huichol and Mazatec shamans in group therapy sessions that for all intents and purposes were shamanic rituals. This was
not entirely a novel turn, as Roquet had been holding ceremonies in the
sierra since the late 1960s,[59] but henceforth these would be the only
contexts in which his patients would receive psychedelics. He no longer
administered the drugs and did not run the sessions. His role was largely

restricted to preparation and post-ceremony therapy sessions. Undertaken in this way, his sessions no longer drew the attention of his critics, because his psychiatric method was so shrouded in indigenous shamanism as to be virtually invisible to the state health agencies that had previously viewed his work with deep skepticism.

We see, then, something of the way in which the connection between indigeneity and the psychedelic experience was overdetermined in these moments. Both Roquet and his critics would link the use of psilocybin and peyote to a form of indigenous mysticism, with the former seeing in this practice a form of expertise that could lead the West out of a cultural morass, and the latter seeing it as just another sign of the backwardness of the Mexican Indian. The drug effects mattered, as they clearly produced bodies that did not quite conform to Western norms of discipline and sobriety, but far more significant was the way that these drugs and their traditional users could simultaneously enchant and disgust serious men in white lab coats.

Even with his detailed record keeping and careful experimentation with drug and dosage, Roquet struggled to demonstrate the efficacy of these drugs in ways that would be compelling to the state. In his case this problem was exacerbated by the fact that he tended to employ multiple drugs and drugs in their natural form (peyote, psilocybin mushrooms), which by their nature contained differing combinations and strengths of the alkaloidal compounds based on the age and point of collection of the plants. That is, the more Roquet embraced shamanic forms of plant knowledge, the less legible he could be to modern psychiatric and pharmaceutical regulatory agencies.

Modern pharmaceuticals relied on a medicalized body and repeatable effects. Psychedelics, which exploded the boundaries of the body and required the skills of an experienced curer to manage (not just the dose, but the entire period of involvement with the drug), simply did not fit the criteria that psychiatry demanded.[60] The fuzziness of the effect was fine for Indians. No, even better, in the minds of the burgeoning antidrug establishment, it was perfect for Indians, because it served to further reinforce the difference between the modern practice of medicine and primitive mysticism.

Roquet's decision to evade further arrest by limiting his psychedelic therapies to the indigenous sphere aligned nicely with his practice as a whole, which had never sought to create distance between the indigenous origins of these drugs and the drugs themselves. He was in this sense the latest in a long line of innovators who saw powerful cures residing in the worlds of his indigenous informants and sought to adopt the cure and not just the plant. When he tried to do this in the sanitized space of a Mexico City clinic, he inspired devotion in his acolytes and rage in his critics. It was either inspired, revolutionary, transformative, or disturbing, perverse, degenerate.

And then, when within a year of being released from jail, he was trekking off to Wirikuta and other sacred indigenous spaces with his patients, no one outside his small circle of admirers paid any attention. In part this was because the drugs were in their natural settings and somehow less jarring to those who had decried their presence in a Mexico City clinic. In part it was because Roquet himself gave up the claim to science when he passed the responsibility for the session to the shamans. Roquet and his patients were now merely fools traipsing through the countryside, easily ignored by serious men of science. And the drugs themselves made more sense as somehow tied to a mystical religious rite. Remote from the urban context of the drug wars, the non-native peyote enthusiasts who joined Roquet on pilgrimages to the sierra were simply a flakey residue of the 1960s, packaged into the form of the new age spiritualist.

CHAPTER ELEVEN

1972

The Exemption

*The manifest desire of some of these groups to remain
Indians is becoming more audible every day, and we must
create the theory and practice that will allow them to
preserve their own identity.*

—Gonzalo Aguirre Beltrán, 1969[1]

On 21 February 1971 the member states of the United Nations agreed
to the Vienna Convention on Psychotropic Drugs, which set out to
impede the flow of psychedelic drugs across international boundaries.
Signatories agreed to adopt the stringent approach to these drugs
already in place in the United States, where peyote and other psychedelic drugs were classified as Schedule I drugs. Under Schedule I peyote
was designated a drug of no therapeutic value, highly subject to abuse.

The agreement created two challenges for the Mexican state. The
first was one of taxonomy. Peyote was outlawed in reforms to the sanitary code in March 1971, but the ban classified peyote as an *estupifi-
cante* (a stupefying drug). The 1971 treaty required the Mexican government to reclassify peyote as a psychotropic drug, which in turn
required an entirely new set of initiatives in the Congress (the treaty was
ratified in 1972, and peyote reclassified in 1973), as well as a new classificatory language that linked peyote, mescaline, psilocybin mushrooms, and LSD in a category of drugs "of little or no therapeutic value,
which, because of their susceptibility to abuse, constitute a particularly
serious problem for public health."[2]

The second challenge was more vexing. The United States, a leading
proponent of the treaty, had already crafted drug-control laws that
made specific exemptions for peyote when consumed in the context of

indigenous rituals. There the rights of the NAC to practice peyotism were enshrined in state and federal laws and had been validated by court rulings in several states. This followed a larger trend in the Americas, where the language of indigenous rights was increasingly gaining traction in the political arena. Just two years earlier the International Labor Organization (ILO) had adopted Convention 169, which specifically enshrined an indigenous right to self-determination, and in the weeks leading up to the signing of the treaty attendees at the Symposium on Inter-Ethnic Conflict in South America signed the Declaration of Barbados, a manifesto calling for Indian liberation.[3] It only made sense, then, that signatories to the Vienna Convention agreed to make an exception for indigenous peyotists.[4]

As far as peyote was concerned, the wording of the exemption made a clear distinction between the derivative drug (mescaline), which would be fully covered by the Convention, and the plant from which that drug originated. According to Article 32.4, "a State on whose territory there are plants growing wild which contain psychotropic substances from among those in Schedule 1 and which are traditionally used by certain small, clearly determined groups in magical or religious rites, may, at the time of signature, ratification or accession, make reservations concerning these plants."[5] Peyote here gains a legitimacy as a right only if it grows wild (that is, uncultivated, collected by a people whose agriculture reveals their backwardness), is consumed by small groups that can be clearly distinguished from others, and in settings that demonstrated that these groups lived at the margins of the modern world. In these settings it could not really be construed as a drug, or even as a psychedelic. It was a sacrament worshipped by an otherworldly people.

The problem for Mexicans was that the exemption made little sense in a society where peyote was not merely a marker the backwardness of a small number of indigenous communities but stood in for much larger threats to the nation: both the possibility that Mexican youths would fall under its spell and the threat that Mexico's significant population of indigenous peoples might never be brought into the modern world, placing the very project of Mexican nationhood at risk. Moreover, there was little precedent in Mexico for claims that the state should respect the cultural or religious rights of indigenous peoples to practice their customs, especially when it came to something like a legal right to consume a dangerous drug. In a state that had long been committed to a series of modernizing projects in which the rights of indigenous peoples to remain indigenous had been inconceivable (and a state that earlier in the century had undertaken a scorched-earth war against organized religion), a formal indigenous right to peyotism did not make a great deal of sense.

Nothing like the NAC existed in Mexico, nor would such an evangelical movement with its clear links to narratives of personal recovery make sense in those communities where peyotism was practiced in Mexico. Even Fernando Benítez's version of the romantic, pastoral Huichol (this will be discussed in chapter 12) did not position peyotism as a right in a fashion that resonated with practices north of the border.[6] Mexico also lacked any legal basis for considering claims to rights based on indigeneity, having expunged all consideration of indigenous peoples as separate castes more than a century earlier, in the 1857 Constitution. Mexico's 1917 Constitution made room for claims based on class identities (peasants and workers), but did not allow for claims based on ethnic difference, and over the course of several decades of reform those who advocated for indigenous rights were marginalized or silenced within a state committed to an assimilationist modernizing project.[7] Moreover, the forms of judicial independence and federal-state differences that allowed claims for individual rights to succeed in the US did not exist in Mexico.

It should thus be unsurprising that when the Mexican Senate ratified the Vienna Convention in December 1972, it made no provision to exempt indigenous peyotists from Mexican sanitary and criminal law.[8] This placed indigenous peyotists in a significant bind. Though they might practice their rituals in the sierra with little interference from the state (there was virtually no police presence in their communities), Huichols faced threats of detention and confiscation both in Wirikuta and along their sacred pilgrimage. They were most vulnerable on their return home, when many pilgrims carried hundreds of peyote buttons. Passing through the numerous towns on their four-hundred-kilometer-route, they cut unmistakable figures in their ritual dress with their bundles of peyote. Unarmed and anything but threatening, they made easy targets for police agents looking for cheap victories in the war on drugs. In the years after the 1971 ban several hundred kilos of peyote were confiscated from individuals along the sacred route. The overwhelming majority of those arrested were Huichol pilgrims.[9]

These arrests generated significant criticism, some of it from unlikely sources. While otherwise deeply concerned about peyote use, Mexico's new addiction-treatment specialists generally argued that the police should leave the pilgrims alone. Distinguishing "ceremonial" use in Huichol communities from peyote use among non-Indians, Guido Belsasso and others repeatedly argued that indigenous drug users were of a different kind. Non-Indian bodies became intoxicated, degenerated, and were placed in physical danger by these drugs. In traditional settings, however, where peyote was integrated into long-standing practices and the truths it produced channeled through carefully stage-managed rituals, indigenous bodies were not placed at risk. The new drug-addiction specialists even argued that in these settings, peyote might have a therapeutic value that was not available to non-indigenous peyotists.[10]

This also spoke, though imperfectly, to the rural-urban divide. Peyote consumed by urban youth, in a context where dangers lay all around, represented something far more dangerous. The speed of urban life and the consciousness needed to navigate its physical dangers, along with the fact that urban youths lived in a world of strangers in which they were invariably confronted with the danger of physical aggression from others who were not similarly embedded in a religious ritual, only added to the dangers presented by peyote intoxication. In rural settings one might be in danger of falling off a cliff or stumbling on a rocky trail, but the social setting of peyote consumption and its attendant rituals mitigated risk to such an extent that peyotism could be safe.

That said, their willingness to tolerate indigenous peyote use was often informed by a darker view of indigenous peoples. Dr. Demetrio Mayoral Pardo of the CEMEF concluded that peyote use among Indians should be tolerated because groups like the Huichols were so locked in a static form of cultural backwardness that there was no point trying to change them. Others speculated that indigenous people were likely so chromosomally damaged by their drug usage that it made no sense to help them.[11] In a similar vein, at one point in 1973 Belsasso proposed that the CEMEF study ritual drug use among indigenous peoples to ascertain the long-term effects of drugs like peyote and marijuana. Others at the CEMEF (including Pedro Ojeda Paullada, who worked in the PGR) worried that such studies would draw the attention of the army or the federal police but agreed that indigenous peyotism and marijuana use offered an ideal means to study the long-term deleterious effects of marijuana and peyote.[12] In these discussions indigenous peyotists emerge as interesting test cases rather than as victims of drug abuse in need of help. The echoes of Tuskegee and the Guatemalan syphilis experiment are impossible to miss.[13]

. . .

Other efforts to protect Huichol peyotism were not so problematic. During the 1960s a growing number of anthropologists, most of them foreign, turned their attention to the Huichols, describing them in terms that were almost diametrically opposed to the negative renderings one sees in bureaucratic accounts of poverty and primitive recalcitrance in the sierra. For the most part the Mexican state was a shadowy presence in this new generation of ethnography. As a rule, foreign writers were not terribly interested in the modernizing project and sought as much as possible to describe a Huichol subject untainted by modernity. By contrast, for a generation of young Mexican anthropologists—especially those with appointments within the INI—the negative specter of the Mexican state increasingly hung heavily over their work. Not merely concerned with the evident failures of the modernization program, many younger researchers found themselves increasingly uneasy with what felt like a necrotic, self-dealing bureaucracy, which had long since abandoned the idealism of the 1930s for bureaucratic authoritarianism. Their unease grew stronger in the aftermath of the 1968 Tlatelolco massacre.

Punctuated by the 1970 publication of *De eso que llaman antropología mexicana* (which included contributions from Arturo Warman, Margarita Nolasco, Guillermo Bonfil Batalla, Mercedes Olivera, and Enrique Valencia), the new generation demanded reforms that would shake the INI out of its bureaucratic funk.[14] Though much of their critique of the agency centered on *caciquismo* and paternalism—on the ways that the INI had come to serve federal bureaucrats while doing little good in actual indigenous communities—their critique was also framed by a growing tendency to question the assimilationist policies of the state. Openly skeptical of nationalist claims that for decades had done little more than justify one-party rule, they insisted that Mexico was a plural nation, that indigenous peoples had an inherent right to self-determination, a right to practice their cultures unmolested by government agents, missionaries, and anthropologists, and a right to freedom from the condescension of Mexico City elites.[15] Inasmuch as colonialism in its various and persistent iterations had made it impossible for indigenous peoples to either enjoy their rights as citizens or protect their traditions, self-determination would give indigenous peoples the power to determine for themselves the extent to which they would participate in the national community, and the extent to which they would withdraw from that community and its system of laws in order to maintain their integrity as distinct peoples.[16]

These claims struck at the heart of the nationalist project in Mexico. It made sense to nationalists that, in a country long characterized by *mestizaje*, the state should work to liberate Indians from their traditions and provide them with the benefits of modern citizenship. Indeed, an earlier generation of Marxist social scientists, who were committed to the erasure of antiquated identities and the fomentation of class consciousness among a properly constituted peasantry, believed the defense of indigenous identities was retrograde, segregationist, even racist. These attitudes were deeply entrenched in the federal bureaucracy, and it would take nearly a decade for anything resembling an embrace of indigenous self-determination to gain any significant traction within the federal government.

In the meantime, the leading edge of Mexican scholarship on indigenous peoples began to shift. Salomón Nahmad Sittón's 1972 *El Peyote y los huicholes* was one of the first texts to openly propose a new direction in Indian policy.[17] Nahmad Sittón (who was director of the INI Coordinating Center in the sierra between 1967 and 1969 and later director of the INI) situated this short book as a celebration of the Huichols as a distinct people within Mexico. In a gesture that was rather unusual for the time, he made this case by drawing on the work of three foreign researchers (Peter Furst, Barbara Myerhoff, and Otto Klineberg). He began with the following words:

> Since the beginning of this century the Huichols, an indigenous group that maintains and preserves its traditions, cultural forms and social organization with singular purity have proven especially attractive to the field of ethnology. The Huichol has a deep pride for his own culture and fights against any intromission that tries to violate his traditional life.[18]

Nahmad Sittón described Huichol territory as a region of refuge, where the extremely high level of monolingualism signaled a culture that remained separated from others despite a generation of efforts to link them to the national community. This made the Huichols a minority culture, dominated and oppressed.[19] They resisted change. Even the Revolution had done little to change life in the region. As such, they were perfect expressions of the phenomena Gonzalo Aguirre Beltran described in his influential essay *La política indigenista en América Latina*. "The manifest desire of some of these groups to remain Indians is becoming more audible every day, and we must create the theory and practice that will allow them to preserve their own identity."[20]

El Peyote y los huicholes presents the Huichols as a mystical people, united in the worship of the holy trinity of maize, peyote, and deer. They are inhabitants of a sacred landscape that ranges from San Blas, Nayarit, through the sierra and to Wirikuta in San Luis Potosí. Their peyotism distinguishes them from other Mexicans, in part because the way they consume the cactus is profoundly distinct. According to Klineberg (who penned his essay in 1934), even the youngest Huichols have a high tolerance for peyote, and no one in the community faces adverse effects. (Klineberg theorizes that this is in part due to the fact that Huichols eat their peyote when it is fresh instead of after it has dried.)[21] Peyote use is thus safe for the Huichols because of the distinct nature of their practices, and not because the cactus itself is harmless.[22]

This distinction is critical. By the early 1970s social scientists could point to a wealth of evidence that peyote was not dangerous when used by indigenous actors. Repeated studies among the Navajos demonstrated that when used by NAC members in therapeutic and religious settings, peyote had a largely positive effect with no negative side effects.[23] Nahmad Sittón and his collaborators made different arguments based on their observations among the Huichols, in part because the therapeutic practices associated with Huichol peyotism were not easily distinguished from their larger cosmology. As for potential dangers, however, they forcefully argued that when consumed in this setting, peyote caused no ill effects. Still, in both cases the scholars making these arguments insisted that there was something particular to the indigenous context that made peyote safe to use. None of these researchers made the more expansive argument that peyote also posed no danger to non-Indians. Whether they did this because they did not want to run afoul of antidrug laws, or because their project was limited to a defense of indigenous peyotism, the indirect effect was to reinforce the view that peyote was in fact dangerous and that indigenous use of peyote was a sign of their immutable alterity. Either they were already so damaged by their peyote use that it did not matter that they were allowed to continue, or their culture so different as to be incommensurable with that of non-Indians. More troubling still was the implication that their bodies were so different from white bodies that a drug too dangerous for the latter was not dangerous for the former. Nowhere did they allow for a simple proposition: that peyote was not dangerous, especially in the hands of experienced users, regardless of their race.

. . .

Around this time, the term "Wixárika" increasingly supplanted the term "Huichol" in popular use. Wixárika is often used to refer both to the language spoken in the region and the community (El pueblo Wixárika). Mexico's Comisión Nacional para el Desarrollo de Pueblos

Indígenas (CDI, or National Commission for the Development of Indigenous Peoples, which is the successor to the INI) uses this and the term "Wixáritari" (technically the plural of Wixárika) somewhat interchangeably. In keeping with that shift, I use that term in the remainder of this chapter.

Indigenous self-determination posed a series of significant challenges for the Mexican state. Unlike in past eras, when modernizing elites imagined they were acting on an inert, largely silent subject (a subject to be transformed into a citizen, and who had to be taught what citizenship entailed), self-determination required an indigenous voice. It required a representative of the community who could articulate that community's demands, represent that community before the state, and provide a living exemplar of authentic tradition. This was a more complex task than at first it might seem. In Mexico, non-indigenous intermediaries have long sought to speak on behalf of or through supposedly indigenous voices to capture some of the resources doled out by the state, especially when either the corporate categories surrounding indigeneity or new initiatives targeting indigenous peoples have created opportunities for those who speak with an indigenous voice.[24] Self-determination enlarged these opportunities. Church officials funneled requests to repair their buildings through indigenous voices. State and local officials often sought out representatives of the Wixárika community as cover for their own demands. In once notable instance, a disgruntled former INI employee working in the Sierra Huichola even created a fake indigenous rebellion under the banner of the Grupo Guerillero "Manuel Lozada" to promote his personal agenda (which included a vendetta against the individuals who were responsible for his firing).[25]

This was not what federal officials had in mind when they embraced indigenous self-determination. For those committed to ending the authoritarianism in the INI, it was critical that the new networks they forged embody a democratic ethos, that they give voice to actual indigenous demands. And for the bosses in the PRI,[26] who viewed the INI as an instrument that they could use to maintain political quiescence in the countryside, imposters only made their work harder. For them, the new indigenista politics would be of value only if it helped them cultivate networks of indigenous power brokers, empowered by federal institutions, who would be granted to power to control the distribution of resources provided by the central state in return for the promise that they would *traer gente* (literally "carry people") for the one-party state.[27]

By the early 1980s the INI was funneling resources to a variety of PRI-affiliated political organizations in the sierra with this project in mind. This included the Consejo Supremo Huichol (CSH), and later the Unión de Comunidades Indígenas Huicholes de Jalisco (UCIHJ). Both were essentially founded by federal officials to cultivate local power brokers who could act as interlocutors between Wixárika communities and the state. As one of the principal channels through which the INI distributed funds for "cultural rescue," these organizations could symbolically fulfill the demand that the state respect an indigenous right to self-determination while using funds provided by that state to purchase loyalty.[28] Through these programs the INI, working with the CSH and UCIHJ, provided funds to help Wixárika pilgrims travel to Wirikuta and supported efforts to overcome obstacles erected by property owners, who built fences along the route and denied pilgrims the right to pass (some of these obstacles were bypassed by using automobiles to make the journey). Other funds were devoted to defending pilgrims from arbitrary arrest and confiscation of their peyote, which remained a source of constant concern through the 1980s.[29] Notwithstanding the good this did, these efforts were embedded within a larger project that was mainly characterized by new forms of caciquismo. Leaders used the patronage they received from the federal government to extend their authority locally, enriching themselves in the process.[30]

More than this, these organizations, along with the new bureaucracies created at the state level during these years, were grounded in a series of logics that played a significant role in determining the contours of *official* indigeneity in Mexico. Wixárika in this context came to be closely identified with cultural purity, with the idea that this was a community that had for centuries resisted any type of intervention from the outside and that was impenetrable to outsiders, who could not understand the inner logics of Wixárika identity and represented a threat to the Wixárika by their very presence in their communities. Peyotism, instead of being a sign of backwardness to be erased, was recast as a cosmology that could not be understood by outsiders. In this iteration of peyotism, those who stood at the intersection of outside and inside (members of Wixárika organizations and state officials who originated in the community) were the linchpins of communal survival.

This version of indigeneity erased a rather long history in which some outsiders had observed, participated in, and been welcome within Wixárika communities, replacing it with a purified version of the Wixárika in which the community would remain a mystery to all outsiders. This suited both government authorities, who could frame the peyote exemption in terms of Wixárika otherworldliness, and those who were empowered through the process to act as gate keepers. Working within the state, individuals like Francisco López (a Wixárika from San Andrés Cohamiata who became a director general of the Comisión Estatal Indígena in Guadalajara) used their newfound authority to secure access to state services and claim larger shares of federal and state budgets for their community, all the while claiming that their principal interests lay in protecting their communities from outsiders and preserving their traditions.

López works within what is for all intents and purposes a spoils system. His ability to claim to be the authentic representative of the Wixárika community has clear material consequences and incentivizes certain forms of monopolistic behavior. As a critical conduit for state aid to Wixárka communities, it makes sense that he argues for a radical version of indigenous sovereignty, one in which outsiders are unwelcome in Wixárika communities and at their ceremonies.[31] He mobilizes the language of self-determination to advocate for a very particular version of Wixárika purity that aligns with the drug prohibitions pursued by the Mexican state since the 1970s. He insists that the Wixárika oppose the use of peyote by outsiders and believe its use by outsiders should be considered a crime. He likewise insists that outsiders should be prohibited from both the sierra and Wirikuta. In making these claims, he articulates a fixed notion of what can and cannot be sacred in the Wixárika universe. Everyone must return to their traditional ceremonial centers to properly take part in community rituals. They must use peyote only under traditionally sanctioned circumstances. The Wixárika, like their landscapes, must remain pure.[32]

López speaks a language that resonates among some Wixárika. When he insists that outsiders can never truly enter their world, and that those who observe or seek to participate in their rituals are at best unwelcome interlopers and at worst dangerous fools, he speaks to a form of ethnic pride that distinguishes the Wixárika from outsiders by highlighting the foolishness of those who attempt to mimic their customs.[33] He does not, however, speak for all Wixárika. Two hundred kilometers away from his office, on the outskirts of Tepic, another Wixárika community has been welcoming outsiders into its midst since the 1990s. Zitakua, a barrio on the edge of the Nayarit state capital built largely by residents of El Nayar displaced from their homes during the construction of the Aguamilpa dam,[34] represents a stunning example of a self-built community in which refugees from the sierra reshaped their indigenous identities in an urban environment.

From its very founding Zitakua's survival has been based on principles that are markedly different from those that govern the world of Francisco López. Sitting on prime real estate overlooking the city, Zitakua occupies land that had already been subdivided into lots for a mestizo *colonia* when members of a growing Wixárika community in the area staked their claim. Believing the site was sacred because of a large boulder shaped like the head of a sheep that lay at its center, in 1988 the artist José Benítez Sánchez convinced Nayarit Governor Celso Delgado to give it to them. On 2 October of that year residents began constructing a tuki near the boulder in the now christened community of Zitakua. Struggling at the margins of the city, and reliant on a variety of sympathetic outsiders for its survival, Zitakua was from the very start integrated into a world that did not operate according to the monopolistic logics seen elsewhere in the sierra. Ignored by the INI in its early years because it did not resemble a traditional Wixárika community, and largely cut off from the spoils of official indigeneity, they shaped a version of Wixárika identity in which outsiders (and in particular nonstate actors), who could help the community with their injections of capital, were not viewed as a threat to their traditions.

Zitakua quickly became something of a tourist attraction, as well as a site where local government officials could demonstrate their support for the local Wixárika community.[35] It has remained that way ever since, one of the few tourist attractions in the otherwise sleepy state capital. And for locals like Rotelio Carillo, who fashions himself a *mara'akáme*, the community has offered the means to negotiate the insertion of certain forms of commerce and witnessing into an ancient ritual, providing material benefits to an otherwise precarious community. Carillo is one of several people in the community who have refashioned these traditions, inviting tourists to observe ceremonies and making artesania available for purchase. Zitakua preserves its ethnic identity in part by obeying the dictates of the market, monetizing its exoticism in order to protect it.[36]

With our current tendency to privilege ideas about cultural purity and authenticity, it might be tempting to suggest that what Carillo does is somehow impure, as compared to López's earnest attempts to defend authentic Wixárika identity, though I think this would represent a gross oversimplification of what distinguishes López from Carillo. Locked in a system in which Wixárika peyotism is a source of fascination and wonder to outsiders (as it has been for more than a century), Carillo

and López occupy different subject positions within a larger constella-
tion of indigenous self-determination in Mexico. López's is more in
keeping with Mexico's traditions of corporate politics and speaks to a
practice in which the authentic indigenous community and its authentic
leaders must be legible to the state as such in order to obtain state
patronage. Carillo is a product of the informal sector and has been part
of a process in which indigenous actors have translated the recent vogue
for things Wixárika into sources of sustenance for their communities.
He needs to be authentic, but more in the eyes of the tourist than in the
eyes of the state. At the end of the day, both perform versions of indigeneity that are profoundly rooted in the twin phenomena of indigenous
self-determination and the larger public's fascination with Wixárika
peyotism. López protects his community by keeping you out, and Carillo protects his by inviting you in.

. . .

Though they might disagree on the finer points of Wixárika sacred life,
there is one issue on which Carillo and López almost certainly agree: If
the Mexican state is to truly respect the cultural self-determination of the
Wixárika, it must act to defend a series of key sacred sites that lie outside
of the sierra from destruction. While Tee'kata is in the Sierra Huichola,
Huaxamanaka, Tatei Aramara, Xapawiyeme-Xapawiyemeta, and
Wirikuta are not, and their protection presents distinct challenges.
Access to these areas during the latter half of the twentieth century was
increasingly difficult, as fencing and other obstacles made pilgrimages
more and more difficult. At the same time, as popular fascination with
the Wixárika grew, tourists increasingly made their way to these sites,
often leaving garbage and stealing offerings to keep as mementos. Lacking title to these lands, the Wixárika had no way to protect their most
sacred spaces from desecration.

Facing waves of complaints from Wixárika leaders about the precariousness of these sites, in the late 1980s the INI began negotiating with
local officials in several states to have these places designated as sacred.[37]
In some cases it was relatively easy to accomplish this task. Tatei Haramara, a small site on an island just off the coast from San Blas, which plays
a central role in Wixárika origin stories, could be protected at little cost to
anyone. On 1 December 1990, San Blas became the first site in Mexico to
be declared sacred. In creating this designation, the governor of Nayarit
promised to restrict access to the site to protect it from gawking tourists.[38]
He likewise promised to give indigenous authorities a role in maintaining

the site, though he stopped short of promising sovereignty. Here (where it would have been easy, given that the site has little value) and elsewhere (where it might have been more difficult given preexisting land titles) no state or federal official ever gave serious consideration to granting Wixárika authorities sovereignty over their sacred places.[39]

Located in a region with untapped mineral wealth, Wirikuta would not be designated a sacred place. Federal and state officials instead opted for the creation of an ecological reserve.[40] Peyote was placed on the Mexican government's endangered species list at the end of 1991, and three years later state authorities in San Luis Potosí declared Wirikuta to be a "Protected Natural Area." As a part of this arrangement, the INI secured permission from the governor of San Luis Potosí to grant the Wixárika and those they approved unrestricted preferential access to 182,108 acres in the state, where they could conduct ceremonies and gather peyote.[41]

As these agreements were negotiated, Wixárika authorities proposed a series of initiatives that would give them limited sovereignty in Wirikuta, but they were repeatedly rebuffed by state and federal officials, who instead began a pilot program with the *ejidatarios* in and around Wirikuta in 1994, which put conservation in local hands. Under this plan, mestizo campesinos from three ejidos in Real del Catorce (San Antonio de Coronados, Tanque de Dolores, and Las Margaritas), working with representatives from several government agencies, created a *sistema de vigilancia communitario* (community vigilance system) to protect a region increasingly seen as under threat from despoliation by tourists, bio-prospectors, and others.

These and subsequent regulations set a clear precedent for the management of Wirikuta. Though the system would allow the Wixárika access to the reserve and keep others out, local ejidatarios and police would serve as the guardians of Wirikuta. Issued credentials as ecological guards by the Procuraduria Federal de Protección al Ambiente (PROFEPA, or the Attorney General for Environmental Protection), local ejidatarios would charge tourists an entry fee, make them sign a promise to respect the zone and its rules, and prevent the removal of peyote for business or narcotrafficking purposes. They would also ensure that Wixárika pilgrims only took a small quantity of peyote from the reserve.[42]

. . .

This was a classic purifying exercise. Under the principles that governed the new ecological preserve, Wirikuta was to be solely an indigenous space. And yet, by the time these rules were enacted Wirikuta had long since ceased to be solely a sacred place to the Wixárika. Real de Catorce was by then a center for new age spirituality and new religious movements, a diverse community of believers who were deeply committed to both the sacredness of Wirikuta and to the ritual consumption of peyote as a part of their own religious practice.[43] In the new legal and ecological landscape, these worshippers of peyote would be labeled not simply as lawbreakers, but as dangerous outsiders whose interest in the peyote found in Wirikuta put the survival of the Wixárika at risk.

The new rules thus created a gap between the law and long-standing practice that local authorities quickly began to exploit. When Teodoro Almaguer Bernal took over as municipal president in Real de Catorce in 2000, he accused the ecological guards of being narcos and arrested the ejidal authorities in Las Margaritas. The ejidatarios in turn claimed that he was muscling in on the region through the local police, who were demanding bribes from new age tourists in Wirikuta.[44] These conflicts simmered for years, as each side made repeated accusations that the other was trying to corner the market on a commodity that was doubly profitable (access could be sold, and those who obtained access could be extorted with the threat of jail).

One of the more notable subsets of these lawbreakers were the "imposters dressed as Huichols," many of whom traveled with Wixárika pilgrims and participated in their rites in Wirikuta.[45] Believing that both the guides and the foreigners were flouting the law and stealing cactuses from Wirikuta (and that the Huichol guides were probably getting paid for their work), in June 2004 the new municipal president of Real de Catorce, Roman Castillo Alvarado, arrested two of the foreigners and demanded that Wixárika authorities "explain why some Huichols help these people by lending or renting them [ceremonial Huichol outfits]."[46]

Identified as imposters by their white skin, clear eyes, and brown hair, these outsiders were confounding on several levels. State officials easily identified them as frauds, who attempted to use the cover of Indian dress to hide their illegal activity. Some Wixárika authorities also disputed the outsiders' right to be in Wirikuta, adopting a language of indigenous purity which, oddly enough, resonates more clearly with the history of state policy than it did with the history of local practices (some Wixárika had a history of allowing non-indigenous guests to accompany pilgrims to Wirikuta and take part in their ceremonies). This nuance, however, has never been easily legible to the state. A white-skinned foreigner in Huichol dress could only be an imposter.

In addition to arresting non-Indians for possessing even small quantities of peyote,[47] the new guardians of Wirikuta surveil Wixárika pilgrims, who now face arrest if they collect more than one hundred plants.[48] On at least one occasion authorities from San Luis Potosí used the pretext of limiting the collection of peyote plants to interrupt a Wixárika ceremony within the sacred hunting grounds, resulting in accusations that the government had treated participants poorly.[49] According to complaints, the police interrupted a ceremony and insulted the participants, treating them like "criminals." They broke the sacred circle, disrespected Grandfather Fire, and during a three-hour ordeal desecrated the sacred offerings. When the police returned the following day, they again "violated" a sacred ceremony, recording pilgrims with a video camera. Pilgrims were told that they risked arrest for their wanton destruction of the peyote plants, even though, as the pilgrims insisted, they were simply harvesting the peyote in the same fashion as they had for three thousand years. In their complaint the Wixárika lamented that the "narcos" and "multinational agroindustry" enjoyed total impunity even as they put the region at risk, while the police persecuted pilgrims, who did no harm at all to Wirikuta.[50]

This last claim reflected perhaps the most troubling development in the battle over Wirikuta to that point. Though conservationist in its outward claims, the project of ecological preservation always allowed for some economic development in the region. Overseen by the Secretaría de Medio Ambiente y Recursos Naturales (SEMARANAT, or the Ministry of the Environment and Natural Resources), government officials allowed bio-prospecting in the region in the early 2000s and even (in contravention of Mexican law) approved the export of several hundred peyote plants by foreign researchers.[51]

. . .

Amid continuing protests from Wixárika authorities over what seemed to be violations of the spirit behind the reserve's creation, in November 2008 the federal government announced the Pacto de Hauxa Manaka para la Preservación y Desarrollo de la Cultura Wixárika (the Pact of Huaxa Manaka for the Preservation and Development of the Wixárika Culture).[52] Aside from giving federal recognition to five sacred places (Tatei Haramara, Tee'kata, Xapawiyeme-Xapawiyemeta, Huaxamanaka, and Wirikuta), the pact promised to "undertake the necessary actions to protect and preserve the historical continuity of the sacred places and pilgrimage routes of the Wixárika People." Negotiated with an organization called the Gobernadores Tradicionales Wixárika and la Unión Wixárika de Centros Ceremoniales de Jalisco, Durango y Nayarit A.C. (UWC-CJDN), the pact established the UWCCJDN as the arbiters of Wixárika authenticity and sovereignty, in that it committed its signatories to "preventing the Wixárika and/or persons outside their culture from using elements of [the sacred places] for purposes contrary to the ceremonies and traditions of the Wixárika people, except in cases that have been previously agreed to under strict consensus." "Tradition" here was now fixed as a notion that outsiders should be banished from Wixárika spaces and that a relatively small group of certified religious authorities would determine what in fact constituted authentic ceremonial uses of peyote. President Calderón donned Huichol attire in announcing the pact (this, evidently, did not make him an imposter), calling Wirikuta a "patrimony of humanity" and the "pride of all Mexicans."

Though they declined to give the UWCCJDN any specific authority over development in the region in the pact, the federal government did promise that they would be consulted in any development programs in Wirikuta (a promise reiterated in San Luis Potosí's new Ley de Consulta Indígena).[53] Imagine their surprise, then, when just months later the government granted a series of mining concessions comprising around 140,000 hectares in Wirikuta to the First Majestic Corporation. Seventy percent of the concessions were in the Natural and Cultural Reserve within Wirikuta, and 42.75 percent in an area that had been designated a zone of "traditional use," meaning only activities that satisfied basic needs could be undertaken.

Completely frozen out of the decision process, the UWCCJDN immediately organized on local, national, and international levels to protest the concessions. Their protests were custom-made for early-twenty-first-century activism, pitting an innocent stone age people against multinational mining companies. Between 2010 and 2014 Wixárika activists traveled to New York, Vancouver (where they protested at board meetings of First Majestic), and elsewhere, repeatedly making a case based on domestic and international law against the concessions. Domestic and foreign documentarians publicized their plight further, as did activists in Mexico.[54]

The defenders of Wirikuta relied on a very specific performance of Wixárika indigeneity. The Wixárika were a primeval people whose devotion to the desert connected them to the mystical origins of humankind, and whose defense of Wirikuta represented a powerfully symbolic statement about the value of the sorts of mystical environmentalism the

Wixárika seemed to exemplify. They were the last guardians of peyote, and as such, the "last guardians of the planet." If the peyote disappeared, so too would they be doomed (and by extension the rest of us). Take, for instance, a letter written by the Regional Wixárika Council for the Defense of Wirikuta to President Calderón on 9 May 2011:

> You are kidnapping and want to assassinate our mother, The Earth, which you have threatened, and seek the forced disappearance of an entire people, the Wixárika People. . . . [I]t will be infinitely cheaper to cancel these concessions than to lament the ecological, spiritual and social tragedy that digging and extracting the entrails of Wirikuta could provoke. . . . Wirikuta is the heart of our essence. If it ends, we die as a people.[55]

In these texts the Wixárika are frozen in time. The community (and not a small number of them, but the entire community) makes the annual pilgrimage, and the essence of who they are will not survive the destruction of the desert. It is a powerful, romantic image, a story of a looming tragedy that Mexicans and the world must stop by opposing two different rapacious mining companies (by this time a second Canadian company, Revolution Resources, also had a claim in the region). And the rescue of this place somehow extends to the rescue of the world, not just because the Wixárika claim this to be the center of the vital energy of the universe but because their supporters repeat this claim, insisting that this place is miraculous, mystical, a site of great energy. As the guardians of that sacred energy, the Wixárika are indistinguishable from the landscape and equally in need of protection.

. . .

That this campaign against the mines succeeded in getting most of the concessions canceled in 2012 offers us tangible evidence of the power of a certain version of indigeneity.[56] That it relied so heavily on a uniform and deeply orientalist vision of a community that is in fact quite diverse may be a sign of the limitations of that version of indigeneity. Aside from the fact that this version of the Wixárika can slide almost seamlessly into the deeply racist way in which mestizo authorities from Real de Catorce to Nayarit dismiss "huicholitos" as naïve, unsophisticated primitives, we are also left with a version of both Wirikuta and peyote that erases the fact that for quite some time this place and the cactus have assumed a sacredness to a burgeoning national and international collection of peyote devotees.

The seemingly imminent threat of ecological collapse places those "imposters" and "tourists" in a very difficult position. Many claim to worship peyote as sacred, and they undertake their rituals in a fashion that belies any claim that they might be damaging themselves (many, in fact, try to replicate Wixárika rites as closely as possible, and there is no evidence that any of them have been harmed), yet none of this matters. The Mexican state remains resolutely opposed to peyote use by non-Indians.

This poses a problem for members of a growing number of groups, organized under names like Mancomunidad Amerikua India Solar (MAIS), Gran Fraternidad Universal, La Nueva Mexicanidad, El Fuego Sagrado, and even the Iglesia Nativa Americana de México (INAM, the Mexican variant of the NAC).[57] Members of these communities embrace peyote as the means of discovering their own indigenous pasts and offering radical critiques of the present. They have developed specific rituals, often syncretic, sometimes modeled on Wixárika ceremonies, sometimes modeled after the NAC, and sometimes sui generis, and have sought to codify and replicate those rituals over time.[58]

Though still relatively small, these groups have grown steadily in size and number since the 1980s and are part and parcel of a broader phenomenon in Latin America in which people who had been raised to think of themselves as mestizos or ladinos have increasingly asserted their newly politicized indigenous selves in gestures that seek to upend the postcolonial logics of their societies.[59] They are also part of a continuing trend in which young Mexicans with little concrete connection to indigeneity discover it as a part their political identities in part by participating in peyote ceremonies.[60] Though the participants are mainly urban and in some ways quite distant from what Mexicans would have traditionally considered indigenousness, they reclaim indigeneity as a way of situating themselves within and against the forces of neoliberal globalization.[61]

Members of these groups may not be able to claim the sort of racial heritage that the Wixárika claim in Wirikuta, but their practices and claims suggest that their belief in the sacredness of peyote should not be dismissed as somehow inauthentic.[62] Yet this is not how the Mexican state views the issue. Non-Wixárika peyotists cannot claim a religious right to consume the cactus within or outside of Wirikuta. The Mexican state has consistently refused to recognize any group that does not have a clearly defined and ancient custom as legitimate peyotists. This means, for instance, that the five thousand members of the INAM, who first petitioned the Secretaría de Gobernación for recognition of their church in 1994, still to face. The threat of arrest for practicing their religion.[63]

There are many reasons we might find this troubling. It amounts to a defense of a racial exclusion based on a prior claim to space, a claim that if normalized could be used by other groups to very problematic ends. It also positions the Wixárika as impossibly fragile, imperiled by any changes in the land. Aside from the obvious falseness of this proposition (the Wixárika have survived within changing landscapes and despite genocidal state policies for centuries), it once again reinforces the role of a paternalistic state as the savior of a fragile people, a people who are ultimately unable to defend themselves.

North American audiences might also be baffled by the fact that the Mexican state is so definitive in denying the link between members of groups like la Nueva Mexicanidad and the INAM to indigeneity. By the measures in place in the US, the vast majority of members of these groups would easily qualify for membership in the NAC and thus have a legal avenue for their peyotism. This claim, however, makes less sense in Mexico, where nationalists have for the better part of a century positioned mestizaje as the fusion of indigeneity and whiteness in a way that created a new self (and thus was neither indigeneity nor whiteness). Mestizaje was the process through which a modern nation was created, the model for citizenship in postrevolutionary Mexico. Most of those who are now turning to movements like the INAM and la Nueva Mexicanidad grew up in settings where indigenous Mexico was remote (and disdained).

This then frames the absurd juxtaposition of the plight of the INAM and the NAC. North of the border, the federal government's insistence on a racial qualification for membership in the church operates as an easy shorthand. Relatively few people could ever meet those criteria, making it possible to stigmatize white peyotists while carving out a limited legal space for Indians to consume peyote. South of the border, Native American Church members from the US have successfully claimed to be so profoundly removed from civilization that Mexican prosecutors declined to prosecute them for peyote possession.[64] And yet the larger legal logics of the NAC cannot be translated to Mexico, because if they were, the vast majority of Mexicans would qualify for membership in the church (this could not be good for Wirikuta!). This is where the line is drawn, not just with the INAM but with any other non-Wixárika peyotist group in Mexico. Peyotism here is a sign of one's distance from civilization, a claim that comes with a larger series of expectations that the Indian perform his or her alterity according to a well-worn script. Those who are in fact within civilization (like *gente de razón* of another era) had better stay on the right side of the line.

Restrictions to Wirikuta are thus written around two competing and ultimately troubling iterations of indigeneity. Because peyote is illegal, Wixárika indigeneity conveys a cultural right to consume something that others will not be able to consume. Illegality was in the first instance established by the danger peyote posed to non-Indian bodies. Given that this view is now largely discredited, illegality is now tied to an ecosystem under threat and a claim that the destruction of that environment is tantamount to genocide. Prohibitions that were originally designed to protect non-indigenous bodies from the danger of peyote now protect peyote from the danger of non-indigenous bodies.

CHAPTER TWELVE

2011

Tom Pinkson

I fought back with all my might. It wasn't a physical battle, it was a psychic and spiritual one. I was fighting for my soul.

—Tom Pinkson[1]

It is August 2011, and I find myself sitting in the office of Tom Pinkson, a therapist in San Rafael, California. I have come to Pinkson because he wrote a book about how Huichol shamans transformed his view of the world and his practice, and I suspect that Pinkson thinks of himself as a sort of white shaman. He confirms this and then proceeds to confound me. He comes across as extraordinarily earnest and seems uninterested in the material acquisitiveness and cultishness with which most of us identify Carlos Castaneda (mention his name and my anthropologist friends roll their eyes). Pinkson has embraced psychedelia as a part of a therapeutic practice in which he tries to understand powerful forces, energies, flows that connect us to one another and to the universe. He talks to me about quantum physics, about the worlds that we are completely unable to see because of our weak powers of perception. He wants access to some of this perceptivity because he believes it can play a central role in the healing process. Because I am attempting to think through the relationship between those outsiders who went on pilgrimages and their Wixárika hosts, I pay close attention when he describes these journeys as events that entail a "dissolving of boundaries." Tom feels that he has been adopted by his teacher, Eligio, that he has become an honorary member of the community. I know that this is a problematic claim, and I want to dismiss Pinkson as a fraud. Instead, I find that I rather like him.

Pinkson in the latest in a long line of refugees from modernity, the mostly young Mexicans and North Americans, who since the late 1960s have embraced a language associated with indigeneity that allowed them to abandon the bourgeois values and authoritarianism they believed had brought their societies to the brink of collapse. Though the products of a seemingly stable social milieu (if the Cold War world could ever be described as that), they rejected the sensibilities with which they were raised—the political, religious, and social norms and institutions of their societies, the soulless, cold, and false nature of the contemporary world. The latest in a tradition that dates at least to Louis Lewin, they sought transformative experiences, or, as Jay Winter might put it, "minor utopias."[2]

Pinkson is a psychedelic enthusiast, but he is not simply that. If he were merely interested in the drug experience, he could have embraced other substances and allied himself to a growing community of scientists who work with MDMA, psilocybin, mescaline, and LSD. That community, which includes prominent figures like Rick Doblin and David Nutt, has gained some legitimacy with the scientific establishment and drug-regulatory agencies through research that relies on pure synthetic drugs, produced in laboratories and tested in carefully designed drug trials. Their research demonstrates the potential therapeutic drug effect of psychedelics for a range of conditions, including PTSD (MDMA), depression (psilocybin), and end-of-life anxiety (LSD). Inasmuch as their work has become legible as medicine, it has done so by denaturing and decontextualizing these drugs, so that their plant origins are virtually impossible to detect, as are the contexts of their traditional use. By contrast, to Pinkson's way of thinking, that context is as important as the peyote itself.

. . .

Wixárika peyotism occupies a distinct position in this story. Cast one way, the rites and traditions associated with peyotism were a sign of backwardness. Cast another, they represented an antidote to the ills associated with modernity—to the alienation and despair of the modern city, the empty striving and falseness that seemed to characterize Mexican and North American society, the way that moderns were profoundly out of balance with the natural and spiritual world. Indeed, even as federal and state officials sought to obliterate Wixárika traditions during the Plans Lerma and Huicot, idealistic sojourners to the sierra (a tradition that eventually included Pinkson) embraced the Wixárika as a living relic of simpler (and perhaps better) times. They were said to "worship the forces of nature," were natural artists who (with the aid of peyote) could undertake herculean tasks.[3] They were organic democrats who chose their leaders fairly and without conflict. Their authorities served honestly, selflessly, and without any remuneration.[4] They saw through the phoniness of their mestizo neighbors, and with good reason perceived them as "false and exploitative people."[5] They lived in a world without gluttony, wrath, and envy, where sexual sins were confessed, where there were no secrets—a world characterized by the "purity of man."[6] Theirs was a "mystical, magical world, of philosophers and poets, of strange beings that live the canyons and pure, nomadic, spiritual men embedded on the plateaus. [They are] members of a communal society: practitioners of an original and true socialism."[7]

There is a direct line between these musings and the man who would become the single most iconic figure of the new age, Carlos Castaneda. The connection begins with the multiplication of journalistic and ethnographic accounts romanticizing the Wixárika during the mid-1960s, many of which were made possible by the new roads and airstrips being built in the region. Among the visitors who made their way into the region were the anthropologists Barbara Myerhoff and Peter Furst and Mexican journalist Fernando Benítez. These three figures, who were among the most important translators of Wixárika customs to the wider world, all relied on a single shaman/artist named Ramón Medina Silva, who lived on a small plot of land near Guadalajara, for much of their information about the Wixárika.[8] Castaneda seems to have learned about Medina Silva—who was one of the chief inspirations for Don Juan and whom he never met—through Furst and Myerhoff, who were his contemporaries in the graduate program in anthropology at UCLA. *The Teachings of Don Juan* began as his master's thesis.

The Teachings begins with a chance meeting with a powerful Yaqui sorcerer named Don Juan Matus at a Nogales bus stop in 1960. Carlos, who wanted to learn about peyote, is repeatedly tested by Don Juan until he encounters a transparent black dog named Mescalito. This encounter convinces the shaman that Castaneda has been chosen to be an apprentice in the ways of the shaman. In subsequent months he spends many hours learning from Don Juan, talking to coyotes, shapeshifting, and ultimately learning to fly (this is recounted in a later book). Moreover, after many arguments with Don Juan, Carlos becomes convinced that these experiences were not in fact hallucinations. They were a "separate reality."

Written as deeply immersive ethnography, *The Teachings* was specific enough to give Don Juan a recognizable form to Castaneda's readers

(Indian, rural, Mexican, cut off from industrial modernity, mystical) but also sufficiently vague as to allow readers to map their own dreams and aspirations onto the text (this had the added advantage of making it impossible for skeptics to falsify his claims). The story seems to take place in northern Mexico, but it could be almost anywhere. Don Juan seems real but is somehow ephemeral, a shape-shifter who secreted his way into Castaneda's life and who would not reveal himself to others. Even his identity as a Yaqui sorcerer seems to be a trick, a clever cover made up to allow Don Juan to hide from prying eyes (there is no tradition of peyotism among the Yaquis).[9]

This was the ultimate charm of Castaneda. He was forever the trickster, brushing aside the empiricism of anthropology in search of deeper meaning, of a world that the narrow evidentiary norms of the social sciences could never capture. Truth, in the sense that professional scholars use the term, was of no interest to him. Furthermore, in denying the metaphorical nature of the trip and performing a version of indigeneity that combines the romance of the mystical primitive with bellicose individualism, he tapped directly into a series of desires that would inform new age spirituality. It was an ethos that rejected the rigid and corrupt religious, social, and political norms of modern life and offered an escape that was not merely metaphorical but literal.[10] Peyote itself was a useful means to reject the greed, individualism, militarism, self-interest, the dishonesty of Cold War society and return to something more pure, more honest.

As Ageeth Sluis notes, Castaneda's shaman is a hypermasculine, hyperindividualized warrior, an avatar for young alienated males who felt crushed into conformity by an unjust system.[11] Through Don Juan, Castaneda had found the means to reject social norms, with the added benefit of the ability to inhabit a world in which he was empowered to also reject the very reality of his quotidian existence. Though expressed through a different language, it was a fantasy that resonated with any number of other countercultural figures of the late 1960s and early 1970s, from Easy Rider's Captain America to Dirty Harry.[12]

. . .

Thanks to the Benítez-Furst-Myerhoff-Castaneda chain, Ramón Medina Silva and his father-in-law, José Ríos Matsuwa, came to be synonymous with Wixárika shamanism among new agers.[13] Prem Das (a.k.a. Paul C. Adams) was one of the first to follow Myerhoff and Furst to the homes of Medina and Ríos. Das apprenticed with them beginning in 1971 and married a Wixárika woman during his time in Mexico. Das traveled around the US selling Wixárika artifacts to support himself during these years, at times taking Ríos with him to attend monthlong seminars on shamanism. It was during one of those visits in 1979 that he took the hundred-year-old Ríos along with Medina's widow, Guadalupe (Medina was killed in a brawl in 1971, leaving Ríos and the extended family as the principal interlocutors for outsiders looking for shamans), to meet Stanislav Grof and Joan Halifax at Esalen, where he performed a series of all-night ceremonies. Grof described Ríos as "one of the most extraordinary spiritual teachers and human beings we have ever met." "Don José always ingested before the ceremony a large bud of peyote cactus that helped him to transcend the limits of ordinary sense perception and to 'see with the mind's eye . . . the interconnectedness of all things, seen and unseen.'"[14] Das, who claimed that he was considered a shaman by the Wixárika, regularly took North American tourists on spiritual visits to the region around Álica, Nayarit, and Wirikuta through the 1980s.[15]

It was also Ríos whom Larain Boyll visited in 1973, and whom she credited with curing her infertility. For many years following her "cure" she worked with Guadalupe and her sister Andrea Ríos in an enterprise that brought tourists to Álica and other Wixárika sites in search of sacred energies. Boyll claimed that she too became a shaman after a six-year apprenticeship with Guadalupe, during which, among other things, she learned to use shamanic power to cure AIDS.[16]

Boyll and Das may have shaded the truth in claiming to be proper Wixárika shamans based on the teachings of individuals who were not even recognized as such by other Wixárika, but in comparison to those who followed in their footsteps, their misrepresentations (or perhaps misunderstandings) seem almost quaint. Ken Eagle Feather (a.k.a. Kenneth Smith), author of multiple books on the "Toltec Path," and "executive director for *Therapeutic Discovery,* a medical science research institute, in Richmond, Virginia,"[17] claims "Don Juan Matus, a Yaqui Indian seer" (and Carlos Castaneda's fictional teacher) as his own teacher.[18] His shamanic teachings bear no resemblance to any Mexican tradition, yet he insists that he has been personally trained by Mexican Indians.

And then there is Brant Secunda. Originally from Brooklyn, Secunda was inspired to look up peyote at the New York Public Library after reading Castaneda in high school. Learning that it was principally associated with the Wixárika, he set out for Mexico on his eighteenth birthday, where he allegedly undertook a thirteen-year apprenticeship in the sierra with none other than the (by then) 110-year-old Don José (Ríos)

Matsuwa. In his rather fanciful telling of his first encounter with Ríos, three days after hiking into the sierra he became impossibly lost and lay down to die. He was awakened by a man who had begun to kick him. The man had been sent to find him by a village shaman (Ríos, one supposes) who had dreamed about his presence. Ríos then taught him their secrets and adopted him as a grandson.[19] After he returned to the US, Secunda established the Dance of the Deer Foundation for Shamanic Studies in Santa Cruz, California, which has for several decades organized events where he reads his patients' energies and heals them in locales as varied as Mount Shasta, Crete, and in the sierra around Álica. Prices range from $200 to $1500 per trip.[20]

Brant falls squarely into a category of people who have been accused of appropriating indigenous cultures for their own benefit. Though he is in some ways tied to a long tradition in which non-indigenous folk have drawn on indigenous iconography in their art and work, broad acceptance of an indigenous right to cultural self-determination has transformed the way most of us understand people like Secunda. We have shifted how we situate culture away from conceiving of it as a diverse set of relatively mutable practices in which the boundaries between one culture and another are often shifting and toward something to be defined, owned, and determined authentic or inauthentic. Given that these claims are also made in a globalizing context in which the bric-a-brac of cultural production are increasingly monetized, with the greatest rewards going to the most purely authentic and artisanal, the claim to cultural rights situates culture itself as property. These rights authorize some people to speak on behalf of a culture, adjudicating what is authentic and what is false, and raise the possibility that outsiders who seek to adopt certain cultural practices are appropriating without due authorization.[21]

This claim has special resonance in contexts where a history of colonialism and asymmetrical power relations have long allowed members of one group (typically of European ancestry) to lay claim to the heritage of another group (typically colonized peoples) in ways that exacerbate inequality, and Secunda seems like a pretty good example of this problem. He has been the object of scathing criticism from those who claim that he has appropriated and refashioned Wixárika shamanism for his own profit, giving virtually nothing back to the community.[22] And, to be sure, much of the criticism seems well deserved. Inasmuch as he has turned Wixárika identity into a commodity (his shaman chocolates are exactly that), or laid claim to some deep connection to indigeneity to market himself as a healer without actually having any historical claim to membership in a community, he does seem to have appropriated and then marketed something that is not his and distorted our image of the Wixárika in the process. In the words of one critic:

> I lived in a Huichol village with Don Jose Matsuwa's granddaughter. She, and all the other Huichol's I lived with consider Brant a charlatan, and more than that, they call him "El Diablo" . . . "The Devil."
> This doltish white American is a charlatan, exploiting my people's ancient traditions while making unsubstantiated claims. There's a reason why Wikipedia took his page/entry down on the basis of fraud and self-promotion. I knew someone who was about to give this phony $6,000 for the "honor" of camping out with him.[23]

. . .

I am drawn to these comments at least in part because they conform to my preexisting inclination to dismiss with a disgusted wave of my hand the likes of not just Brant Secunda but Prem Das, Larain Boyll, Ken Eagle Feather, and Carlos Castaneda. I laughed out loud when I read a letter in which Weston La Barre called Aldous Huxley a "noodlehead,"[24] and found the attacks on Castaneda very satisfying. La Barre also took aim at Castaneda, calling *The Teachings* a "pseudo-profound deeply vulgar pseudo-ethnography,"[25] and claimed that his entire apprenticeship was made up in the UCLA library. Richard de Mille and Jay Fikes wrote several books detailing his lies and cynicism in great detail, condemnations that rang even more true as Castaneda grew rich from his catalog and cultivated what seemed to many to be a bizarre cult in his Southern California compound.[26]

I was also immediately sympathetic to Joan Townsend's reading of the neoshaman as someone who takes on the trappings of traditional shamanism but substitutes a highly individualized obsession with self-actualization for the much more community-focused practice of traditional shamanism.[27] The accusation that all these figures are "playing Indian," practicing cultural tourism, and committing ethnocide makes sense to me.[28] If Captain America was a fool and a cautionary tale (did he not meet his end in a most unfortunate fashion?), Castaneda and his lot are snake-oil salesmen.

And yet this is also where I begin to doubt myself, fearing both that I have failed to understand what drew these individuals to peyote and that I may be flattening out the shamans in ways that only reinforce much more troubling forms of orientalism. The very terms of the conversation—concepts like "authentic," "appropriation," and "charlatan"—are rooted in a series of assumptions about purity and difference that work to make the white shamans legible only as objects of derision. Both the West and the Wixárika must remain stable signifiers of difference for these concepts to have purchase, with the Wixárika never changing, never appropriating Western practices or embodying a plurality of cosmologies, and the West remaining a stable signifier of rationality, science, and order. All those who seek to transgress are simply playing at being Indian while at heart remaining subjects of the West. This, for instance, is one of the reasons we focus on the material desires of Das, Boyll, and Secunda while ignoring those of their informants. By marketing indigeneity, they prove their position within the West. And instead of being strategic actors engaged in a transaction, their informants become at best victims of asymmetrical power relations and at worst false representatives of a marginalized culture.[29]

Then there is the problem that it is not exactly clear what is being appropriated. If we accept that Carlos Castaneda made up Don Juan in the library, we are forced to confront the fact that his supposed appropriations were based (likely in their entirety) on a fiction. His Don Juan Matus never existed. This raises obvious questions about Ken Eagle Feather, who claims to have apprenticed with Castaneda's sorcerer teacher. Prem Das studied first with Ramón Medina Silva, who Phil Weigand and Jay Fikes dismiss as inauthentic.[30] Boyll and Secunda learned from Das and in turn from Medina Silva's father-in-law, widow, and sister-in-law, all of whom lived outside of the traditional Wixárika ceremonial centers, did not teach their charges rituals that could be clearly identified as traditional Wixárika rites, and seem to have been willing collaborators who saw these relationships as a means to pursue their own interests.[31]

From a purely ethnographic standpoint, there is some legitimacy to the question of whether the shamanism practiced by Medina, Ríos, and their extended family resembled the traditions practiced elsewhere. It seems it did not, at least not entirely, and because of this, Furst, Myerhoff, Benítez, and others may have been guilty of mistakenly allowing Medina and his family to stand in for the whole. That said, these debates do not speak to the question of whether Medina et al. were really shamans. To answer this question, we need to dig a little further.

The term *shaman* has always been a form of shorthand used in the West, a catchall for people who in other contexts might be considered traditional healers, mystics, singers (in the case of the Wixárika), and tenders of sacred knowledge. While within communities these roles are

often differentiated, for outsiders fascinated with alternative epistemologies the shaman captures most of the important distinctions between
the individualistic Western self and the communally-oriented other. This
distinction, however, misses one key point. As Donald Joralemon and
Ben Feinberg note, while the shaman is a healer who holds sacred
knowledge, they also tend to operate in the intersection between the
inside of a community and the outside. Their knowledge is specialized,
not held by all in the community, and in many shamanic traditions the
way that individual shamans demonstrate their power is through their
capacity to claim status in the world beyond their communities. They
must possess a certain quick-footedness, especially when their rituals
involve psychedelic drugs. They do not simply recite the old texts. They
produce new texts over the course of their rituals, healing in ways that
sometimes focus on the restoration of communal balance and at other
times focus on the individual. Shamans in a variety of Mexican traditions have welcomed outsiders into their ceremonies precisely because
their ability to cure those outsiders elevates their status within and
beyond the community. Medina, who relied on outsiders to help sell his
artwork, was precisely this sort of shaman.[32]

Shamans thus operate not so much at the center as along the margins
of their communities, connected to inside and outside worlds, their status dependent in part on their capacity to translate each for the other.[33]
This is why shamanism is not a practice that easily moves between
authentic and inauthentic or pure and impure. It is instead relational,
built around transactions that elevate the shaman as they cure the sick
or restore the community. Their very identity as shaman is the product
of the recognition they receive because of their skill in these transactions.[34]

Medina might thus have been a poor example of the traditional
Wixárika singer/curer in the ethnographic sense, and scholarship that
made him representative of something larger would have missed the
multiple roles that curers, singers, and others charged with tending to
sacred traditions played in these communities; but one misses the larger
story of shamanism and its relationship to Western epistemes if we dismiss him as inauthentic or impure. Medina, and Ríos and the rest of his
family, were recognized as shamans in Álica and among the outsiders
who ventured there in search of shamanic teaching (this in spite of
Medina's insistence that he was merely an apprentice). The distinctions
that might have led other Wixárika to challenge his knowledge and

power made little difference to those who found in Medina a powerful mystic with specialized knowledge of other worlds.

. . .

If we are to rescue Medina from inauthenticity, perhaps we should do the same for his students, the white shamans. If in their moments of intercultural exchange Medina, Ríos, and his widow and daughters gained the privilege afforded to interlocutors and artists, it may be that their apprentices did something more than simply appropriate a series of symbols and then profit from them.[35] They also gained a language and set of practices that helped them to articulate their unease with the Cold War West, language that conjured up a world unseen by the naked eye and that was infinitely more magical and powerful than that imagined by the rational, ordering practices of their world. And peyote was critical, at least at first. The peyote-aided mystical experience was an antidote to the inauthenticity of Western life.[36]

To be sure, the peyotism practiced by the white shamans was nothing like the thing it copied. Without question, it tended to be an individualistic practice impossibly divorced from the communal experience of Wixárika peyotism.[37] Still, when we describe this difference through the concept of appropriation or inauthenticity, we are in turn required to fix the thing being appropriated in ways that erase the long history of insider-outsider transactions within Wixárika shamanism. Instead of finding a complex terrain in which two parties engage in an (admittedly asymmetrical) transaction—one gets paid, sells their art, perhaps enjoys elevated status in their community, and may even secure opportunities to travel abroad and extend their social networks, while the other gets the opportunity to brush up against sacred knowledge and perhaps experiences something cathartic and transformative—we are left with a much flattened image that reinscribes the boundaries between the Indian and the West.

But these boundaries were exactly the point. Those who ventured to the sierra, who studied with or aspired to become shamans, were doing everything they could to transgress these boundaries, to enter a realm where their bodies, their consciousness, their relationship to reality could be disrupted. This, of course, is why peyote was so critical. Put simply, in the midst of their hallucinogenic experiences with their shaman-teachers, man who possessed knowledge and dominated nature became man possessed by knowledge, dominated by nature, man who must surrender to the power of the unseen world, faintly aware of a truth that lies just beyond the grasp. In these moments nature overwhelmed man, inverting the very logics of modernity.[38]

It should be unsurprising that the white shamans used the language of indigeneity to describe these experiences. And yet, in part because what they created here was so distant from the ethnographic "truth" of Wixárika experience, we might consider the differences between the white shamans and their erstwhile teachers as a reason to suggest that they did not appropriate anything so much as they identified with an enduring symbol of the romantic other. In a way, the fantasy of indigeneity they mobilized was a product of the Western imagination. It has long fueled the dreams of those seeking an escape from the universalizing, rationalizing, ordered West and into the specificity of the other.[39]

Our ability to find acts of appropriation in these transactions is limited by the fact that the concept of Wixárika deployed by the white shamans is a simulacrum, a copy for which there is no original.[40] Neither the white shamans nor their audience were concerned with the thing they copied in the sense of ethnographic truth. They preferred truthiness, plausibility that was sufficiently nonspecific that it need not be verified. It needed to feel right, to align with their expectations of what the mystical other should be, without getting sufficiently specific to either disrupt their fantasies about the forms of mysticism they favored or allow the messiness of poverty and marginalization to intrude. What the white shamans wanted was a pure mystic, living outside of time, free of the stain of European colonialism, connected to ancient forms of knowledge, the spirit world, and energy flows of the universe, and deeply connected to the earth. They preferred a subject who was remote, almost inaccessible, not only because that made their narratives impossible to falsify, but because they wanted a subject profoundly off the grid, untainted by electricity, television, any form of connectedness. They wanted Don Juan.

The distinction between this and an act of pure appropriation may seem academic. In denouncing those instances in which nonindigenous peoples have laid claim to indigeneity to their own benefit while further marginalizing indigenous peoples, critics rightly point out the ways in which colonial regimes of knowledge are reinscribed through acts of appropriation. And some of the white shamans have clearly done just that. My concern, however, is with the way in which we flatten out highly variegated experiences if we reduce all of these acts to simple appropriation. Is there room for us to imagine both indigeneity and whiteness as fantasies, whose long histories are more entwined than the discourse of appropriation allows? Is it possible to introduce the idea of cultural exchange here, to recognize that beliefs, values, and practices move across cultural boundaries even as those exchanges sometimes reinscribe those boundaries?[41] Is it possible that, in our rush to dismiss them, we have miscast the white shamans—that the way they deploy the trope of indigeneity can offer us insights into a history in which Western subjectivity has been less stable than it might seem?

. . .

This reading of the white shamans also makes it easier for me to understand Tom Pinkson. He wants me to believe that he had a transcendent experience among the Wixárika, that he found a form of connection and understanding with his teachers that puts the lie to claims of immutable cultural difference between the Wixárika and the Western subject. Trained as I am to wonder about the possibility of cross-cultural understanding, this is the position of which I am most skeptical. I want to think that he did not understand what he was experiencing, that he has been the worst kind of tourist, the one who tells you that people are the same wherever you go.

And yet this representation of Pinkson does not quite capture his project. For Tom it is both the plant in its original form and the people who have used it from time immemorial that matter. Pinkson believes his transformative experiences among his teachers in Wirikuta enhanced his capacity to see, to understand his own powers, and ultimately to heal his patients. Tom is clearly a sensitive, intelligent man, who has spent a lifetime in the helping professions. His own journey into his career was somewhat circuitous but always informed by his sense that he had an unusual capacity for understanding and empathizing with others. He feels that he has always been able to see and feel things that others cannot. He does not quite say it this way, but Tom thinks he has a gift, and that it was his effort to fully realize this gift that brought him first to a series of spiritual practices rooted in the Native American traditions in the US and ultimately to the Wixárika.

Tom believes that most of what we think about ourselves as bodies and minds are simply fictions we use to order the world. He argues that the human form is porous, that the physical boundaries we assume are simply a function of the limits of our ability to perceive through the senses. Tom believes in the unseen thing, in the power of the thing that cannot be touched. His book is filled with stories of learning things about people simply by touching their bodies, of forms of communication with humans and animals that go well beyond our cognitive capacities. He asks me to expand my mind and tells me that though he had a sense of his abilities before he went to the sierra, it was during his travels with Wixárika shamans to Wirikuta that he realized just how powerful these forces were. He is connected to the universe.

When he relates his apprenticeship, Tom repeats the mantra of many of the white shamans. Though an outsider to the sierra, with little Spanish and no ability to speak the language, he found teachers, to whom he returned again and again. He began by observing from a respectful distance. Once his teachers decided he had shown an appropriate level of respect, they invited him into their world. He offered up what he could, the car he had rented for the drive to Wirikuta, whatever other support he could offer. And after a long period of initiation, slow acceptance, he was allowed to take part in the peyote hunt. At first he was a novice, could not do it, but after following the advice of his teacher and closing his eyes, he came to the point where he was ready. The peyote revealed itself to him, and he became an insider. Tom was then able to take the insights he gained, the new vision he had attained, and integrate them into his own therapeutic practice, curing his patients in California in ways that drew from the cures he experienced in Mexico.

Peyote is clearly an actor in this story. Peyote allows Tom to experience a series of perceptual shifts that put the lie to the bourgeois body as "atomized, completed, and the locus of social control, reductive analysis and fixed meanings."[42] Moreover, Tom also reports feeling an intense connection to the other participants in the peyote ceremonies he witnessed in the sierra. In part this is the common experience of the ritual, the dancing, the chanting, the feeling of night in the desert, but he feels that the common psychedelic trip connected him to those who shared the experience in profound ways—that it was a shared experience in which he was deeply connected to the other participants despite their great cultural differences.[43]

Peyote ceremonies have a capacity to produce a sense of connection in ways that are more profound than most rituals. Bodies undertaking the trip together, from the initial feeling of nausea to the immense feeling of well-being and then hallucinating together—the aural and visual and other sensory experiences framed by the sounds and sights as manipulated by the teacher (darkness, fire, drumming, chanting, dancing, singing, the smell of burning substances)—often feel connected to each other, at least in part because the drug itself seems to cause boundaries between the self and other to dissolve. These effects are accentuated by the sha-man-guide, who often uses gesture and sound (instead of language) to force participants to align to his demands and expectations. Powerfully mimetic, these experiences have the capacity to create a strong sense of connection among people from diverse backgrounds.[44] Stanislav Grof indicates as much when relaying his experiences with Ríos, which he described as a moment of clear connection produced through a night-long experience of drumming, chanting, and music. "For those of us who did not understand Don José's chanting in the Huichol language, the ceremony seemed to resemble others we had done in the past."[45]

Grof connected to the ceremony and to Ríos through the ways his chanting evoked his own memories. Resemblance, mimesis, bodies coming together through the sensuous experience of drumming, chant-ing, and the common hallucinogenic trip had the capacity to produce a sense of both familiarity (it could "resemble others we had done in the past") and foster a powerful sense of connection among all participants in a peyote rite, especially when that rite took place during pilgrimages to Wirikuta, where all participants were somewhat displaced and most unfamiliar with the experience. Even most of the Wixárika on a pilgrim-age might have taken this journey only once or twice before (if ever), and the shamans guiding that journey thus play a particularly critical role in initiating all present into a special form of knowledge. All, in some ways, were being introduced to the sacred space and sacred knowledge, connecting to each other while making sense of the rituals through reference to what they resembled, and in the process connect-ing to their pasts and to each other. In dynamic settings like this, outsid-ers could very easily feel like they became a sort of insider. It was a contextual connection, one that was unlikely to last beyond the rite itself, but it was nonetheless a powerfully felt connection.

Connection also leads to adoption, which is a critical part of Tom's narrative (as it is with others who aspire to be white shamans).[46] Though it may seem strange that Pinkson was adopted in spite of a language barrier, this act was preceded by a series of mimetic practices that went far beyond language, understanding. These moments were character-ized by a very powerful experience in which he followed the lead of his teacher through the immersion of his body within the peyote ceremony.

Tom begins as the naïve outsider and becomes a shaman in his own right, an insider, in a process that ends with that adoption. This is the kind of thing that drives the anthropologists crazy (though some also tell adoption stories), as it erases the fact that the Western body essentially remains a Western body, replete with the privilege that comes with that status, even as that Western body now also lays claim to one of the few sites of power available to the other. Still, even if this is true, if we focus on Tom's failure to understand this problem, we could miss something that might be just as important. Adoption, for Tom, is a deeply transgressive act, the moment in which he could reject the universalistic, rationalistic, and hopelessly narrow worldview of the capitalist West and cross over into the particular. Whether he really succeeds in doing this is a question for Tom. Whether we would ever be willing to believe that he had done so is a more troubling question for the rest of us.

Crossing is a common theme in the history of race in the Americas. Sometimes called passing, it is a reminder that subaltern subjects have a long history of refusing to stay in their place, of challenging racial hierarchies by strategically moving from one category to another. Whether described as upward mobility, double-agenting, or something else, their actions remind us of the permeability of social categories. We do not, however, generally allow people like Tom Pinkson the luxury of shifting from one category to another. We assume that as a white, bourgeois male, he can only inhabit the category that purports its own universality. He risks criticism, mockery, dismissal, or condemnation for longing to be adopted into a Wixárika family. It may be that we criticize him because he has appropriated something, or misrepresented something, but given his modest circumstances and earnest beliefs, it is a little difficult to make this claim stick. It is, I suspect, Pinkson's refusal to stay in place that prompts our unease. Westerners are more comfortable with those who cross from the particular (Indianness) into the universal (whiteness). We have trouble with people who want to go in the other direction, because if they could, they would confound the racial hierarchies that order our worlds.

Race, Space, Time

Not everyone who was displaced by the building of the Aguamilpa dam wound up in places like Zitakua. One rather small community of valley residents had the opportunity to be relocated to higher ground on the edge of the newly formed lake. Founded in 1989, Potrero de la Palmita is difficult to get to. One needs to travel by motor launch across the lake, a twenty-minute ride from the dam, and then climb a steep embankment to enter the village, which is home to about five hundred people. For many years the principal access to the community came via small plane, which meant infrequent visits by government officials. This was not entirely to the displeasure of residents. According to Eligio López, the sometime local boss, federal and state officials are largely unwelcome in the community and have been driven out on many occasions. They have left behind the built landscape of the modern state—health clinics, schools (their sides painted with murals that depict Dora the Explorer, Winnie the Pooh, and peyote cacti), basketball courts, and government buildings (constructed with local labor, on land donated by the community)—but only rarely the bureaucrats to staff them. López tells stories about driving government doctors out of the village with pride, a reminder that this newly built Wixárika community is autonomous from the state, even if it owes its existence to the modernization projects of that very state. A combination of local solidarity, isolation from infrastructure, and the weakness of that state has allowed them to shape their lives in a manner that is to their own choosing.[1]

Lately that choosing has involved a decision embrace ecotourism, with the hope that a growing number of sympathetic visitors would make the four- to five-hour trip from Puerto Vallarta to witness the ceremonial and artistic life of an authentic Wixárika community. According to López, visitors can witness peyote ceremonies, watch artesania being made, take part in art-making workshops, and be introduced to Wixárika cosmologies. While in Potrero de la Palmita, visitors can stay in one of four cabañas constructed in the community, which were opened in 2010. They were built with the help of the CDI.

This is a sanctioned indigenous space. Hoping that ecotourism would spawn economic development not just in Potrero de la Palmita but in nearby communities, federal and state officials have supported the project from the start. The new construction and reconstructed spaces are designed to be welcoming to outsiders and suitable for art workshops and public performances. The state also created signage designating the community (which rests in the municipality of El Nayar) a sacred place. It is now Tawexikta, Lugar del Sol, a Centro Ecoturístico. Federal law further sanctions the continued practice of peyotism in the community, protecting its residents when they take part in pilgrimages, and ensuring that they face no penalties for the peyote they bring back to Potrero de la Palmita. Plastic buckets can be found in various parts of the community, where samples of peyote brought back from Wirikuta are kept alive. Protected by a cloak of legality (as Wixárika, they are entitled to collect and use peyote), Potrero de la Palmita offers ecotourism plus—a chance to get close to nature and psychedelia at the same time.

López understands that this is a business, and while he clearly distinguishes between insider and outsider, he is also willing to provide the tourist with an immersive experience. If you want to try some peyote, he is happy to share, telling you that it is a miracle drug, good for his rheumatism, aching joints, and problems in the head. López will also invite tourists to learn how to make Wixárika yarn paintings and other crafts and provides them with accommodations that evoke enough rusticity to feel authentic but not so much that tourists feel uncomfortable. He also endeavors as much as possible to keep the community prepared for visitors. Should they receive notice that a boatload is setting out from the dam, loudspeakers announce their impending arrival so that local artisans can prepare their goods for sale.[2] Through this orchestrated performance of Wixárika identity, tourists "experience Huichol life" and "peek into the lives of the native tribe by witnessing their ritual dances or shopping directly from Huichol women for their intricate artisan work."[3]

Though the cabins, which are operated by a group of twenty-six women and three men who form the Grupo Turístico Tawexikta, were given an award from the Ministry of Tourism for excellent service, quality, and cleanliness in 2012,[4] business has on the whole been a little slow. Potrero de la Palmita is somewhat off the beaten path, and for all their accolades, some tourists have complained that inadequate screens and plentiful bugs have resulted in an experience that was a little too authentic. Moreover, it is not at all clear that everyone in the community embraces these developments. López and his family seem to have benefited from the cabañas and live in the best house in the village, with solar panels, electric lights, and evidently the only phone in town. Their walls are nicely stuccoed, unlike the exposed brick walls of their neighbors. Others in the community are either indifferent or actively hostile—the presence of outsiders never being something uniformly welcome in Wixárika communities.

And still, the ecotourist initiative goes on, acting by its very existence as a powerful symbol of the ways that the sanctioned spaces for indigeneity, the press for economic development, and neoliberal globalization have come together to produce the odd positioning of peyote within modern drug-control regimes. Community residents are displaced, certainly, and always wary of the state, yet they are beneficiaries of the twin forces of ecotourism and indigenous self-determination, which have created opportunities in which some in the community have been able mobilize a symbolic repertoire that other poor Mexicans cannot. Peyote is not simply licit here. It lies at the heart of a state-supported development project.

. . .

There is perhaps no starker juxtaposition to the state-sanctioned peyote ecotourism of Potrero de la Palmita than the story of the Church of the First Born, a small peyote church in Tulsa, Oklahoma, founded in the early 1920s. Like so many peripheral phenomena, we have only the thinnest of records attesting to existence of this church and the life of its African American founder, John Jamison. While traveling in Oklahoma during the spring of 1931, Mrs. Maurice G. Smith of the Bureau of Indian Affairs met his daughter Mabel, who was then a member of a rapidly disintegrating congregation. John Jamison was already five years dead, having perished in 1926 "as a result of concussion of the brain after being struck by a 'half-crazed negro.'"[5] Smith never explains the precise reason for the attack, but we are elliptically led to believe that it must have had something to do with the church.

Jamison's parents had been allotted, and he grew up surrounded by Indian communities in Lincoln, Oklahoma. As a child he learned the local vernacular, grew close to many of his neighbors, and was invited to participate in the peyote ceremonies of the local church. In and of itself, this seems hardly remarkable. Rural Oklahoma in the early twentieth century was its own kind of melting pot, with displaced indigenous peoples and African Americans living side by side and producing novel cultural and ethnic forms (as well as conflicts about lineage that persist to this day),[6] and peyote churches in this era tended to be evangelical, welcoming not just individuals from other indigenous communities but non-Indians as well. Given his own history of displacement, Jamison may have felt a sense of belonging not just in the camaraderie of the ceremony but in the ways it articulated a separate space for indigeneity, an identity that challenged the racial and social hierarchies that otherwise characterized everyday life in rural Oklahoma.

Jamison was welcomed in the peyote religion, but only to a point. According to his daughter, some members of the peyote churches resented the fact that he was taking up "the old Indian religion." Here as elsewhere the claim to ancient origins would be a tool used to limit who could and could not claim an authentic connection to the peyote religion, though it was clear that what Jamison faced was not so much rejection as ambivalence among his fellow peyotists. Some accepted him as participant, while others insisted he could never belong.

Jamison left Lincoln County at some point prior to 1920 and moved to Tulsa, where he decided to replicate the ceremonies he had witnessed in the countryside. Mabel is certain of the timing in her conversation with Smith, as she insists that the peyote church in Tulsa predated the 1921 race riot. The date would have been indelibly marked in her memory, as it would have been for most members of Tulsa's African American community. The riot offered a visceral reminder of the precariousness of urban existence for Tulsa's blacks, an experience that might have underscored the attractiveness of alternative epistemologies, free of the racial violence of everyday life.

To be sure, Jamison's church was that sort of space. It was a small church, made up entirely of African Americans and Indians, where members could participate in healing ceremonies that eschewed white authority, led either by Jamison or an Indian member of the church. According to Mabel, the curing was critical, as people were drawn "by the healing and doctoring which Jamison sometimes attempted just as the Indians do." Though spatially reorganized for an urban setting, Jamison did as much as he could to replicate the ceremony as he had known it. Services took place all night, in an Indian tipi. There was drumming, sacred dishes, rattles, and medicine feathers. Jamison even dressed in an Indian costume sometimes, though he also made "use of the white man's hymns and bible" and there was no ceremonial smoking of cigarettes, as well as little use of cedar smoke. These modifications angered some of his erstwhile allies in the Indian community, as they believed them to be unsanctioned modifications of the conventional ritual.

Jamison met with no success in attempting to incorporate his church in Oklahoma, and this may have been one of the sources of his downfall. The government's hostility toward peyote also discouraged some of his black congregation. Never particularly large, the members of the church grew suspicious when the government banned the transportation of peyote. According to Mabel, this is why many quit the church. This response intrigued Smith: "this attitude on the part of the negroes is double interesting in view of the rebellious attitude which the Indians displayed under the same circumstances, and their resort to illegal procedures to obtain peyote."

Peyote, as we have seen, existed within a legal netherworld during these years. Forbidden by some state laws and under pressure from federal authorities, it nonetheless circulated freely on many Oklahoma reservations, as it seems to have done also among white scientists, New York socialites, and European intellectuals. In each case, the spaces chosen for the practice of peyotism were critical. Since peyote was not illegal in Europe, research laboratories, or cosmopolitan centers, white enthusiasts had little to fear. Members of the Native American Church were somewhat less protected but built informal distribution networks and were protected by the space of the reservation, where state and local authorities could not enforce their laws. Despite the earnestness of his belief and the formality of his rituals, John Jamison faced an entirely different set of challenges. Oklahoma's ban could cover the urban spaces of Tulsa, a city where the black minority already faced forms of violence that were both quotidian and extreme. Facing repression, black, urban peyotists gave up their religion and in so doing marked peyote as an Indian thing.

. . .

The tragedy of the Church of the First Born—like the long legal battles over bona fide use some decades later, the racialization of drug laws, the absurdist farce in which mestizo ecological guards surveil Wixárika pilgrims to ensure that they conform with authorized/authentic practices, and ultimately the advent of peyote-based ecotourism—serves to remind us of the ways in which peyote has been implicated in the production of racial categories since Europeans first came across this cactus.[7] Race in these stories is also invariably linked to specific spaces where racial identities are codified and those deemed inauthentic excluded: the laboratory versus rural Oklahoma, a house in Palm Springs versus a hogan in Needles, Mexico City versus Wirikuta and Potrero de la Palmita. Indigenous actors can enter the spaces reserved for the dominant racial position (whiteness in the US, a ladinized version of whiteness in Mexico)—Tulsa, Mexico City, Palm Springs, the laboratory—though in those spaces they are continually reminded of their subordinate status. Whites, by contrast, as representatives of universality, of modernity, commit acts of betrayal when they seek to enter those spaces reserved for the specificity of indigeneity. They are heretics, charlatans, hippies, frauds. Worse still, they have appropriated something from the other.

Some benefit from that boundary. The legal rights of indigenous peyotists in the US and Mexico are now enshrined in law, and in limited cases provide an opportunity for economic development. Setting aside questions of whether or not the Wixárika and members of the NAC are forced to perform a certain version of indigeneity in order to remain legible, this is obviously a positive development. That the Peyote Way, the white shamans, and others face sanctions for their peyote use is where our problem lies. Medical arguments against peyote have long since been debunked, and the ecological argument forces us to impose tortured racial boundaries on space, especially in the US, where some NAC members argue that they should have exclusive access to the peyote gardens of south Texas in spite of the fact that their own traditions of peyotism are no more ancient than those of some non-indigenous groups. If we accept this reasoning, we allow ecological scarcity to erase long and complicated histories while simplifying and hardening the distinction between Indian and non. We also inadvertently make it easier for others to argue that scarcity and ecological vulnerability justify their own racially purifying exercises.

Blackness has played a somewhat peripheral role in the twentieth-century history of peyote (it was more prevalent in Inquisitional texts, where we see slaves and free people of color using peyote in their religious and curing ceremonies with some frequency),[8] which may be one reason why the story of John Jamison stands out. We are reminded through his church that there is a larger history of racial exclusions built into the story of peyote, and while the specific spaces and experiences of the Church of the First Born spoke principally to the experience of a formerly allotted African American in post-riot Tulsa, peyote had a similar effect here as it did elsewhere, cleaving the Indian off from non-Indians by limiting sanctioned peyote use to indigenous spaces.[9]

While the African American members of the Church of the First Born might simply have been unlucky to practice their religion in a space that was both unsanctioned and unsafe, their story also highlights the ways that the history of peyote is as much about the banishment of non-indigenous bodies from the mystical realm as it is the story of the relegation of indigenous bodies to that realm. Jamison was erased, first literally and then figuratively, his church reduced to a footnote, and his acolytes rendered as timid, naïve, and perhaps a little crazy. They were unlike Indians because they did not defend their peyote church as assiduously as Indians did theirs, and the fact that the defense was made impossible both by their urban precariousness and the active hostility of their erstwhile indigenous allies was forgotten.

. . .

I began this project with an assumption that I would find that the category "Indian" acquired profoundly different meanings as we crossed the border. The different histories of the American and Mexican states suggested as much. Moreover, substantial differences across space and time are impossible to miss. In the US peyotism was part of an evangelical religion, a pan-indigenous cultural form that connected otherwise distinct communities through a common practice. It has been the subject of constitutional challenges here since the 1920s, and has been successfully defended as a First Amendment right for members of the Native American Church. US government officials and missionaries undertook extensive efforts to eradicate peyotism on the reservations at various points during the first half of the century, and peyotism itself was a relatively novel practice.

No such constitutional right exists in Mexico, and until relatively recently nothing approximating the Native American Church existed there. Furthermore, in Mexico peyotism is much more closely tied to a specific set of communities and bound up in the history of those communities. Government officials paid little attention to their peyotism prior to the 1960s, and even then treated it as a phenomenon likely to wither away with the advent of modernity. Peyote, then, seemed to offer an excellent opportunity to demonstrate how certain concepts of race do not cross the border.

In the end I am not sure I can make that argument. Over a long period of time in both Mexico and the US we see similar logics deployed, similar affective responses, and ultimately the creation of remarkably similar legal regimes around peyote use. Some of those similarities might be understood as the product of forces external to both the US and Mexico (for instance, the 1971 Vienna Treaty on Psychotropic Drugs, which embraced an exemption for indigenous uses of medicinal and sacred plants) or as the product of US pressure on Mexico (Mexican drug laws are often drafted in part to conform to demands coming from the US). Others cannot be so easily explained.

In Mexico peyote has had the power to elicit curiosity, disgust, and enchantment since Europeans first took note of the cactus. It has long been implicated in sentiments that shaped the contours of the category "Indian," especially inasmuch as the Indian symbolized something that was almost diametrically opposed to whiteness (the term used in Mexico is *mestizaje*, though mestizaje as deployed within Mexican nationalism has long subsumed the indigenous past into a largely Europeanized present).[10] Peyote did not so much carry these sentiments with it as it crossed the border as it generated a remarkably similar set of associations in the US over the course of the twentieth century. For the most part these responses rendered indigenous peyotism as somehow normal and nonindigenous peyotism as a problem to be addressed. It is a world where Eligio López can enjoy the full protection of the law while Anne Zapf lurks in the shadows, and where John Jamison has no place whatsoever.

Notes

INTRODUCTION

1. Ignacio Sendejas, *Metodo Curativo*, Monterrey, 13 August 1833. Archivo Municpal de Monclova, Coahuila, Fondo Siglo XIX.

2. On the place of peyote in colonial Mexico more generally, see (among others) Alexander Dawson, "Peyote in the Colonial Imagination"; G. Aguirre Beltán, *Medicina y magia;* Martin Nesvig, "Peyote, Ever Virgin."

3. Peyote was one of the yerbas commonly sold in *tianguis populares*. See Ricardo Pérez Monfort, *Yerba, goma, y polvo,* 30. See also Richard Evans Schultes, "Peyote—An American Indian Heritage from Mexico," 202–4; J.S. Slotkin, "Peyotism, 1521–1891"; José Domingo Schievenini Stefanoni, "La prohibición de la marihuana en México, 1920–1940"; Olga Cárdenas de Ojeda, *Toxicomania y narcotrafico,* 25–27; Ricardo Pérez Monfort, "El veneno 'paradisiaco,' 152–55; Luis Astorga, *El siglo de las drogas,* 20–23.

4. See Isaac Campos, *Home Grown,* 81–102; Pérez Monfort, "El veneno 'paradisiaco,'" 143–210.

5. There was some question about the actual presence of the devil. See Fernando Cervantes, *The Devil in the New World.*

6. On the Native American Church (NAC), see Weston La Barre, *The Peyote Cult;* Omer C. Stewart, *Peyote Religion: A History* (esp. 239–45); Barbara Myerhoff, *Peyote Hunt: The Sacred Journey of the Huichol Indian;* Peter T. Furst, ed., *Flesh of the Gods;* Thomas C. Maroukis, *The Peyote Road;* Stacy Schaefer, *Amada's Blessings.*

7. James A. McCleary, Paul S. Sypherd, and David L. Walkington, "Antibiotic Activity of an Extract of Peyote," 247–49; A. D. Bloom et al., "Chromosome Aberrations among the Yanomamma Indians," 920–27; Michael C. Mithoefer et al., "Durability of Improvement in Post-Traumatic Stress Disorder Symptoms"; Tom Csordas, "Word from the Holy People," 284.

8. Robert L. Bergman, "Navajo Peyote Use: Its Apparent Safety"; John Calabrese, *A Different Medicine*, 13. On particularity, see Dipesh Chakrabarty, "Postcoloniality and the Artifice of History."

9. See Allan Pred, *The Past Is Not Dead: Facts, Fictions, and Enduring Racial Stereotypes* (Minneapolis: University of Minnesota Press, 2004); Diana Michele Negrín, *Colores Mexicanos;* Philip Deloria, *Indians in Unexpected Places;* Kenneth Mills, *Idolatry and Its Enemies*, 212–14, 269; Stephan Palmié, "Other Powers"; Diane Nelson, *A Finger in the Wound*, 129; Rebecca Earle, "Indians and Drunkenness in Spanish America." See also María Josefina Saldaña-Portillo, *Indian Given.*

10. See Clyde Haberman, "LSD-like Drugs Are out of the Haze and Back in the Labs," *New York Times*, 15 May 2016; Teri S. Krebs and Pål-Ørjan Johansen, "Lysergic Acid Diethylamide (LSD) for Alcoholism"; "End the Ban on Psychoactive Drug Research"; David E. Nichols, "Differences between the Mechanism of Action of MDMA, MBDB, and the Classic Hallucinogens"; David Nutt, "A Brave New World for Psychology." See also Rebecca Earle, "'If you eat their food . . .'"; Alfred Crosby, *The Columbian Exchange: Biological and Cultural Consequences of 1492* (New York: Praeger, 1972).

11. See for example Remón Medina Silva, "How One Goes on Being Huichol," 199; Havelock Ellis, "Mescal: A New Artificial Paradise."

12. See Tom Csordas, "Introduction: The Body as Representation and Being-in-the-World." See also Todd Gitlin, "On Drugs and Mass Media," 32; Bryan Turner, "The Body in Western Society"; Sehta M. Low, "Embodied Metaphors: Nerves as Lived Experience," in Csordas, *Embodiment*, 139–62; Pierre Bourdieu, *Outline of a Theory of Practice*, 72; Thomas J. Csordas, "Embodiment as a Paradigm for Anthropology."

13. I first heard this term from Higinio González to refer to psychedelic enthusiasts.

14. See Thomas J. Csordas, "The Rhetoric of Transformation in Ritual Healing"; Thomas J. Csordas, "Medical and Sacred Realities."

15. See Wolfgang Schivelbusch, *The Tastes of Paradise* (New York: Vintage, 1992); David T. Courtwright, *Forces of Habit.*

16. Ben Highmore reminds us that affect is truth, the loss of control, the inability to remain calm. "Bitter Aftertaste: Affect, Food, and Social Aesthetics," 118. See also Gonzalo Aguirre Beltán, *Medicina y magia*, 159; Robert Crewe, "Brave New Spain."

17. It is, in this sense, an "actant." See Jane Bennett, *Vibrant Matter.* See also Thomas Ots, "The Angry Liver," 22–24.

18. We might consider obedience here as a performance in which we cannot assume that disciplined bodies reflect disciplined minds. See for example Derek Sayer, "Everyday Forms of State Formation."

19. Affect begins with the peyote user's perception (the visual, aural, and olfactory response), which then becomes a bodily response (the warm feeling of enchantment, the tensing of the body and discomfort or disgust), and then cognition (an effort to turn affective responses into meaning). Emotions then become, as Gilles Deleuze suggested, the product of a "violent collision of mind and body." See Deleuze, *Essays Critical and Clinical*, 123–25; Elspeth Probyn,

"Writing Shame," 77–80; Bourdieu, *Outline of a Theory of Practice*; Jon Beasley-Murray, *Posthegemony: Political Theory and Latin America*. See also Highmore, "Bitter Aftertaste," 118; Patricia Clough, "The Affective Turn: Political Economy, Biomedia, and Bodies," 207–9; Zoltan Kovecses, *Metaphor and Emotion;* William Reddy, *The Navigation of Feeling*. An excellent examination of the role that indigeneity plays in the construction of the Western Self can be found in Fernando Coronil, "Beyond Occidentalism."

20. See Sianne Ngai, "Merely Interesting."

CHAPTER ONE

1. Richard Burton also mentions peyote in his *Look of the West,* originally published in 1862. See Jan G. Bruhn and Bo Holmstedt, "Early Peyote Research"; Govind J. Kapadia and M. B. E. Fayez, "Peyote Constituents." See also J. M. Coulter, "Preliminary Revision of the North American Species of Cactus, Anhalonium, and Lophophora."

2. Carl Lumhotlz, *Unknown Mexico,* vol. 1, 358; G. A. Bender, "Rough and Ready Research—1887 Style." See also Stacy Schaefer, *Amada's Blessings,* 37.

3. The article in the *Druggist's Bulletin* was a reprint of an article published in April 1887. J. R. Briggs, "'Muscale Buttons.'" Both Slotkin and Prentiss and Morgan later question Briggs's account, claiming that it was likely not peyote that he had ingested.

4. Quoted in Daniel M. Perrine, "Visions of the Night," 16.

5. Alkaloids are the naturally occurring, nitrogen-based chemical compounds that typically produce physiological responses in humans. Bruhn and Holmstedt, "Early Peyote Research," 353–90.

6. Some historical accounts indicate that Lewin was traveling in the US in 1886, but the timing for the arrival of the buttons at Parke Davis suggest it must have been 1887. Bruhn and Holmstedt, "Early Peyote Research," 360–62.

7. Coulter, "Preliminary Revision," 91–132.

8. It was briefly marketed as a sleep aid by German pharmaceutical company Boeringer and Sons in the late 1890s. See Perrine, "Visions of the Night." See also Francisco López-Muñoz et al., "The History of Barbiturates." Bruhn and Holmstedt, "Early Peyote Research," 364.

9. Anhalamine was isolated by Kayder in 1899. He and Lewin insisted that there were two distinct species, one containing mescaline and the other pellotine. In time most botanists would conclude there was only a single species, *L williamsii*. See United Nations Division on Narcotic Drugs, *Bulletin;* Perrine, "Visions of the Night."

10. Louis Lewin, *Phantastica*. See also H. H. Rusby, "Mescal Buttons."

11. Heffter, 1898, quoted in Perrine, "Visions of the Night," 44.

12. Manuel Urbina, "El peyote y el ololiuhqui," 32. See also Perrine, "Visions of the Night"; James Mooney, "The Mescal Plant and Ceremony." On Mooney more generally, see L. G. Moses, *The Indian Man*.

13. D. W. Prentiss and Francis Morgan, "Anhalonium Lewinii," 577; E. E. Ewell, "The Chemistry of the Cactaceae"; Mooney, "The Mescal Plant and Ceremony," 7–11.

14. Perrine, "Visions of the Night."

15. In the testimony Wiley does recount that they had previously done toxicity tests on guinea pigs and other small animals. United States House Committee on Indian Affairs, *Peyote: Hearings Before V Subcommittee of the Committee on Indian Affairs of the House of Representatives H.R. 2614 to Amend Sections 2139 and 2140 of the Revised Statutes and the Acts Amendatory Thereof, and for Other Purposes* (Washington: Government Printing Office, 1918), 52–53.

16. Prentiss and Morgan, "Anhalonium Lewinii," 577–85. On the distinction between Indians and Caucasians in this regard, see "Let's Eat a Mescal Button," *Sunday Herald* (Boston), 3 November 1895.

17. Prentiss and Morgan, "Anhalonium Lewinii," 577–85.

18. Prentiss and Morgan, 579–80, 584.

19. Prentiss and Morgan, 577–85; Havelock Ellis, "Mescal: A New Artificial Paradise."

20. "Let's Eat a Mescal Button."

21. "Let's Eat a Mescal Button."

22. Mooney, "The Mescal Plant and Ceremony," 7–11.

23. Mooney, 7–11.

24. Mooney, 7–11.

25. Mooney, 7–11.

26. S. Weir Mitchell, "Remarks on the Effects of Anhelonium Lewini."

27. Ellis, "A Note on the Phenomena of Mescal-Intoxication."

28. Ellis, "Mescal: A New Artificial Paradise," 141.

29. Ellis, "Mescal," 134.

30. Ellis, "Mescal," 135.

31. Ellis, "Mescal," 136.

32. Ellis, "Mescal," 137.

33. Ellis, "Mescal," 138.

34. Ellis, "Mescal," 141.

35. Ellis, "A Note on the Phenomena of Mescal-Intoxication," 1542.

36. "Paradise or Inferno."

37. "Paradise or Inferno."

38. See for example Huntington Cairns, "A Divine Intoxicant." On this tendency more generally, see Londa Schiebinger, *Plants and Empire;* Londa Schiebinger, "West Indian Abortificants."

CHAPTER TWO

1. *Estudio relativo al peyote* (México: Instituto Médico Nacional, 1913), 51–52.

2. On the research done in Mexico prior to the 1880s, see for example Isaac Campos, *Home Grown,* esp. chap. 4; Pérez Montfort, "El veneno 'faradisiaco'"; Froylán Enciso, *Nuestra historia narcótica.*

3. Xavier Lozoya, *La herbolaria en México.*

4. Juan Manuel Noriega, "Curso de historia de drogas." See also Juan Pablo García Vallejo, "Breve historia de la legislación de drogas en México."

5. Juan Manuel Noriega's 1902 "Curso de historia de drogas" was canonical in this regard. On the history of drug regimentation and laws during this era, see for example Luis Astorga, *El siglo de las drogas*. See also Pérez Montfort, *Yerba, goma y polvo;* Pérez Montfort, "El Veneno 'Faradisiaco'"; Enciso, *Nuestra historia narcótica*. For an excellent treatment of this shift over time, see Pamela Voekel, *Alone before God*.

6. I discuss this in Dawson, "Peyote in the Colonial Imagination." See also R. Crewe, "Brave New Spain."

7. Peter T. Furst, "Myth as History, History as Myth."

8. Manuel Urbina, "El peyote y el ololiuhqui." Lumholtz first published work on the Huichols in *Scribner's* in 1894. He published what would be for many decades the authoritative text on this community, *Unknown Mexico/ Mexico desconocido*, in 1902. Diguet, a chemical engineer sent to Mexico in the 1890s by the French *Compagnie du Boleo*, published "La sierra du Nayarit et ses indigénes" in 1899. Diguet also explored the medical uses of peyote extensively in "Les cactacées utiles du Mexique," published posthumously in 1928.

9. They tended to downplay ongoing conflicts with mestizo communities and haciendas. See Michele Stevens, "'. . . As Long as They Have Their Land.'"

10. Guadalupe Ocotán (Ratsisarie) is an annex of San Andrés, cleaved off when Nayarit claimed it as part of its state instead of Jalisco in 1873. Similarly, Tuxpan de Bolaños (Tutxipa) is an annex of San Sebastián.

11. Stacy B. Schaefer, "The Cosmos Contained."

12. Schaefer and Furst, "Introduction," in *People of the Peyote,* 1–25.

13. Particularly Padres José Ortega and José Arlegui. See for example J. Ortega, *Historia del Nayarit*.

14. Carl Lumholtz, *Unknown Mexico*, vol. 2, 213. See Lumholtz, *Unknown Mexico*, vol. 1, 6–9, 148, 177–79, 245–49, 357–59, 374–75. On Lumholtz, see Charles Bowden, "Learning Nothing, Forgetting Nothing: On the Trail of Carl Lumholtz"; Michele M. Stephens, *Under the Eyes of God,* 310–14. More generally, see Stacy B. Schaefer, "The Crossing of Souls"; Peter Furst, "To Find Our Life"; Peter Furst, *Hallucinogens and Culture;* Barbara Myerhoff, *Peyote Hunt;* Susana Valadéz, "Dreams and Visions from the Gods"; Fernando Benítez, *En la tierra mágica del peyote,* Ramón Mata Torres, *Los peyoteros;* Juan Negrín, *Acercamiento histórico y subjectivo al Huichol;* Johannes Neurath, *Las fiestas de la Casa Grande;* Jay C. Fikes, *Unknown Huichol;* J. C. Fikes et al., eds., *La mitología de los Huicholes;* Phil Weigand, *Estudio histórico y cultural sobre los Huicholes.*

15. On this tendency, see also Ales Hrdlicka, "Physiological and Medical Observations," 250–51.

16. "Peyotes: Datos para su estudio," 206; *Estudio relativo al peyote,* 1913, 7–9, 36–37.

17. Urbina, "El peyote y el ololiuhqui," 25. They all draw from Padre Arlegui, *Cronica de la provincia de Zacatecas,* part 2, cap 7, 154–55. See also José Ramírez, "Lectura de turno."

18. Ramírez, "Lectura de turno," 235. See also *Estudio relativo al peyote.*

19. *Estudio relativo al peyote,* 12.

20. José Ramírez, "Peyote." Ricardo Pérez Montfort, "Fragmentos de historia de las drogas," 143–210, esp. 166.

21. Noriega, "Curso de historia de drogas," 506–12.

22. Noriega, "Curso de historia de drogas." R. Rosendo Corona, an engineer for the state of Jalisco who in 1898 traveled to Santa Catarina (one of the central Huichol sites), compared the effect of peyote to marijuana intoxication, *Estudio relativo al peyote*, 15. Campos demonstrates that these were not simply elite beliefs but shared by poor people as well. See Campos, *Home Grown*, 124–81.

23. *Estudio relativo al peyote*, 36–37.

24. Urbina, "El peyote y el ololiuhqui," 33. Degeneration was a more general fear. See for example Pablo Piccato, *City of Suspects:*, 51. Ricardo Pérez Montfort and Isaac Campos both argue that the moralizing about marijuana centers on class and race, though Campos notes that popular and elite views of the effects of madness were remarkably similar during this period. See Pérez Montfort, *Yerba, goma y polvo*; Campos, *Home Grown*, esp. 155–81. See also José Domingo Schievenini Stefanoni, "La prohibición de la marihuana en México, 1920–1940."

25. *Estudio relativo al peyote*, 10.

26. *Estudio relativo al peyote;* Ramírez, "Lectura de turno." For a larger consideration of the meaning of drunkenness in these contexts, see Rebecca Earle, "Indians and Drunkenness in Spanish America."

27. This was one reason that they drew guidance from a short essay published by Walter Dixon in the *British Medical Journal* in 1898. An extract from the essay, which describes a fairly simple solution produced from peyote, was published in the *Anales* of the institute in 1899: "Peyotes: Datos para su estudio," 205–6. See also Urbina, "El peyote y el ololiuhqui" and *Estudio relativo al peyote*. See also Walter E. Dixon, "A Preliminary Note."

28. *Estudio relativo al peyote*, 61.

29. *Estudio relativo al peyote*, 60.

30. *Estudio relativo al peyote*, 59–60.

31. *Estudio relativo al peyote*, 50, 53–54.

32. *Estudio relativo al peyote*, 55–56.

33. *Anales Instituto Médico Nacional* 5 (1903): 133–34; *Estudio relativo al peyote*, 50.

34. *Estudio relativo al peyote*, 51. "Peyotes: Datos para su estudio," 212.

35. *Estudio relativo al peyote*, 57.

36. *Anales Instituto Medico Nacional* 5 (1903): 133–34.

37. *Anales Instituto Médico Nacional* 7 (June 1905): 187–92.

38. *Anales Instituto Médico Nacional* 7 (June 1905): 187–92.

39. *Estudio relativo al peyote*, 51–52.

40. "Peyotes: Datos para su estudio," 213–14.

41. *Anales Instituto Médico Nacional* 5 (1903): 62–63.

42. *Anales Instituto Médico Nacional* 5 (1903): 62–78.

43. *Anales Instituto Médico Nacional* 5 (1903): 62–78.

44. Antonio A. Loaeza reported this on 30 September 1901. *Anales Instituto Médico Nacional* 5 (1903): 144–45.

45. "Informe," 28 February 1902, *Anales Instituto Médico Nacional* (1902): 236.

46. *Anales Instituto Médico Nacional* 5 (1903):, 23.

47. *Anales Instituto Médico Nacional* 5 (1903): 138, 162–64. "Informes de los trabajos ejecutidos en el Instituto Médico Nacional, durante el mes de Enero de 1905," *Anales Instituto Médico Nacional* 7 (1905): 52.

48. Noriega, "Curso de historia de drogas."

49. *Estudio relativo al peyote,* 60.

50. Urbina, "El peyote y el ololiuhqui," 45.

51. *Estudio relativo al peyote,* 62–63.

52. Ignacio de la Peña Páez, "El estudio formal," 54; Lozoya, *La herbolaria en México.*

53. García Vallejo, "Breve historia."

54. See for example Cassiano Conzatti, "Las plantas heróicas mexicanas"; B. P. Reko, "Alcaloides y glucósidos en plantas mexicanas." See also Clemente Robles, "Acción fisiológica del clorhidrao de peyotina," 215–20.

55. On this, see Campos, *Home Grown;* Pérez Montfort, *Yerba, goma y polvo;* Enciso, *Nuestra historia narcotica,* esp. chap. 3.

56. Olga Cárdenas de Ojeda, *Toxicomania y narcotrafico,* 25–27.

57. This became the basis for all subsequent reforms to the sanitary and penal codes, up to 1971. *Enervantes* become *estupificantes* in the 1949 sanitary code. Cárdenas de Ojeda, *Toxicomania y narcotrafico,* 25–27.

58. See "Estudio del reglamento de narcóticos," May–June 1930; SP/SJ/3/5, AHSSA, Mexico City (*SJ* in this instance stands for "Sección Juridica Consultiva"); Ricardo Pérez Montfort "Historias primigenias"; Pérez Montfort, *Yerba, goma y polvo.* More broadly, see Jordan Goodman et al., eds., *Consuming Habits.*

59. Oficio 9, 12880, 27 April 1928, in Maximo Martínez, *Las Plantas medicinales de Mexico,* 215–20.

60. In the 1934 sanitary code, coca, cocaine, and cannabis are included as enervantes, banned, but peyote and mescaline are not included. See *Diario Oficial* 85:53 (31 August 1934): 1194–95. In the 1934 sanitary code under *Drogas enervantes* (Article 406) there was no mention of peyote (Departamento de Salubridad Pública, *Codigo Sanitario de los Estados Unidos Mexicanos,* 1934). Peyote was included the following year as one source of drug addiction, along with heroin, cocaine, morphine, and marijuana, but was not banned. "Reglamento de toxicómano: Proyecto de reglamento interior para el Hospital Federal de Toxicómanos," June 1935; SP/SJ/43/15, AHSSA, Mexico City.

61. It was manufactured as a tonic and sold as Le Peyotyl by a Genevese pharmacy in the early 1930s. See United Nations Division on Narcotic Drugs, *Bulletin,* 25–26.

CHAPTER THREE

1. NARA RG 75, E 764, Box 1.

2. W. Ketcham, Director, to the Secretary of the Interior, 9 March 1911, NARA RG 75, E 764, Box 1.

3. Alejandro Camino, "El peyote: Derecho histórico"; "History, Use and Effects of Peyote," *Indian School Journal* 12:7 (May 1912): 239–41, NARA RG 75, E 764, Box 1. On earlier prohibition efforts, see *Peyote: An Abridged*

Compilation from the Files of the Bureau of Indian Affairs, prepared by Dr. Robert E. L. Newbern, Chief Medical Service, under the Direction of Chas. H Burke, Commissioner (Lawrence, KS: The Haskell Institute, 1922), 5–7; Schaefer, *Amada's Blessings,* 98–99; Stewart, *Peyote Religion,* 128–47.

4. Chief Special Officer William Johnson to the Commissioner of Indian Affairs, en route El Paso, TX, 4 May 1909, NARA RG 75, E 764, Box 1. See also W. Ketcham to the Secretary of the Interior, 9 March 1911, NARA RG 75, E 764, Box 1.

5. Chief Special Officer to Commissioner of Indian Affairs, 11 September 1909, NARA RG 75, E 764, Box 1. Johnson to Commissioner of Indian Affairs, 15 January 1910, NARA RG 75, E 764, Box 1.

6. George Hoyo, Superintendent, Otoe Agency (OK), to Henry Larson, Chief Special Officer, 11 November 1916, NARA RG 75, E 764, Box 1; W. Ketcham to the Secretary of the Interior, 9 March 1911, NARA RG 75, E 764, Box 1.

7. See for example F. A. McKenzie, *"Pussyfoot" Johnson,* 67–90; "W. E. Johnson Dies; Dry Crusader, 82," *New York Times,* 3 February 1945, 11.

8. See "Mescal Bean Taken up by Sioux and Poncos," *Omaha World Herald,* 26 February 1912; Jacob Bried to Edward Ayer (Phoenix), 10 March 1916; Mrs. Delavan L. Pierson, "Indian Peyote Worship," *Southern Workman,* April 1915, 242; Gertrude Seymour, "Peyote Worship—An Indian Cult and Powerful Drug," *Red Man,* June 1916, 345–46. All found in Correspondence of the Chief Special Officer Relating to Peyote, 1908–1918, NARA RG 75, E 764, Box 1. On these racial fears, see in particular Paul Gootenberg, *Andean Cocaine,* and Campos, *Home Grown.*

9. Walter Roe of Winnebago, NE, to Rev. Wilbur Crafts, DC, 21 November 1908, NARA RG 75, E 764, Box 1.

10. The Shanghai Conference was attended by thirteen nations and led to the creation of the International Opium Commission, which had thirteen member states (Mexico was not included). This was the first major international cooperative effort to control the flow of opium and cocaine, and was formalized at the end of the First World War. See I. Bayer, H. Ghodse, "Evolution of International Drug Control"; Paul Gootenberg, "Cocaine's Long March North"; David P. Stewart, "Internationalizing the War on Drugs."

11. Superintendent, Shawnee Indian School, Shawnee, OK, to Chief Special Officer Larson, 12 November 1916, NARA RG 75, E 764, Box 1.

12. Johnson to Commissioner of Indian Affairs, 15 January 1910, NARA RG 75, E 764, Box 1.

13. Pierson, "Indian Peyote Worship," 244. See also L. E. Sayre, of University of Kansas, to A. R. Snyder, Potawatoni Agency, 5 May 1915, NARA RG 75, E 764, Box 1. See also Seymour, "Peyote Worship," 347.

14. Superintendent, Shawnee Indian School, Shawnee, OK, to Chief Special Officer Larson, 12 November 1916, NARA RG 75, E 764, Box 1.

15. See for example the testimony of the Utah state chemist Harman Harms in 1917, United States House Committee on Indian Affairs (*Peyote,* 37). See also *What about Peyote* (New York: Home Mission Council of North America, presented with the Thirty-fourth Annual Report of the Indian Rights Association, 1916), NARA RG 75, E 178; Pierson, "Indian Peyote Worship," 241;

Seymour, "Peyote Worship: An Indian Cult and a Powerful Drug," *The Survey* 36:7 (13 May 1916): 183; Secretary to Mrs. Mary Roe, Colony, OK, 22 January 1915; Mary Roe to F. H. Abbott (Board of Indian Commissioners), 3 April 1914, NARA RG 75, E 764, Box 1.

16. "Peyote" in *The Native American* 14:27 (5 July 1913): 379–80. See also G. A. Watermulder, "Mescal: A Menace to the Indians," address to the Mohank Conference, 14–16 October, 1914, published in *Southern Workman*, December 1914, 681–87, NARA RG 75, E 764, Box 1.

17. Secretary Abbott to Mrs. Roem, New Haven, CT, 7 April 1914; Secretary Abbott to Mary Roe, 24 March 1914, NARA RG 75, E 764, Box 1. See also Rev. G. A. Watermulder, "Mescal"; F. H. Daiker, "Liquor and Peyote a Menace to the Indian," in the Thirty-second Annual Report of the Lake Mohonk Conference; Mrs. Delavan L. Pierson, "American Indian Peyote Worship," *Missionary Review of the World*, March 2015; Seymour, "Peyote Worship," 345–47; Walter Roe of Winnebago, NE, to Rev. Wilbur Crafts, DC, 21 November 1908; correspondence from Red Cliff Indian Agency, Bayfield, WI, 16 October 1914; "Peyote Injurious to Utah Indians," *Indian School Journal*, June 1916; "Peyote" in *The Native American* 14:27 (5 July 1913): 379–80; Francis Blast to Rev. Father W. J. Ketcham, 18 December 1916, NARA RG 75, E 764, Box 1.

18. Pierson, "American Indian Peyote Worship," 202; Elsie Kenton, Supervisor, to Commissioner of Indian Affairs, detailing observations of recent visit to Field Matrons in Oklahoma, 29 August 1911, NARA RG 75, E 764, Box 1. See also Charles Shell, Cheyenne and Arapaho Agency (OK), to Mr. W. Johnson, US Special Officer, Salt Lake City, 22 June 1909, NARA RG 75, E 764, Box 1.

19. Pierson, "Indian Peyote Worship," 244. See also L. E. Sayre, of University of Kansas, to A. R. Snyder, Potawatoni Agency, 5 May 1915, NARA RG 75, E 764, Box 1. Statement of Dr. Richardson, Yankton Agency, about death of David Stricker Jr. (believes it is an overdose of mescal buttons), 10 January 1917. Charles Shell, Cheyenne and Arapaho Agency (OK), to Mr. W. Johnson, US Special Officer, Salt Lake City, 22 June 1909, NARA RG 75, E 764, Box 1.

20. G. A. Watermulder, "Mescal," 681–87.

21. Superintendent, Osage Indian Agency (OK), to Commissioner of Indian Affairs, 24 December 1908, NARA RG 75, E 764, Box 1.

22. Gertrude Seymour, "Peyote Worship," 345–46.

23. Hoyo to Henry Larson, Chief Special Officer, Denver, 11 November 1916, NARA RG 75, E 764, Box 1.

24. Jacob Bried to Edward Ayer (Phoenix), 10 March 1916. Correspondence of the Chief Special Officer Relating to Peyote, 1908–1918. See also *What about Peyote.*

25. Watermulder, "Mescal," 681–87.

26. Watermulder, "Mescal," 681–87.

27. Pierson, "Indian Peyote Worship," 242.

28. Fears of Mexican influence are reasserted around these ideas time and time again. See for example "Mexicanizing Indian Education," *The Christian Century*, 11 October 1934, NARA 75 (178), Box 18.

29. J. S. Slotkin, "Peyotism, 1521–1891," 202–30.

30. Schaefer, "The Peyote Religion and Mescalero Apaches," 140–41. See also Stewart, *Peyote Religion.*

31. Unclassified notes in Office Files of Commissioner John Collier, 1933–1945, NARA RG 75, E 178. See also Schaefer, "The Peyote Religion and Mescalero Apaches"; Mooney, "The Mescal Plant and Ceremony"; Stewart, *Peyote Religion;* La Barre, *The Peyote Cult;* Morris E. Opler, "The Use of Peyote by the Carrizo and Lipan Apache Tribes." It is also possible that it was first introduced into the US by the Mescalero Apaches, who already practiced peyotism by the 1870s and who may have learned it during their raids on Rarámuri (then known as Tarahumara) communities in Chihuahua. However, since their tradition bore no traces of Christian influence, it is unlikely that they influenced the Oklahoma peyote cults. See Schultes, "Peyote—An American Indian Heritage from Mexico," 199–201; Ruth Shonle, "Peyote—Giver of Visions."

32. Morris E. Opler, "A Description of a Tonkawa Peyote Meeting."

33. Parker's life is explored in William T. Hagan, *Quanah Parker, Comanche Chief.*

34. Chief Special Officer Henry Larson to Commissioner of Indian Affairs, 9 December 1916, NARA RG 75, E 764, Box 1.

35. See Chief Special Officer Henry Larson to R. P. Stewart, US Attorney, in Deadwood, CO, 15 April 1915, NARA RG 75, E 764, Box 1. See also *Peyote: An Abridged Compilation,* 24.

36. Schaefer, *Amada's Blessings,* 98–99.

37. See for example A. R. Snyder, Potawatomi Agency, KS, to Henry Larson, Chief Special Officer, Denver, 6 May 1915; Edwin Minor, Superintendent, Kickapoo Training School, Germantown, KS, to Henry A. Larson, Chief Special Officer, Denver, 23 November 1915; Edwin Minor, Superintendent, Kickapoo Training School, Germantown, KS, to Henry A. Larson, Chief Special Officer, Denver, 20 December 1915; Chief Special Officer to Commissioner, 21 April 1917; Chief Special Officer to E. A. Hutchinson, Indian Superintendent, Fort Wachakic, 22 March 1917; J. P. Brandt, Special Officer in Bemidji, MN, to Henry Larson, 11 March 1918, NARA RG 75, E 764, Box 1.

38. On the BIC, see Henry Fitz, "The Last Hurrah of Christian Humanitarian Indian Reform."

39. Stewart, *Peyote Religion,* chap. 8.

40. Congress also held hearings every year between 1912 and 1916 to consider implementing a ban, but never took action. Miscellaneous peyote correspondence during 1915, NARA RG 75, E 764, Box 1. See also United States House Committee on Indian Affairs, *Peyote: Hearings Before a Subcommittee of the Committee on Indian Affairs of the House of Representatives H. R. 2614 to Amend Sections 2139 and 2140 of the Revised Statutes and the Acts Amendatory Thereof, and for Other Purposes* (Washington: Government Printing Office, 1918), 42.

41. George Vaux Jr. to Abbott (cc to Sec of Interior), 24 October 1914, NARA RG 75, E 764, Box 1.

42. See Department of Agriculture, Bureau of Chemistry, "Service and Regulatory Announcement No. 18," issued 8 May 1915, *Peyote: An Abridged Compilation* 23.

CHAPTER FOUR

1. United States House Committee on Indian Affairs, *Peyote,* 16.

2. Chief Special Officer to Commissioner of Indian Affairs, 20 April 1917, NARA RG 75, E 764, Box 1.

3. Loose papers, NARA RG 75, E 764, Box 1.

4. He mentioned specifically the Mission, Sioux, Cheyenne. Arapaho, Havasupai, Apache, Kiowa, Comanche, Osage, Kickapoo, Omaha, Winnebago, Potawatomi, Sac and Fox, Santee, Shawnee, Otoe, and Missouri. See United States House Committee on Indian Affairs, *Peyote,* 5.

5. United States House Committee on Indian Affairs, *Peyote,* 13.

6. United States House Committee on Indian Affairs, *Peyote,* 20.

7. United States House Committee on Indian Affairs, *Peyote,* 16.

8. United States House Committee on Indian Affairs, *Peyote,* 16.

9. United States House Committee on Indian Affairs, *Peyote,* 16.

10. United States House Committee on Indian Affairs, *Peyote,* 19.

11. This comes from Brosius's submission to the 1918 hearings, which includes a publication from the Thirty-fourth Annual Report of the Indian Rights Association, 14 December 1916, titled *The Ravages of Peyote* (United States House Committee on Indian Affairs, *Peyote,* 19).

12. These last quotes come from the submission of Mrs. Roe and were included in an article titled "Mescal, a Menace to the Indians" (United States House Committee on Indian Affairs, *Peyote,* 44–46).

13. United States House Committee on Indian Affairs, *Peyote,* 24, 27–30, 35, 135.

14. United States House Committee on Indian Affairs, *Peyote,* 44.

15. United States House Committee on Indian Affairs, *Peyote,* 28. See also statement of Harvey Wiley, 21 February 1918. See also statement of Roswell P. Angier of Yale, office files of Commissioner John Collier, 1933–1945, NARA RG 75, E 178.

16. Father William Ketcham, Director Catholic Indian Missions, to Congressman John Tillman, 26 February 1918. See also the article submitted by the proponents of the ban, titled "Mescal, a Menace to the Indians," which contains a litany of complaints (United States House Committee on Indian Affairs, *Peyote,* 44–46).

17. United States House Committee on Indian Affairs, *Peyote,* 122–23.

18. United States House Committee on Indian Affairs, *Peyote,* 21.

19. United States House Committee on Indian Affairs, *Peyote,* 166.

20. Take for instance Peyote Investigation, statement of Pe-na-ro, Apache, 24 September 1918. See also statement of George Maddox, Comanche, 18 September 1918, NARA RG 75, E 764, Box 1. See also Gertrude Seymour, "Peyote Worship: An Indian Cult and a Powerful Drug," *The Survey* 36:7 (13 May 1916): 181.

21. Transcript of the 1918 hearings, NARA RG 75, E 764, Box 1. See also United States House Committee on Indian Affairs, *Peyote,* 63.

22. United States House Committee on Indian Affairs, *Peyote,* 68–74; transcript from the 1918 hearings, NARA RG 75, E 764, Box 1.

23. United States House Committee on Indian Affairs, *Peyote,* 146–48.

24. On the larger legislative struggle and the role of Owen, see Stewart, *Peyote Religion,* esp. 213–21.

25. See for example Francis La Flesche to George Vaux, Chairman of Board of Indian Commissioners, 14 October 1916, United States House Committee on Indian Affairs, *Peyote,* 88.

26. United States House Committee on Indian Affairs, *Peyote,* 18.

27. Among others, Otto Wells, Comanche spokesman, defended peyote as "the best medicine that any person could take for his stomach" (United States House Committee on Indian Affairs, *Peyote,* 79–80). James Mooney also suggested it saved the life of his interpreter. See various, in NARA RG 75, E 764, Box 1.

28. Declaration of members of the Mexican Kickapoo tribe, Shawnee, OK, 15 July 1909, NARA RG 75, E 764, Box 1.

29. United States House Committee on Indian Affairs, *Peyote,* 149.

30. United States House Committee on Indian Affairs, *Peyote,* 79–80. See also interview between Arthur Bonnicastle (interpreter and spokesman for the Osage delegation of Osage agency) and the Secretary of the Board of Indian Commissioners, 15 January 1916, NARA RG 75, E 764, Box 1.

31. Transcript of the 1918 hearings, NARA RG 75, E 764, Box 1.

32. Transcript of the 1918 hearings, NARA RG 75, E 764, Box 1.

33. Transcript of the 1918 hearings, NARA RG 75, E 764, Box 1.

34. Quoted in Stewart, *Peyote Religion,* chap. 8.

35. Transcript of the 1918 hearings, NARA RG 75, E 764, Box 1.

36. "Discussion Concerning Peyote," April 1935. From Hearings of House Committee on Appropriations in Charge of Interior Department Appropriation Bill for 1936, office files of Commissioner John Collier, 1933–1945, NARA RG 75, E 178.

37. The IRA was passed in 1934.

CHAPTER FIVE

1. Mrs. Delavan Pierson, "American Indian Peyote Worship," *Missionary Review of the World,* March 1915, 203.

2. Kevin Feeney, "Peyote, Race, and Equal Protection."

3. There were extensive descriptions of the ceremonies in the testimonies of 1918, as well as in missionary publications and other reports. See for example *Peyote: An Abridged Compilation,* 11. This ceremony is described in great detail elsewhere, including Stewart, *Peyote Religion,* and Thomas C. Maroukis, *The Peyote Road.*

4. Albert Hensley, Winnebago, NE, to Commissioner of Indian Affairs, 9 October 1908, NARA RG 75, E 764, Box 1. See also Stewart, *Peyote Religion,* 157; Pierson, "American Indian Peyote Worship," 203.

5. Mooney to Joseph B. Thoburn (Secretary of the OK Historical Society), 16 June 1921; Mac Haag to Joseph B. Thoburn, 27 June 1921, NAA catalogue no. MS 7300 (James Mooney).

6. Mooney to Joseph B. Thoburn, 2 September 1921, NAA catalogue no. MS 7300 (James Mooney).

7. *Peyote: An Abridged Compilation*, 13. The same claims are repeated in Bulletin 21, "Peyote," published by the Office of Indian Affairs in 1929, NARA 75, E 178.

8. *Peyote: An Abridged Compilation*, 8, 25–30.

9. *Peyote: An Abridged Compilation*, 1.

10. *Peyote: An Abridged Compilation*, 1–2.

11. *Peyote: An Abridged Compilation*, 12.

12. *Peyote: An Abridged Compilation*, 13.

13. *Peyote: An Abridged Compilation*, 17.

14. *Peyote: An Abridged Compilation*, 13.

15. *Peyote: An Abridged Compilation*, 11.

16. Kansas in 1920, Iowa in 1925, Nevada in 1921, Montana in 1923, North Dakota in 1923, Wyoming in 1920, South Dakota in 1923, New Mexico banned peyote in 1928. Donald Collier, "Peyote: A General Study of the Plant, the Cult, and the Drug," *Survey of Conditions of Indians in the United States*, written in April 1932, bibliography revised in 1937, NARA 75, E 178.

17. A thorough analysis of Collier's career can be found in Karin Rosemblatt, *The Science and Politics of Race*.

CHAPTER SIX

1. Bulletin 21, "Peyote" Department of the Interior, Office of Indian Affairs, 1929, NARA RG 75, E 178.

2. Chief Annie's Tommy and nine members of the Goshute tribe (Ibapah, UT) to Collier, 1 November 1937, NARA RG 75, E 178. See also Joseph Chez, Utah AG, to Collier, 6 January 1938, NARA RG 75, E 178; AG of Utah to John Boyden, US District Attorney in SLC, 1 February 1939, NARA RG 75, E 178.

3. E. A. Farrow, Superintendent Paiute Agency, Cedar City, UT, to Mr. Annie's Tommy, 2 November 1937, NARA RG 75, E 178.

4. E. A. Farrow, Superintendent Paiute Agency, Cedar City, UT, to Collier, 25 January 1938, NARA RG 75, E 178; Collier to Joseph Chez, Utah AG, 12 January 1938, NARA RG 75, E 178.

5. See Andrés Guerrero, "The Construction of a Ventriloquist's Image"; Carmen Martínez Novo, "Managing Diversity."

6. Bulletin 21,"Peyote," Department of the Interior, Office of Indian Affairs, 1929, NARA RG 75, E 178. *Mission Almanac* for 1941, NARA RG 75, E 178.

7. This would include Stewart, *Peyote Religion*; Maroukis, *The Peyote Road*; Garrett Epps, *Peyote vs. the State*.

8. Donald Collier noted in particular opposition among the Winnebagos, where it had been introduced in 1901. Collier, "Peyote: A General Study of the Plant, the Cult, and the Drug," *Survey of Conditions of Indians in the United States*, April 1932, bibliography revised in 1937.

9. Adalbert Thunder Hawk, Council Secretary, Rosebud Tribal Council (SD), to the Commissioner of Indian Affairs, 15 May 1936, NARA RG 75, E 178; anonymous, Western Shoshone Agency, NV, to Commissioner of Indian Affairs (the letter is not signed and, though written as if from the council, is written on the letterhead of the Office of Indian Affairs Field Service), 6 March

1929, NARA RG 75, E 178. Rev. G. E. Lindquist alleges much of this in a report for the Home Missions Council in 1937, reprinted in *Mission Almanac* for 1941, NARA RG 75, E 178.

10. John Collier to Weston La Barre, 10 June 1937, NAA La Barre Box 5. See also Donald Collier, "Peyote: A General Study of the Plant."

11. Subcommittee of House Committee on Appropriations Hearings, 1936, 689–96; "Discussion Concerning Peyote" from Hearings of House Committee on Appropriations in Charge of Interior Department Appropriation Bill for 1936, April 1935, 689; Charles West, Acting Sec. of the Interior, to Elmer Thomas, Chairman, Committee on Indian Affairs in US Senate, 18 May 1937, NARA RG 75, E 178.

12. "Discussion Concerning Peyote" from Hearings of House Committee on Appropriations in Charge of Interior Department Appropriation Bill for 1936, April 1935; Collier to Richard Evans Shultes, 26 February 1936, NARA RG 75, E 178.

13. Among the evidence, he then submits for the record a copy of Petrullo's *Diabolic Root* (which argues that the peyote religion is "the natural and final recourse of a subjugated people") and an extract from Alexandre Rouhier, *Le Peyotl*. "Discussion Concerning Peyote" from Hearings of House Committee on Appropriations in Charge of Interior Department Appropriation Bill for 1936, April 1935, NARA RG 75, E 178.

14. See clipping from 1941 *Mission Almanac*, NARA RG 75, E 178.

15. "Discussion Concerning Peyote" from Hearings of House Committee on Appropriations in Charge of Interior Department Appropriation Bill for 1936, April 1935, NARA RG 75, E 178.

16. See illegible name, Mennonite Mission, Thomas, OK, to Collier, 6 August 1935, NARA RG 75, E 178; "Does Uncle Sam Foster Paganism?" *The Christian Century*, 8 August 1934, NARA RG 75, E 178, Box 18; *The Christian Century*, 11 October 1934, NARA RG 75, E 178, Box 18.

17. H. Bruce, Superintendent, Potawatomi Agency, KS, to Commissioner of Indian Affairs 25 June 1935, NARA RG 75, E 178.

18. This included SD, ND, ID, MT, NE, IO, WY, NM, CO, and UT. Charles West, Acting Sec of the Interior, to Elmer Thomas, Chairman, Committee on Indian Affairs in US Senate, 18 May 1937, NARA RG 75, E 178.

19. "A bill to prohibit the transportation of anhalonium in certain cases, and for other purposes," NARA RG 75, E 178. See also Documents on Peyote: Senate Bill 1399, 8 February 1937, and Departmental Report, 18 May 1937, NARA RG 75, E 178. See also Schaefer, *Amada's Blessings*, 98–99.

20. In a letter to Collier, dated 1 April 1937, R. E. Schultes points out the "peyote was removed from the genus Anhalonium in 1896 and has never been replaced in this genus!" (NARA RG 75, E 178). The NAC also flooded Washington with opponents of the bill. See for example Superintendent of Shoshone Indian Agency, WY, to Collier, 18 May 1937, NARA RG 75, E 178.

21. He testified in favor of prohibition in 1918 but now opposed bill 1399.

22. All the testimony is found in Documents on Peyote, Senate Bill 1399, 8 February 1937, and Departmental Report, 18 May 1937, NARA RG 75, E 178.

See also Richard Evans Schultes, "The Appeal of Peyote." See also Weston La Barre to Collier, 10 August 1938, NARA RG 75, E 178.

23. Charles L. Tranter, MD, "Peyote—New Dope Menace," *PIC*, 8 December 1942 (Tranter is the head of the Association for Prevention of Peyotism).

24. Malcolm Easterlin, "Peyote—Indian Problem No. 1," *Scribner's Commentator* 11:1 (1941): 77–82. See also Ruth Sheldon, "Indians—Our Minority Problem," *Scribner's Commentator* 9:2 (December 1940). In a letter from Collier to Charles Fahy, Assistant Solicitor Gen of US, 5 December 1941, Collier calls them Nazi propaganda, NARA RG 75, E 178, Box 19. See also Karl Menninger of the Menninger Clinic, Topeka, KS, to Collier, 20 July 1938, NARA RG 75, E 178.

25. These were qualitative judgments and have been repeatedly challenged. See for example Stanton Peele, "Addiction as a Cultural Concept"; Peter E. Nathan et al., "History of the Concept of Addiction"; Virginia Berridge and Griffith Edwards, *Opium and the People;* Dwight B. Heath, "Drinking Patterns of the Bolivian Camba."

26. Superintendent, Santa Fe Indian School (NM), to Collier, 6 December 1934, NARA RG 75, E 178.

27. Francis Cayou (Omaha) and Edgar McCarty (Osage) Hominy, OK, of the NAC, to Collier, 17 October 1934, NARA RG 75, E 178.

28. This comes from a long document describing the development of peyote religion in Navajoland, circa 1940, 8–9, NARA RG 75, E 178.

29. "Girl Dies after Peyote Meeting," *The Eagle* (Fallon, NV), 18 May 1940. The story recounts the death of a thirteen-year-old Indian girl named Viola Leef from Mina after a peyote meeting. She had TB, and the coroner concluded it was a death from tuberculosis.

30. Howard Gorman (Vice Chairman, Navajo Tribal Council), "The Growing Peyote Cult and the Use of Peyote on the Navajo Reservation," 18 May 1940, NARA RG 75, E 178. See also the pamphlet *What about Peyote*, New York, Home Mission Council of North America. The pamphlet was produced by the National Fellowship of Indian Workers during the summer of 1940, NARA RG 75, E 178.

31. Gorman, "The Growing Peyote Cult," 9–10. See also statement of Millie Cicsco, Lukachukai, AZ, 9 May 1939, NARA RG 75, E 178.

32. Frank Sorrelman of Lukachukai, aged thirty, spoke positively of the impact of peyote, but all others were extremely negative. Gorman, "The Growing Peyote Cult," 8–10.

33. Gorman, "The Growing Peyote Cult," 11–12.

34. Gorman, "The Growing Peyote Cult."

35. See clipping from 1941 *Mission Almanac*, 12, NARA RG 75, E 178.

36. Collier to Secretary Ickes, 6 December 1940, NARA RG 75, E 178.

37. R. C. Williams, Assistant Surgeon General, to Collier, 15 January 1945, NARA RG 75, E 178.

38. Collier to Secretary Ickes, 6 December 1940. See also Collier to Indian Office Personnel, 15 January 1941, NARA RG 75, E 178.

39. Collier to Mr. Stewart (Superintendent, Navajo Service), 10 March 1944; Collier to Mr. J. W. Stewart, Superintendent, Navajo Service, AZ, 7 April 1944, NARA RG 75, E 178.

40. Thomas Premo and six others, members of the Shoshone Business Council Western Shoshone Agency, Owybee, NV, to Collier, Commissioner of Indian Affairs, 14 January 1939, NARA RG 75, E 178; statement by Adelbert Thunder Hawk, Secretary, Rosebud Tribal Council (1939?), NARA RG 75, E 178. Member of Rosebud community to Collier, 22 September 1941, NARA RG 75, E 178. See also Margaret Schuyler Sternbergh, Reno, to Collier, recalling a conversation he had with Trantor on 22 and 26 May 1943, NARA RG 75, E 178; Charles Tranter, MD, to S. L. Rowe, Director General of the Pan American Union (DC), 6 December 1941, NARA RG 75, E 178; see also Don C. Foster, Supt., Carson Indian Agency, Stewart, NV, to Collier, 12 December 1942, NARA RG 75, E 178.

41. "Drive to Outlaw 'Dream Buttons,'" *New York News*, 30 November 1941. See also clipping from 1941 *Mission Almanac*, NARA RG 75, E 178; "Sent to an Artificial Paradise by the Evil Cactus Root," *Milwaukee Sentinel*, 12 July 1941. See also the pamphlet *What about Peyote*, New York, Home Mission Council of North America, NARA RG 75, E 178; Dr. W. Prosser, "The Effects of Peyote and Narcotics upon Heath," *National Fellowship of Indian Workers* (January–February 1940), NARA RG 75, E 178. See also Rev. R. H. Harper's series of articles in 1940 for the *Christian Indian*; Charles L. Tranter, "Peyote—New Dope Menace," in *PIC*, 8 December 1942, 6–9; Dr. Walter Bromberg and Charles Tranter, "Peyote Intoxication," *Journal of Nervous and Mental Disease* 97:5 (May 1943): 518–27. See also two articles from the *Pocatello Tribune*, one titled "Blame Peyote for Tragedies" and the other "Police Chief Hints at Use of Drug," 22 June 1942, NARA RG 75, E 178; C. Graves, Supt. of Fort Hall Agency (ID), to Collier, 16 July 1943, NARA RG 75, E 178.

42. "Button Button," *Time*, 18 June 1951, NAA La Barre, Box 8.

43. La Barre to the editors of *Time*, 4 July 1951, NAA La Barre, Box 8.

44. J. S. Slotkin to La Barre, 3 July 1951; "Statement on Peyote," 1951, 582–83, NAA La Barre, Box 8.

45. Audrey Simon of *Time* to La Barre, 25 July 1951, NAA La Barre, Box 8.

46. Willis De Jaques, "America's Newest Dope Horror," *Man to Man*, July 1952.

CHAPTER SEVEN

1. From the testimonials offered by a group of Roquet's patients who appeared at a hearing overseen by Deputy Carlos Sansores Pérez in the Salon Verde of the Mexican Congress on 28 December 1974. From the Papers of Norma Roquet.

2. Portions of this chapter and chap. 10 are drawn from Alexander Dawson, "Salvador Roquet, María Sabina, and the Trouble with Jipis.".

3. Awyn W. Knauer and William Maloney, "A Preliminary Note"; Erich Guttmann, "Artificial Psychoses"; Erich Guttmann and W. S. Maclay, "Mescalin and Depersonalization"; Alexander Rouhier, *Le Peyot,*; Kurt Beringer, *Der Meskalinrausch* ; Samuel W. Fernberger, "Observations on Taking Peyote"; Samuel Fernberger, "Further Observations in Peyote Intoxication"; F. Wertham and M. Bleuler, "Experimental Study"; Heinrich Klüver, "Mescal Visions and

Eidetic Vision," *American Journal of Psychology* 37:4 (October 1926): 502–15; Huntington Cairns, "A Divine Intoxicant." See also UN Division on Narcotic Drugs, *Bulletin on Narcotics*, 24. In a 1944 study of medicinal plants in Mexico, Maximo Martínez reported that recently Juan Roca of the Instituto de Biologia had begun a study of peyote as a heart tonic. Martínez, *Las plantas medicinales de México*, 215–20.

4. Some did attempt to understand the links, including Humphrey Osmond. See Humphrey Osmond, "Peyote Night." See also Erika Dyck, "Peyote and Psychedelics on the Canadian Prairies." See also Fannie Kahan, *A Culture's Catalyst*.

5. The first article published on their work was H. Osmond and J. Smythies, "Schizophrenia: A New Approach. Osmond also attended ceremonies of the NAC in Saskatchewan. See Kahan, *Culture's Catalyst;* Osmond, "Peyote Night," 112. See also Erika Dyck, *Psychedelic Psychiatry;* Stephen Siff, *Acid Hype*, particularly chap. 2; Sarah Shortall, "Psychedelic Drugs."

6. The experiment took place on 2 December 1955 and was intended for the BBC Program *Panorama*, but was not broadcast.

7. See "Paradise or Inferno," 390; Robert Charles Zaehner, "The Menace of Mescalin." Huxley drew on Hindu imagery, Zen Buddhism, and William Blake, among others, in *The Doors of Perception* (New York: Perennial, 1990 [1954]).

8. Quoted in Alfonso Perabeles, "Salvador Roquet."

9. Janine Rodiles, *Una terapia prohibida,* 112–14. See also Roquet, unpublished memoir (from the Papers of Norma Roquet).

10. Quoted from Roquet's unpublished memoir (from the Papers of Norma Roquet, n/d).

11. The Social Services Institute for State Workers.

12. Salvador Roquet et al., "The Existential through Psychodisleptics: A New Psychotherapy," 9–11 (from the Papers of Norma Roquet).

13. Alberto Villoldo, "An Introduction to the Psychedelic Psychotherapy of Salvador Roquet," 45; Rodiles, *Una terapia prohibida,* 116–17.

14. Salvador Roquet, "Operación Mazateca: Estudio de hongos y otras plantas alucinogenas mexicanas. Tratamienio psicoterapeuitico de psicosintesis," 1971 (from the Papers of Norma Roquet).

15. Roquet, "Operación Mazateca." See also Juan García Carrera, *La otra vida de María Sabina* (Mexico City: Talleres Esfuerza, 1986), 38–39.

16. Rodiles, *Una terapia prohibida,* 120–21. Sabina ran the velada Gordon Wasson wrote about in "Seeking the Magic Mushroom," *Life,* 13 May 1957. She later attracted a great deal of attention as the most iconic representative of psychedelic indigenous shamanism in Mexico during the 1960s.

17. Benjamin Feinberg, *The Devil's Book of Culture,* 127–37, 188–90. See also Donald Joralemon, "The Selling of the Shaman."

18. In *La otra vida de María Sabina,* Juan García Carrera quotes Sabina as feeling bitterness toward Roquet at the end of her life because she believed he abandoned her after the mid-1970s and grew rich from her knowledge while she suffered. Photos from 1979 suggest that he did continue to visit at least until the end of the decade.

19. Perabeles, "Salvador Roquet."

20. Roquet, "Operación Mazateca." There is an interesting corollary in Weston La Barre, "Primitive Psychotherapy."

21. La Barre, "Primitive Psychotherapy"; Alexander and Dorothea Leighton "Elements of Psychotherapy in Navaho Religion." See also Thomas J. Csordas, "Embodiment as a Paradigm for Anthropology."

22. He draws the term from Agustin Palacios, Santiago Ramirez, and Gregorio Valmer, *Psicoanálisis, La técnica,* 242–43. On the misreading, see Thomas J. Csordas, "The Psychotherapy Analogy and Charismatic Healing"; Janice Boddy, "Spirits and Selves in Northern Sudan"; Janice Boddy, "Spirit Possession Revisited."

23. On the dissonances, see Thomas J. Csordas, "Ritual Healing"; Thomas J. Csordas, "Medical and Sacred Realities"; John Calabrese, "Spiritual Healing and Human Development"; Kevin Feeney, "The Legal Basis for Religious Peyote Use."

24. Salvador Roquet and Dr. Jaime Ganc, "Factores estudiados y evolución de la técnica psicoteraeutica con el uso de los psicodislepticos," in Roquet, "Operación Mazateca."

25. An interesting discussion of this can be found in Paul Gootenberg and Isaac Campos, "Toward a New Drug History of Latin America."

26. Roquet makes these claims in a variety of settings, including Roquet et al., "The Existential through Psychodisleptics," 22, and his unpublished memoir. He also alludes to it in Perabeles, "Salvador Roquet."

27. Villoldo, "An Introduction," 49.

28. See Roquet, "teoria, " in "Operación Mazateca." See also Roquet and Ganc, "Factores estudiados."

29. Roquet and Ganc, "Factores estudiados." See also Perabeles, "Salvador Roquet."

30. Armando Carlock, "Salvador Roquet Pérez, psiquiatra especialista en psicosíntesis," *El Nacional,* 19 September 1969. See also Roquet's unpublished memoir.

31. Even Sabina made the accusation. For a larger discussion of this issue, see, among others, Jean Comaroff and John Comaroff, *Ethnicity, Inc.;* Michael Forbes Brown, *Who Owns Native Culture?*

32. Richard Yensen, *Hacia una medicina psiquedélica,* 59.

33. The experience was recounted in Humphry Osmond, "Peyote Night."

34. Leary experimented primarily with psilocybin, mescaline, and LSD. See Lattin, *Harvard Psychedelic Club,* particularly 85–148. See also Nathaniel J. Hiatt, "A Trip Down Memory Lane"; Andrew Weil, "The Strange Case of the Harvard Drug Scandal."

35. Rodiles, *Una terapia prohibida,* 123.

36. Rodiles, *Una terapia prohibida.*

37. Alvaro Estrada, *Huautla en tiempo de hippies,* 107.

38. Here I draw most directly from Kwame Anthony Appiah, *The Ethics of Identity* (Princeton, NJ: Princeton University Press, 2005).

39. Roberto Assagioli also used the term but somewhat differently. See Roberto Assagioli, *Psychosynthesis.* The following descriptions of the practices in the clinic are drawn from Roquet, *Operación Mazateca;* Perabeles, "Salvador

Roquet"; Roquet et al., "The Existential through Psychodisleptics"; A. Villoldo "An Introduction," 45–58; Walter Houston Clark, "'Bad Trips'" May Be the Best Trips," *Fate*, April 1976.

40. Roquet, "teoria."

41. Villoldo, "An Introduction," 45.

42. This is in some ways a version of "set and setting," as pioneered by Al Hubbard in the 1950s, though for Hubbard the setting was supposed to be soothing. See Dyck, *Psychedelic Psychiatry*, 90–99.

43. See Javier Mancera Fuentes to Director Federal Seguridad, Mexico City, 19 March 1971, AGN, Dirección Federal de Seguridad. Expediente Personal Rafael Estrada Villa, Versión Pública, Legajo 4, folio 190 to 192.

44. This approach was relatively common in LSD therapy in the US at the time, based on the theory that the patient should be overwhelmed by the experience. See Shortall, "Psychedelic Drugs and the Problem of Experience."

45. Rivea Corymbosa and Ipomea Violacea are two types of Ololiuqui.

46. Villoldo "An Introduction," 45–50.

47. Roquet, "Operación Mazateca." See also Clark, "'Bad Trips.'"

48. Rodiles, *Una terapia prohibida*, 37.

49. Roquet et al., "The Existential through Psychodisleptics," 60–65.

50. Roquet et al., "The Existential through Psychodisleptics," 57.

51. Roquet et al., "The Existential through Psychodisleptics," 59.

52. See for instance Juan García Carrera, *La otra vida*, 26–27.

53. Janine Rodiles describes a session with a Huichol shaman in Wirikuta in great detail in her *Una terapía prohibida*, 51–90.

54. On the Mexican response to the hippies, see Eric Zolov, *Refried Elvis*; Estrada, *Huautla en tiempo de hippies*; José Agustín, *La contracultura en México*, esp. 90–92.

55. Fifty-seven percent improved, 28 percent were cured. These statistics are drawn from the random study of 388 files. See Roquet et al., "The Existential through Psychodisleptics." More broadly, see Patricia de Parres, "LSD and hongos para la salud," *Contenido*, August 1972 (from the Papers of Norma Roquet); Salvador Roquet, "En Busca de la aplicación terapeutica de los psicodislepticos" (from the Papers of Norma Roquet). See also Stanley Krippner, "Editorial," *Psychoenergetic Systems* 1 (1976), 103; Smith, "'Bad Trips'"; Salvador Roquet and Pierre Favreau, *Los alucinógenos*.

56. Armando Carlock, "Salvador Roquet Pérez." Similar claims were made in the *JAMA* the following year for LSD. Walter N. Pahnke, et al., "The Experimental Use of Psychedelic (LSD) Psychotherapy."

57. Testimonials offered by a group of Roquet's patients who appeared at a hearing overseen by Deputy Carlos Sansores Pérez in the Salon Verde of the Mexican Congress on 28 December 1974. The session was organized by Gabriel Parra, a friend of the doctor, a lawyer, and a reporter at the Camara de Diputados, in an effort to put pressure on the government to release Roquet after his arrest that year.

58. Perabeles, "Salvador Roquet."

59. See for example Sylvia Sayago, "Las médicas abordan el problema de la drogadicción juvenil," *El Nacional*, 8 September 1970; "Responsibilidad de la

familia," *Novedades,* 7 September 1970; "Llamado a los padres de familia," *El Universal,* 10 April 1970; "Graves Peligros," *El Universal,* 11 July 1969; Dr. Ramón de la Fuente and Dr. Carlos Campillo Serrano, "Desordenes psiquiatricos asociados con el consumo de drogas," 1971 (Consejo Nacional de Problemas en Farmacodependencia) SSA-SP-caja 244- exp. 2; Dr. y Gral. Demetrio Mayoral Pardo, "Toxicomania-Farmacodependencia" CEMEF *Informe,* 1:6 (1973): 4, SSA-SP 266.1.

60. Perabeles, "Salvador Roquet," 25.

61. Roquet and Ganc, "Factores," 41.

CHAPTER EIGHT

1. Plan Huicot, "Resumen del Octavia Reunion celebrada por los representantes de los diferentes organismos que participan en el mejoramiento del area Huicot celebrada en la secretaría de la presidencia el 27 de Febrero de 1971."

2. Alfonso Fabila, "Situación de los Huicholes de Jalisco," 1958 CDI Archive.

3. Alfonso Faliba, *Los Huicholes de Jalisco* (Mexico City, 1959), 10.

4. Fabila, *Los Huicholes de Jalisco,* 12.

5. Fabila, *Los Huicholes de Jalisco,* 13.

6. Fabila, *Los Huicholes de Jalisco,* 14.

7. Fabila, *Los Huicholes de Jalisco,* 8–9.

8. See for example Carlos DeNegri, "María Isabel Hernández," *Excelsior,* 14 June 1965. We also see this in Marcos Cueto, "Appropriation and Resistance."

9. In *La antropología y la burocracia indigenista,* Ricardo Pozas argued the CCIs were established in urban centers under false pretenses, to serve the bureaucrats, because the INI actually opposed critical investigations of Indians.

10. Aside from three schools established in Tuxpan de Bolaños (1963), Ocota de la Sierra (1963), and San Andrés Cohamiata (1965), the INI had almost no permanent presence in the sierra during these early years (INI, "Informe de la visita al CCI de la Zona Huichol de Tuxpan de Bolaños, Jalisco," 1979, CDI, FD 14/16).

11. EUM, Poder Ejecutivo Federal, *Plan Lerma: Asistencia técnica. Operación Huicot* (Guadalajara: 1966), 9, 12 (CDI, FD 18/004). "¿Padecen los Huicholes dos Graves Problemas?" *El Universal,* 17 July 1966; "Eficaz ayuda para los Indios Huicholes," *El Universal,* 3 February 1967.

12. Several Huichol communities were granted land by the federal government during these years. Santa Catarina received 72,720 hectares, as of presidential resolution 9 August 1960. San Andres (3,610 persons) was given 74,940 hectares, 14 September 1965. San Sebastian (2857) was given 240,447 on 15 October 1953. Tuxpan de Bolaños (2,025) was not given land. It seems that almost a decade later most still had not received their land. See "Quieren saber si sus tierras son de Jalisco o de Nayarit," *El Universal,* 24 May 1974.

13. *Plan Lerma 1966,* 88, trans. from Spanish in Negrín, 2014.

14. CCI-Cora Huichol, "Informes," 1966, CDI, FD 18/2. See also "Contra el Aislamiento de los Huicholes se pronunció el Candidato Orozco, en Jalisco,"

Excelsior, 19 November 1970. See also Prof. Diego Vázquez Juárez to Prof. Reynaldo Salvatierra Castillo, 29 March 1966, CDI, FD 18/2. See also COPLAMAR (Coordinación General del Plan Nacional de Zonas Deprimidas y Grupos Marginados), *Programa Integrado 10: Zona Huicot Nayarit,* México, 1978.

15. See for example Alexander Dawson, *Indian and Nation.*

16. See for example Juan Negrín, "Informe General, Taller Escuela Tuapuri," 5 May 1984, CDI, FD 14/005; Ignacio León Pachuco, reporting on visit to CCI-Huichol, Tuxpan de Bolaños, 14–20 December 1985, in "Expediente de la Zona Norte de la Región Huichol," 1986, CDI, FD 14/005. See also Juan Negrín, *Acercamineto histórico y subjetivo al Huichol.*

17. This is not to say they were not racist, but that they thought of themselves as antiracist. For a fascinating discussion of this challenge, see Emiko Saldívar, "'It's Not Race, It's Culture.'"

18. In the Cursos de Capatación para promotores culturales del Centro Coordinador Cora-Huichol, *Programa de Higiene y Primerros Auxilios* (23 May 1967), there is no mention of peyote. We instead see a uniform idea of hygiene and health, with no sense of specific needs or particularities, and under vices are mentioned alcohol, cigarettes, coffee, and "trastornos ocasionados por drogas en general" as things students need to learn about (CCI-Cora Huichol, "Informes," 1967–70, CDI, FD 18/3). See also Guadalupe Santacruz, "Nuestros Indios," *El Sol de México,* 19 April 1968. See also CCI-Cora Huichol, "Informes," 1966, CDI, FD 18/2. See also "Contra el Aislamiento de los Huicholes." Karen Reed also notes that it is informed by a version of acculturation, a desire to bring them into the national economy, in *El INI y los Huicholes,* 80.

19. Centro Coordinador Cora-Huichol, Jalisco-Nayarit, "La medicina social en el area Cora-Huichol" (1971?), CDI, 33.1.

20. "La medicina social en el area Cora-Huichol" (1971?), CDI, 33.1.

21. This included the CFE, CONASUPO, DAAC, INDECO, SAG, SCT, SEP, SIC, SOP, SRH, and SSA Plan Huicot, *Programas de actividades de las dependencias participantes para 1971,* CDI, FD 18/005. Ramón Morones, "Coras, Huicholes y Tepehuanes participaran de la vida nacional," *Excelsior,* 15 December 1970. See also Prof. Miguel Palafox Vargas, *El Plan Huicot: Obra humanista de la revolución* (Tepic: Comite promotor del desarrollo socio economico del estado de Nayarit, 1975).

22. Palafox Vargas, *El Plan Huicot.*

23. José de Jesús Torres Contreras, *El hostigamiento a "el costumbre" huichol: Los procesos de hibridación social* (Zamora: El Colegio de Michoacán, Universidad de Guadalajara, 2000), 342, cited in Negrín, *Colores mexicanos,* 52.

24. In 1970 the Ministry of Health reported over three thousand clinic visits per year.

25. She also gave out 16 large bags of toys. Raul Rodriguez Ramos, CCI-Cora Huichol, "Informes," 1967–70, CDI, FD 18/3.

26. Pedro Ruíz González, *Plan Huicot: Informe de avances,* 1973, CDI, FD 32/001.

27. Consejo Supremo Huichol, Zona Norte de Jalisco, "Programa para la región indígena huichol de la zona norte del estado de Jalisco, 1982–1983," 11 November 1982, CDI, FD 14/003.

28. Arturo Toriz y Alvarez, "Informe de evaluación al CCI de Tuxpan de Bolaños," 15 March 1979, CDI, FD 14/005.

29. Lic. Arturo Toriz y Alvarez, "Informe de evaluación al CCI de Tuxpan de Bolaños," 15 March 1979. Consejo Supremo Huichol, Zona Norte de Jalisco, "Programa para la región indígena huichol de la zona norte del estado de Jalisco, 1982–1983."

30. Consejo Supremo Huichol, Zona Norte de Jalisco, "Programa para la región indígena huichol de la zona norte del estado de Jalisco, 1982–1983."

31. CCI-Huichol, project for the relocation of the administrative offices from Guadalajara to Tepic, January 1983, CDI, FD 14/013. COPLAMAR (Coordinación General del Plan Nacional de Zonas Deprimidas y Grupos Marginados), "Programa Integrado 10: Zona Huicot Nayarit México," 1978; COPLAMAR, "Programa Integrado 9: Zona Huicot Jalisco México," 1978; Raúl Rodríguez Ramos, "Informe de la visita al CCI de la región Huichol Magdalena, Jalisco," May 1982.

32. CONASUPO maintained a rigid monopoly on the marketing of maize and beans, while Tabamex controlled tobacco, and Imecafe coffee.

33. INI, "Diagnostico de las regiones indígenas: Cora, Huichol y Tepahuane," August 1989, CDI, FD 18/15.

34. See for example José O. Avila Arévalo of the INI to Dr. Enrique Valencia V. Subdirector of Social Anthropology, 11 February 1983, CDI, FD 14/003; "Estrategia de operación en la región Indígena Huichola a base de residencies" (1983), CDI, FD 14/005; Ignacio León Pacheco, report of visit to CCI-Huichol, Tuxpan de Bolaños, 14–20 December 1985. Ignacio León Pacheco, "Informe de visita realizada a la zona norte," 14 Feb 1986, in "Expediente de la Zona Norte de la región Huichol," 1986, CDI, FD 14/005; INI, "Diagnostico de las regiones indígenas: Cora, Huichol y Tepahuane," August 1989, CDI, FD 18/15. See also M. Ángel Hernandez Díaz, *Región Huicot: Diagnostico sociodemografico*, 1995.

35. CCI-Cora Huichol, "Informes," 1966, CDI, FD 18/2; CCI-Cora Huichol, "Informe," 1965.

36. Anthony Shelton, "The Girl Who Ground Herself," 451–67; Stacy B. Schaefer, "The Cosmos Contained," 365–66.

37. See for example Prof. Reynaldo Salvatierra Castillo to Caso, 30 June 1965, in CCI-Cora Huichol, "Informe," 1965. See also CCI-Cora Huichol, "Informes," 1967–1970; Diego Vázquez to Salvatierra Castillo, 30 July 1966, CCI-Cora Huichol, "Informes," 1966.

38. Reynaldo Salvatierra Castillo to Caso, 4 December 1965, CCI-Cora Huichol, "Informe," 1965.

39. See 1965 report on a school in Santa Catarina Coexcomatitlán, Reynaldo Salvatierra Castillo to Caso, 4 December 1965, which includes a report by Diego Vázquez Juárez from 30 November 1965, CCI-Cora Huichol, "Informe," 1965, CDI, FD 18/1. See also Raúl Rodríguez Ramos to Caso, 17 March 1970, CCI-Cora Huichol, "Informes," 1967–1970, CDI, FD 18/3.

40. CCI-Cora Huichol, "Informe," 1965, CDI, FD 18/1.

41. Palafox Vargas, "El Plan Huicot"; Ignacio León Pacheco et al., "Informe," 23 February 1985, CDI FD 14/10. See also INI, "Diagnostico de las Regiones indígenas: Cora, Huichol y Tepahuane," August 1989, CDI, FD

18/15; Consejo Supremo Huichol, Zona Norte de Jalisco, "Programa para la región indígena huichol," 11 November 1982, CDI, FD 14/003; Ignacio León Pacheco, report on visit to CCI-Huichol, Tuxpan de Bolaños, 14–20 December 1985, CDI, FD 14/10; Unión de Comunidades Indígenas Huicholes de Jalisco (UCIH-J), "Programa de desarrollo comunal de la región Wixárika de Jalisco," 1995, CDI, FD 14/19. See also Ignacio León Pacheco, "Informe de Visita realizada a la zona norte," 14 February 1986, in INI, "Expediente de la Zona Norte de la Región Huichol," 1986, CDI, FD 14/005.

42. Prof. Jesús Carillo Hernández to Maximo Gonzalez Salvador, 20 November 1983.

43. See Giorgio Agamben, *State of Exception.*

44. Antrop. Gildardo González Ramos to Salvatierra Castillo, 31 March 1966, CCI- Cora Huichol, "Informes," 1966, CDI, FD 18/2. Plan Huicot, "Resumen del Octavia reunion celebrada por los representantes de los diferentes organismos que participan en el mejoramiento del area Huicot celebrada en la secretaría de la presidencia el 27 de Febrero de 1971."

45. "Informe de la visita de apoyo a el CCI de Tuxpan de Bolaños, Jalisco," 1983.

46. Comité Coordinador para el desarrollo de la región Huicot, "Informe de actividades Plan Huicot." 1974; Lic. Arturo Toriz y Alvarez, "Informe de evaluación al CCI de Tuxpan de Bolaños, 15 March 1979.

47. INI, "Informe de la visita al CCI de la zona Huichol de Tuxpan de Bolaños, Jalisco," 1979, 6.

48. Lic. Arturo Toriz y Alvarez, "Informe de evaluación al CCI de Tuxpan de Bolaños," 15 March 1979.

49. Ruben Sanchez Contreras, proposal to move the CCI from Magdalena to Guadalajara, July 1982.

CHAPTER NINE

1. *Peyote: An Abridged Compilation,* 19–20.

2. People v. Woody, 61 Cal.2d 716 (1964).

3. As of 1987 California law called for a maximum ten-year prison sentence for planting, cultivating, or drying peyote, and a maximum of twenty years on second offense. "Religious Use of Peyote Upheld," *Church and State,* November 1964, describes the effect as "demoralizing and degrading."

4. Founded in 1918, the NAC became the Native American Church of the United States in 1944, and the Native American Church of North America in 1955 (to reflect the presence of Canadian chapters within the church). The NAC is an umbrella organization meant to support state level chapters, and is often referred to as the "mother" church. For the sake of simplicity, in this book I use NAC to refer to all iterations of the church.

5. Schaefer, *Amada's Blessings,* 102–4.

6. Arizona v. Mary Attakai, 4098 AZ (1960). Judge McFate's ruling followed developments in Montana (1957) and New Mexico (1959), which had created exemptions for the bona fide use of peyote for religious purposes. See "'Right' to Hallucinate" *Newsweek,* 6 August 1962. See also Csordas, "Ritual

Healing," 3–23; David F. Aberle, *The Peyote Religion among the Navajo;* La Barre, *The Peyote Cult;* Omer Stewart and David Aberle, *Peyotism in the West;* Omer Stewart to Weston La Barre, 18 June 1965, NAA La Barre, Box 8.

7. See Stewart, 1987. J. S. Slotkin, long a member of the church, was even elected to the National Board of Directors of the NAC in 1954. See "Indian Church Names White Man Officer," *Cedar Rapids Gazette,* 25 July 1954, NAA Sol Tax Papers, Box 8—MS 4802.

8. This comes from a ruling US Court of Appeals Case, 10th Cir. (Case No. 6146, 1959).

9. Arizona v. Mary Attakai, 4098 AZ (1960).

10. Members of the church warned one another to keep their records, maintain their charters, and undertake other practices to make their church legible to the state. See Peter Miller and Warren D'Azevedo to Members, Washo Chapter of the NAC NA, 27 August 1964, NAA La Barre, Box 8. See also Jefferson Clitlick, "Making Mincemeat of Minzey," *The Berkeley Barb,* 10–16 August 1973.

11. "Peyote Use Ruled Legal in Indian Rite," *San Francisco Chronicle,* 25 August 1964.

12. In re Grady, 61 Cal.2d 887 (1964).

13. *Desert Sun* (Palm Springs), 28 May 1962, 1.

14. The court in Riverside County has no record of the final disposition of the case, though it seems likely that they ruled it was not a bona fide religious claim. "Judge Studies Peyote Case," *Redlands Daily Facts,* 18 February 1965, 7. An article from 1973 also suggests that Grady ultimately failed in his claim. Jefferson Clitlick, "Making Mincemeat of Minzey."

15. Clitlick, "Making Mincemeat of Minzey."

16. Alan Ginsberg writes about peyote in "Birth" and composed "Howl" after a night walking around San Francisco after taking peyote. Alice Marriot wrote about her experience with peyote in "The Opened Door" in the *New Yorker,* 25 September 1954, 90. David Ebin published *The Drug Experience* in 1961. More broadly, on the fascination with these drugs, see Siff, *Acid Hype;* Jay Stevens, *Storming Heaven: LSD and the American Dream;* Lattin, *The Harvard Psychedelic Club.* On the 1960s more generally, see Todd Gitlin, *Years of Hope, Days of Rage.*

17. She reports a peyote séance in her New York apartment in 1914 in her memoir *Movers and Shakers.* See Marcus Boon, *The Road of Excess,* 229–33. See also Brown, *Who Owns Native Culture?,* 96.

18. Edward C. Burks, "Peyote Peddler at Odds with U.S.," *New York Times,* 23 June 1960. See also Paul Gehard, of the Institute for Sex Research at Indiana University, to La Barre, 26 January 1960. Gehard notes that a beatnik cafe in New York was selling peyote, but that they "decided peyote was too much to gag down" and were now selling mescaline in capsules (NAA, Papers of Weston La Barre, Box 5).

19. "The Drug Scene: A Growing Number of America's Elite are Quietly Turning On," *New York Times,* 10 January 1968; *The Drug Takers* (New York: Time Life Books 1965); "Hippie Regulars on Haight Want Part-Timers to Take a Trip," *New York Times,* 19 August 1967. The link between enhanced sexual pleasure and psychedelic drugs was also explored by Robert Masters in *Play-*

boy, prompted largely by Timothy Leary's claims that "LSD is the greatest aphrodisiac known to man." Masters indicates that most mind-altering drugs are linked to sex. R. E. L. Masters, "Sex, Ecstasy and the Psychedelic Drugs," *Playboy*, November 1967. Masters also examines peyote in *Forbidden Sexual Behavior and Morality* (New York: Julian Press, 1962). See also Karen Joe-Laidler et al., "'Tuned Out or Tuned In.'"

20. Jim Bishop, "The Village Answers God with Psychedelic Church," *Tulsa Daily World*, 22 December 1966. See also Richard Lyons, "Genetic Damage Linked to LSD," *New York Times*, 3 March 1967.

21. Arnold M. Ludwig, "Patterns of Hallucinogenic Drug Abuse."

22. Ludwig, "Patterns of Hallucinogenic Drug Abuse," 12.

23. Ludwig, "Patterns of Hallucinogenic Drug Abuse."

24. Leary v. US (1967). Other drug-based religions suffered similar fates in the years after *Woody*. See for example Clitlick, "Making Mincemeat of Minzey." Other cases where this sort of defense failed included People v. Mitchell, 244 Cal. App.2d 176 (1966), People v. Collins, 273 Cal. App.2d 486 (1969); People v. Wright, 275 Cal. App.2d 738 (1969); New York v. Gary Ward Crawford (1972). The Church of the New Awakening was denied a religious exemption in Kennedy v. Bureau of Narcotics and Dangerous Drugs, 459 F.2d 415 (9th Cir., 1972).

25. North Carolina v. William Robert Bullard III, Supreme Court of North Carolina (1966).

26. "Peyote Possession Hearing Set Today," 15 June 1968 (newspaper clipping, no journal indicated), NAA, Papers of Weston La Barre, Box 8.

27. North Carolina v. William Robert Bullard III, Supreme Court of North Carolina (1966).

28. *Drug Abuse Control Amendments of 1965*, 79 Stat. 226 § 3(a).

29. *Comprehensive Drug Abuse Prevention and Control Act of 1970*, 21 U.S.C. § 812(c), Schedule I(c)(12).

30. See Erich Goode, "Moral Panics and Disproportionality: The Case of LSD Use in the Sixties," 533–43; Erich Goode and Nachman Ben-Yehuda, *Moral Panics*, 81. See also Richard D. Lyons, "Science's Knowledge on the Misuse of Drugs and How They Act Is Found to Lag," *New York Times*, 9 January 1968.

31. Failed challenges came from the Church of the Tree of Life, in San Francisco; Ghost Clan—Mesita, CO; the Church of the Awakening in Arizona; the Neo-American Church (aka Original Kleptonian); Paleo American Church in Warren, VT; Church of the Golden Rule, in San Jose, CA; the Universal Life Church; and the Temple of the True Inner Light. See R. Stuart, "Entheogenic Sects and Psychedelic Religions," *MAPS* 12:1 (2002); Thomas Lyttle, "Drug Based Religions."

32. Targets included the Church of the Awakening—a peyote sect led by Drs. John and Louisa Aiken, whose members were largely white—which began as a study group in 1958 in Socorro, NM, incorporated in 1963. See J. W. Aiken, "Can Drugs Lead You to God?" *Fate Magazine*, 1963. See also M. E. Sonnenrich et al. 1969 "Memorandum of Law in the Matter of: Petition of the Church of the Awakening to Amend 21 CFR 320.3(c)(3)." Hearing in conformance

with 21 U.S.C. 371 (e), Department of Justice, Bureau of Narcotics and Dangerous Drugs, 1 August 1969.

33. See US 79 Stat. 226 Sec. 11; 31 Fed. Reg. 4679–80 (1966), § 1307.31 Native American Church. See also Native American Church of New York v. United States, 468 F. Supp. 1247, 1249, 1251 (1979).

34. *Drug Abuse Control Amendments of 1970, Hearings before the Subcommittee on Public Health and Welfare of the Committee on Interstate and Foreign Commerce,* House of Representatives, 91st Cong., 2d Sess. 117–18 (1970).

35. Public Law 103–344 (H.R. 4230) (1994). Epps (*Peyote vs. the State*) offers an excellent analysis of this case. See also Feeney, "Peyote, Race, and Equal Protection," 65–88.

36. Schaefer, *Amada's Blessings,* 149–50. Marijuana smokers, who likewise placed the churches' claims of peyote as sacrament at risk, were similarly shunned. See for instance Peter S. Miller, "Continuity and Change in Washo Peyotism: A Preliminary Report," 4 December 1964, NAA La Barre, Box 8.

37. A 1979 court ruling in New York affirmed that if he could establish that his church had a bona fide belief in peyote as a god, Alan Birnbaum's Native American Church of New York qualified for an exemption under the law (the case had begun with an exemption granted by the state of New York but later denied by the DEA), Native American Church of New York v. US, 468 F. Supp. 1247, 1251 (1979). It was affirmed in 1980. Another incident (noted in Stewart, 333) involved a white couple in Grand Forks, ND, arrested for peyote in 1984. See also California v. David Rene Marbain, California, First Appellate District, Division Three (motion heard on 11 July 2013 and filed in September 2014). See also Paul Payne, "Minister Seeks Return of Peyote Seized in Santa Rosa," *Press Democrat,* 7 April 2013. Relevant also is the case of Leo Mercado, in Kearny, AZ, a former member of the Peyote Way who fell afoul of the law both because he was delinquent in child support payments and because police found small amounts of marijuana and ecstasy when they raided his home. See Terry Greene Sterling, "A Vision Gone Bust," *Phoenix New Times,* 18 February 1999.

38. Arizona v. Janice and Greg Whittingham, Appellants Court of Appeals of Arizona, Division One, Department A (1973). A similar finding was seen in Oklahoma in Whitehorn v. State, 561 P. 2d 539 (Okla. Cr. App. 1977).

39. J.S. Slotkin is an obvious example, but even more interesting is the anthropologist George Morgan, who was adopted by the Sioux NAC in 1964. See Morgan in *Psychedelic Reflections,* edited by Lester Grinspoon and James B. Bakalar (New York: Human Sciences Press, 1983). See also Schaefer, *Amada's Blessings,* 123–27. Sherry Smith analyzes the similarly illuminating case the American Church of God in Santa Fe, NM, in which the collaboration between native and nonnative peyotists was quite extensive. See Sherry L. Smith, *Hippies, Indians, and the Fight for Red Power,* 43–70.

40. U.S. v. Boyll, 774 F. Supp. 133 (D.N.M. 1991).

41. He counted Neil Cassidy and Timothy Leary among his friends, claimed to have introduced Leary to peyote, and was the artist responsible for the medallions he wore. Trujillo also helped Leary establish the Sri Ram Ashram in Arizona

after the latter was fired from Harvard. My observations about the Peyote Way are based on a visit to the church on 19 August 2011. Many of these observations were confirmed in Eric Tsetsi, "A Remote Arizona Church Offers Followers Peyote-Induced Psychedelic Trips," *New Times*, 8 January 2014.

42. They were hitchhiking to Tucson, and their ride stopped at the ranch.

43. On 11 May 1979 they incorporated the Peyote Way Church of God. The church was formally registered as a nonprofit in 1981.

44. Tex. Health & Safety Code Ann. § 481.111(a).

45. This is also discussed in a letter from Anne Zapf, which can be found in Guy Mount, *The Peyote Book*, 103–6.

46. Their lawsuit assumed greater urgency when several members of the church were arrested on 19 November 1982 in Richardson, TX, and charged with possession of peyote. Peyote Way v. US and Texas, 556 F. Supp. 632 (7 February 1983).

47. Peyote Way v. US and Texas (24 September 1984).

48. Peyote Way v. US and Texas (24 September 1984).

49. Peyote Way v. Meese, 698 F. Supp. 1342 (28 October 1988); Peyote Way v. Thornburgh, 922 F.2d 1210 (6 February 1991).

50. Peyote Way v. Meese, 698 F. Supp. 1342 (28 October 1988). See also Wright, 2007.

51. Peyote Way v. Meese, 698 F. Supp. 1342 (28 October 1988); Peyote Way v. Thornburgh, 922 F.2d 1210 (6 February 1991).

52. Peyote Way v. Thornburgh, 922 F.2d 1210 (6 February 1991).

53. Peyote Way v. Smith and Mattox (24 September 1984).

54. Peyote Way v. Thornburgh, 922 F.2d 1210 (6 February 1991).

55. In Whittingham, Birnbaum, and Boyll. Also, in 2004 the Utah Supreme Court found that the peyote exemption applied to all members of the NAC regardless of race (State of Utah v. Mooney 2004), resulting in the acquittal of James "Flaming Eagle" Mooney and Linda Mooney, non-Indians who had created the Oklevueha Earthwalks Native American Church of Utah (founded 1997), on charges of peyote possession. The federal government continued to press the case, and the Mooneys ultimately agreed to discontinue their use of peyote until they could prove they were members of a federally recognized tribe.

56. UDV v. Ashcroft (2002), 11, citing Boyll (1991), 1336.

57. UDV v. Ashcroft (2002), 11, citing Peyote Way (1991), 1216.

58. The AIRFA revisions of 1994 in some ways supersede this ruling. Under this law members of "traditional Indian religions" and not simply members of the NAC may enjoy the exemption, though they must be members of federally recognized tribes to be eligible. Feeney, "Peyote, Race, and Equal Protection in the United States," 65–88.

59. Maroukis, *The Peyote Road*, 201.

60. The NAC also repudiated the Whittingham case, claiming that "whether the Indian roadman running the ceremony and other Indians present at the ceremony considered the Whittinghams members of that NAC chapter is a factual matter on which the court apparently had no record" (NAC 2002, p. 15, from the amicus brief filed in UDV v. Ashcroft in which members of the NAC sought to distance themselves from the UDV), Feeney, 2014, 65–88. This is an

ahistorical claim and erases people like Amada and Claudio Cardenas, who were not just members; their home was the Texas headquarters of the NAC-NA (Schaefer, *Amada's Blessings,* 103).

61. Morgan's life is discussed in Schaefer, *Amada's Blessings.*

62. Interview with Matthew Kent and Anne Zapf, Peyote Way Church of God, 19 August 2011.

63. Sandor Iron Rope of the NAC made comments to this effect at the Multi-disciplinary Association of Psychedelic Science Conference, on 22 April 2017.

64. See Terry Greene Sterling, "A Vision Gone Bust," *Phoenix New Times,* 18 February 1999. At his 1998 trial Victor Clyde of the NAC of Navajoland testified that peyote was too holy to be cultivated. This gave prosecutors the justification to confiscate Mercado's peyote plants in January 1999. Clyde, however, did not represent a uniform view of Mercado within the NAC. Others came to his defense on various occasions in the late 1990s. See for example Bill McCaddley, "Arizona's Peyote Foundation Raided," *Cannabis Culture,* 1 May 1999.

65. Arizona has an exemption for "bona fide practice of a religious belief" in Title 13–3402.

CHAPTER TEN

1. Dr. Antonio Prado Vértiz, "El peyote (la droga religiosa)," *Novedades,* 12 March 1971.

2. PRG press Release, 22 November 1974, SSP-SP, 264.3.

3. In reforms to Article 217 of the Código Sanitario, 20 March 1971, peyote, hallucinogenic mushrooms, and ololiuqui were classified as *estupificantes.* Armando Bejarmo to Dr. Manuel Altamirano Ferrer, 13 August 1971, SSP-SP, caja 244, exp. 2. See also Consejo Nacional de Problemas en Farmacodependencia, SSP-SP, caja 244, exp. 2. Punishments included prison sentences of between six months to five years and fines between 5,000 and 50,000 pesos. Reforms to the penal code in 1974 also targeted these drugs, increasing punishments and fines. Lic. Rodolfo Chávez Calvillo (representative from the PGR), "Informe," 1971, SSP-SP, caja 244, exp. 2. *Uso y abuso de drogas. Información para maestros* (Mexico City: Secretaría de Educación Pública, 1974), SSP-SP, 295.1.

4. These ties are described in Jesús Aranda, "Nueva denuncia contra Echeverría Alvarez," *La Jornada,* 17 July 2002; "Con la derrota del 68 murió el Maoísmo en México: Emery U.," *Excelsior,* 30 March 1985. See also testimony by Federico Emery Ulloa, 25 July 2002. Toca Penal 344/2006-II, Mexico City, 29 November 2002; Raúl Monge, "Nazar Haro y la psicotortura," *Proceso,* 3 August 2002.

5. *Alerta* published an article on 7 December titled "Hospital para degenerados." See Rodiles, *Una terapia prohibida,* 159–60.

6. This account comes from "24 horas de terror," *Tiempo: Seminario de la vida y la verdad* 66:1699 (25 November 1974).

7. On the domestic origins of Mexico's drug war, see Isaac Campos (*Home Grown*), Froylan Enciso (*Nuestra historia narcotica*), and Ricardo Pérez Montfort (*Yerba, goma y polvo*).

8. See for example "Razzia de hippies en Huautla: Deporta gobernación a 22 de los 84 detenidos," *Novedades,* 12 July 1969; Sara Lovera, "El problema de la drogadicción tiene origen político: Lammoglia," *El Día,* 21 August 1977. Zolov (*Refried Elvis*) writes extensively about the extent to which the hippie was seen as foreign to Mexico.

9. Enrique Marroquín makes up the name *Jipiteccas* in *La contra-cultura como protesta.*

10. On Mexican conservatism, see Eric Zolov, *Refried Elvis;* Jaime Pensado, *Rebel Mexico,* esp. 147–80, 201–34; Jaime Pensado, "'To Assault with the Truth.'" See also "La campaña contra el tráfico de drogas abarcará 4 estados," 7 August 1966; Carlos Ravelo, "La lucha contra las drogas," *Excelsior,* 9 June 1965.

11. In a survey conducted in 1971 at the national preparatory school only 1.2 percent admitted they had used hongos, 1.2 percent had used LSD, while 10.7 percent had used thinner, 10.4 percent marijuana, and 56.6 percent alcohol (SSP, caja 244.2).

12. Beatriz Reyes Nevares, "Las drogas, un nuevo azote para la inteligencia y el vigor juvenil," *Novedades,* 18 March 1969; Samuel Maynez Puente, "Sucedáneos del afecto," *Excelsior,* 26 April 1969.

13. "Llamado a los padres de familia," *El Universal,* 10 April 1970.

14. Juventino Chávez, "El 14 por ciento de la actual juventud capitalina consume drogas y enervantes," *Novedades,* 2 August 1970.

15. "Aumenta el 4% Annual el uso de Drogas en Nuestro Pais," *El Universal,* 11 October 1970.

16. Samuel Bernardo Lemus, "Perniciosos perjuicios de las drugas," *El Universal,* 13 September 1971.

17. Nevares, "Las drogas." See also "Estalla la familia y los hijos recurren a la droga," *Excelsior,* 18 September 1969; Chávez, "El 14 por ciento"; Puente, "Sucedáneos del afecto."

18. See, among others, "Orientando al joven se vence a las drogas," *El Universal,* 17 March 1970; "Señalan el peligro de las drogas," *El Nacional,* 31 July 1970; "Llamado a los padres de familia"; Nevares, "Las drogas"; "Estalla la familia"; Chávez, "El 14 por ciento"; Puente, "Sucedáneos del afecto"; "Señalan el peligro de las drogas," *El Nacional,* 13 July 1970; "Aumenta el 4%."

19. Alfonso Noriega, "Reacciones de adolescente," *Excelsior,* 14 February 1970; "Mexico y E.U. contra el narcotráfico," *Excelsior,* 21 January 1970; Luis Ernesto Cárdenas, "Solo el esfuerzo conjunto de gobernantes y gobernados logrará frenar la drogadicción," *El Nacional,* 11 May 1971.

20. "Batalla contra las drogas," *Novedades,* 27 February 1970; "Orientando al joven se vence a las drogas"; Hector M. Cabildo (who is a doctor and a member of the Sociedad Mexicana de Salud Mental), "Epidemiolgía y prevención de la farmacodependencia," *El Día,* 27 February 1974.

21. He was a UNAM professor and leading figure in Mexican criminology.

22. "Estalla la familia."

23. "Estalla la familia."

24. Aside from Quiroz Cuarón see, among others, Sylvia Sayago, "Las médicas abordan el problema de la drogadicción juvenil," *El Nacional,* 8 September 1970; "Responsabilidad de la familia"; "Llamado a los padres de familia";

Alfred Grosser, "La droga y el vacío" (reprinted from *Le Monde,* Paris), *Excelsior,* 28 September 1969; "Graves peligros," *El Universal,* 11 July 1969; Lemus, "Perniciosos perjuicios de las drogas," 13 September 1971; Alfonso Noriega, "Reacciones de adolescente," *Excelsior,* 14 February 1970; see also Puente, "Sucedáneos del afecto." Vértiz, "Lucha contra las drogas"; Dr. Ramón de la Fuente and Dr. Carlos Campillo Serrano, "Desordenes psiquiatricos asociados con el consumo de drogas," 1971, SSP-SP, caja 244, exp. 2 (Consejo Nacional de Problemas en Farmacodependencia).

25. Dr. Raul Suarez Hurtado, of Nuevo Laredo, Tamaulipas, to President Echevarría, March 1974, SSP, 264.3.

26. Antonio Lara Barragan, "Mitos y dioses en drogadictos," *El Universal,* 22 March 1969.

27. Antonio Lara Barragan, "Toxicomanías, delitos y rebeldías juveniles," 19 March 1969 (from the Archivos Económicos, Biblioteca Miguel Lerdo de Tejada, original newspaper not indicated). On the larger fear, see Shortall, "Psychedelic drugs and the Problem of Experience," 193.

28. "Graves peligros."

29. On the colonial period, see for example Fernando Cervantes, *The Devil in the New World,* 40–41, 84–89; Laura Lewis, *Hall of Mirrors;* Aguirre Beltran, *Medicina y magia;* Dawson, "Peyote in the Colonial Imagination." As for the postrevolutionary period, see Manuel Gamio, *Forjando Patria*; Dawson, *Indian and Nation in Revolutionary Mexico;* Alan Knight, "Racism, Revolution, and Indigenismo."

30. "Llamado a los padres de familia."

31. "El problema de farmacodependencia," Departamento de Psicología Medica, Psiquiatría y Salud Mental, Facultad de Medicina, UNAM, 1971, SSP-SP, caja 244, exp. 2:32, 38–39. See also Grosser, "La droga y el vacío"; Puente, "Sucedáneos del afecto." See also report compiled by Dr. José Carranza Acevedo, of the IMSS 1971, SSP-SP, caja 244, exp. 2 (Consejo Nacional de Problemas en Farmacodependencia).

32. See for example Lemus, "Perniciosos perjuicios de las drogas"; Gerardo Pacheco Santos, "Conocer el lenguage de los farmacodependientes ayuda a ganar su confianza," *El Día,* 14 April 1976; Cabildo, "Epidemiolgía y prevención"; Guillermo Cardiff, "Incultura sexual y drogadicción," *El Heraldo de Mexico,* 14 December 1977; "El problema de la drogadicción juvenil."

33. See for example Alejandro Iñigo, "El Huichol, hermanado con el peyote casi desde que nace," *Excelsior,* 21 May 1970.

34. On moral and physical degeneration, see for example "Farmacodependencia, crisis de nuestro tiempo," *El Día,* 15 April 1975; "Las drogas, aventura mortal," *El Heraldo de Mexico,* 4 July 1980; Angel Perez Isaak, "Alerta la A. Civica Feminina contra drogas y pornografia," *Excelsior,* 11 February 1979.

35. Dr. Antonio Prado Vértiz, "El peyote (la droga religiosa)," *Novedades,* 12 March 1971.

36. The first CIJ was founded in 1969 and opened in 1970. Between 1973 and 1976 CIJ opened twenty-nine centers with a combination of government and private help. Lammoglia was the founding director of the Centro de Trabajo

Juvenil, created as a dependency of the SSP in 1969, which shortly thereafter became the Centros de Integración Juveniles.

37. Personal communication with Norma Roquet, September 2009.

38. Dr. Francisco Alarcón Navarro, Jorge Miranda, and Nicolás Pérez Ramírez, Drogadicción, (n/d, but 1971–1973), SSP-SP, caja 245, exp. 1.

39. Alarcón Navarro et al., *Drogadicción*.

40. Luis Berruecos, "La función de la antropología en las investigaciones sobre farmacodependencia," in Consejo Nacional de Problemas en Farmacodependencia, Informe, 15 March 1974, SSP-SP, 293.2.

41. Report compiled by Dr. José Carranza Acevedo of the IMSS 1971 (Consejo Nacional de Problemas en Farmacodependencia), SSP-SP, caja 244, exp. 2. See also "El problema de farmacodependencia," Departamento de Psicologica Medica, Psiquiatria y Salud Mental, Facultad de Medicina, UNAM, 1971 SSP-SP, caja 244, exp. 2 (Consejo Nacional de Problemas en Farmacodependencia), 32.

42. Consejo Nacional de Problemas en Farmacodependencia, SSP-SP, caja 244, exp. 2. See also Dr. José Carranza Acevedo, *Información a jóvenes,* Consejo Nacional de Problemas en Farmacodependencia, 1972, SSP-SP, 263.3; Programa Nacional de Combate a los Problemas de Drogas, ¿Como Identificar las drogas y sus usarios? (Mexico City: CEMEF and SEP, 1976).

43. *Uso y abuso de drogas,* 18. See also Dr. y Gral. Demetrio Mayoral Pardo, "Toxicomanía-Farmacodependencia," *CEMEF Informe* 1:6 (1973), SSP-SP, 266.1, 4.

44. "Farmacodependencia, crisis de nuestro tiempo."

45. "Llamado a los padres de familia."

46. "No hay centros para rehabilitar a los niños farmacodependientes," *El Universal,* 19 April 1976; Victor Payan, "200,000 Llamadas recibieron en 1979 en los Centros de Integración Juvenil," *Excelsior,* 24 April 1980.

47. This is discussed in José Neme Salum, "Minima, la farmacodependencia en México: Mondragón y Kalb," *Excelsior,* 20 October 1986.

48. Gregorio Dichara González, "La drogadicción en México," in *Conflictos obrero patronales* 1 (1974): 16–17. See also Dr. José Carranza Acevedo, IMSS, to Dr. Rafael Velasco Fernandez, Secretario del Consejo Nacional de Problemas en Farmacodependencia, 26 January 1974, SSP, 293.2; Dr. Hector M. Cabildo Arellano et al., "Investigación sobre el uso de substancias intoxicantes entre los menores y jovenes del distrito sanitario 16," Mexico, DF, September 1971, 13, SSP, caja 259.2; Consejo Nacional de Problemas en Farmacodependencia, "El Problema de Farmacodependencia en México," July 1972, SSP, 263.3; Dr. Guillermo Calderón Narváez, Director of Salud Mental at SSP, "Consideraciones generales en relacion con el problema de farmacodependencia" (1972), SSP-SP, caja 244.2; Chávez, "El 14 por ciento." See also memo from Dr. Carlos Pucheu R., UNAM, to Dr. Rafael Velasco Fernandez, Secretario del Consejo Nacional de Problemas en Farmacodependencia (1974), SSP-SP, 293.2.

49. A 1970 survey in Mexico City asked 3,096 people if they had taken peyote or mezcalina, and not a single person had. Only four said they had taken mushrooms (Cabildo Arellano et al., "Investigación sobre el uso de substancias

intoxicantes). One 1975 report suggests that twenty-one of every one thousand had consumed farmacos (this includes peyote and hongos). Of those who indicated they had taken these drugs, most were irregular users or had stopped using (Segundo reporte de resultados de la investigacion epidemiologica sobre el problema de la farmacodependencia en el Distrito Federal, CEMEF, June 1975, SSP-SP, 295.1).

50. Segundo reporte. See also Dr. Magdalena Labrandero I, Secretaria Técnica, Consejo Nacional Contra Adicciones, "Encuesta nacional sobre el uso de drogas psicotropicas, problemas relacionados con el consumo de alcohol y tabaquismo en Mexico. Protocolo de investigacion," January 1988, SSP, 643.2. One 1980 study found only two people out of thirty-three hundred studied who used peyote ("Aún no de ha practicado una investigación epidemiológica en gran escala sobre drogas," El Día, 28 June 1980).

51. Cristina Diego Fernández, "Las drogas, aventura mortal (III parte)," El Heraldo de México, 2 July 1980; "Las drogas, aventura mortal (V parte)," El Heraldo de México, 4 July 1980; "Niños indígenas y campesinos huyen del hogar for falta de comprehensión," Excelsior, 4 July 1980. See also Martha Robles, "Libertad o drogas. El cerco de la degradación," Excelsior, 3 June 1988. Eduardo A. Hacho, "Drogadicto o alcohólico, 40% del estdiantado de nivel medio," Excelsior, 25 July 1987.

52. See for example Roberto Noriega, "Drogadiccíon entre 10 y 15% de los jóvenes preparatorianos," El Sol de México, 30 Sept 1973; Lepoldo Cano, "Anfetaminas, las drogas de uso común entre los jóvenes," El Universal, 4 July 1979; "Se agudiza el problema de la farmacodependencia," El Día, 8 August 1979; Salvador Castañeda, "A pesar de combatirlo, se incrementa el uso de drogas," Novedades, 14 July 1979; Francisco Jorda Galan, "Es muy grande el número de adictos; jóvenes la mayoría," El Univeral, 10 October 1979; "Aún no de ha practicado una investigación epidemiogica"; Centros de Integración Juvenil, "Estudio epidemiologico en escuelas. Centro Local 'Acapulco,'" December 1981, SSP, 592.8; Centro Mexicano de Psiquiatria, "Investigaciones sobre farmacodependencia en el Estado de Guerrero realizadas por los Centros de Integracion Juvenil" (1985?), SSP, 592.8; Encuesta Nacional de Adicciones, 1990 (based on the 1988 survey of fifteen thousand homes), SSP, 743.1.

53. Many of these figures wrote to the Mexican government to protest his arrest. See Stanley Krippner, "Editorial," Psychoenergetic Systems 1 (1976): 103. See also letter from Ofelia Canales de Hodgins, Department of Physics, University of Virginia, to Echeverría, 3 December 1974. Others included Walter Houston Clark, Professor Duncan Blewett of the University of Regina, Dr. Oscar Rios, research psychiatrist at McGill University, Dr. Harvey Cox, Harvard University, Dr. Carmi Harari, American Psychological Association, Division of Humanistic Psychology, Larry Davis, Medical Director of the Mental Health Center of the Community Hospital of Indianapolis (Papers of Norma Roquet).

54. Salvador Roquet to Dr. Carlos Campillo Saénz, Mexico, 29 November 1974 (Papers of Norma Roquet). See also Roquet et al., "The Existential through Psychodisleptics," 56–57. Walter Houston Clark claimed the police had acted on Guido Belsasso's advice. See Clark, "'Bad Trips.'" More broadly, Roquet believed the psychiatric community in general was against him. See

letter from Roquet to Echeverría from prison, 3 February 1975 (Papers of Norma Roquet).

55. See for example Clark, "'Bad Trips.'"

56. See Javier Mancera Fuentes to C. Director Federal Seguridad, Mexico City, 19 March 1971, expediente Personal Rafael Estrada Villa, Versión Pública, Legajo 4, folio 190 a 192, AGN, Dirección Federal De Seguridad.

57. Roquet's defenders dispute these claims, insisting that Roquet was conducting therapy sessions in Lecumberri, though they concede that some of that therapy was "involuntary." This is most clearly demonstrated in email correspondence with Gabriel Parra, 1 September 2014.

58. See note 4, above. Richard Yensen and Gabriel Parra have reservations about the accuracy of Emery Ulloa's recollections (Richard Yensen, personal communication, Vancouver, 2 September 2014; Gabriel Parra, personal communication, Mexico City, 1 September 2014).

59. Roquet, "En busca de la aplicación terapeutica de los psicodislepticos."

60. Most research on LSD in the US was terminated by 1968. Matthew Oram notes that these experiments were also undermined by the inability of researchers to establish proof of efficacy ("Efficacy and Enlightenment"). See also Shortall, "Psychedelic Drugs"; Stephen Snelders, Charles Kaplan, and Toine Pieters, "On Cannabis, Chloral Hydrate, and Career Cycles of Psychotropic Drugs in Medicine," *Bulletin of the History of Medicine* 80:1 (2006): 95–114.

CHAPTER ELEVEN

1. "Política indigenista en América Latina," *Anuario Indigenista*, Mexico, 1969, 26.

2. Art. 247 of the law. Cárdenas de Ojeda, *Toxicomania y narcotrafico.*

3. Signatories included Scott Robinson, who made a seminal film on the pilgrimage to Wirikuta, and Guillermo Bonfil Batalla, one of the key figures in the critique of indigenismo.

4. Art. 32, § 4. The law was published in *Diario Oficial,* México, 24 June 1975.

5. United Nations, Convention on Psychotropic Substances, 1971, art. 33.4.

6. Fernando Benítez, *En la tierra mágica del peyote.*

7. See Dawson, *Indian and Nation in Revolutionary Mexico.*

8. The convention was signed by Mexico on 21 February 1971 Rafael Hernández González, *El peyote en la Nueva España (un viaje hasta nuestros dias),* thesis for Licenciado en Historia, UNAM, 2000, 184. Currently, under art. 198 of the 1994 federal penal code, anyone convicted of growing peyote faces a prison sentence of one to six years, though 2009 reforms to the health code and penal code permit the ceremonial and cultural use of peyote by indigenous peoples.

9. On 16 March 1998 the Mexican army detained two women, four men, and a ten-year-old child from the Huichol community of San Andrés Cohamiata. They were held in Vallecito, in the municipality of Heujuquilla el Alto, Jalisco, accused of trafficking estupificantes. (See La Ojarasca Supplement, *La Jornada,* 8 April 1998). See also *La Jornada,* 20 February 1996; Hernández

González, *El peyote,* 184; "Operación Cóndor," *El Universal,* 19 August 1978; Enrique Aranda Pedroza, "Imipidió el ejército que llegaran al mercado internacional enervantes con valor de más de 239,000 milliones de pesos," *El Universal,* 22 December 1977; "El combate del cultivo y trafico de drogas," *El Día,* 24 February 1985; informe by Lic. Rodolfo Chávez Calvillo (representative from the PGR), some time in 1971, SSP-SP, caja 244, exp. 2 (Consejo Nacional de Problemas en Farmacodependencia). See also Francisco Ortíz Pinchetti, *La Operación Condor* (Mexico City: Proceso, 1981), 74–75. In 1990 Prem Das was arrested along with a group of North Americans in Tepic with forty kilograms of peyote (Phil C. Weigand and Jay C. Fikes, "Sensacionalismo y etnografía").

10. See joint memorandum from Guido Belsasso and John C. Kramer (Special Action Office for Drug Abuse Prevention), 5 September 1972, SSP-SP, caja 259.2; Dr. Francisco Alarcón Navarro, Jorge Miranda, and Nicolás Pérez Ramírez, *Drogadiccíon* (written sometime 1971–73), SSP, caja 245 exp. 1; Segundo Reporte de Resultados de la Investigacion epidemiologica sobre el problema de la faramcodependencia en el Distrito Federal, CEMEF, June 1975: 1–2, 79. SSP, 295.1; Teresa Gurza, "Las drogas, recurso terapéutico pervertido en el uso clandestino," *El Día,* 8 April 1976; Centro Mexicano de Estudios en Salud Mental, *La familia ante el problema de las drogas, una program de la familia para la prevención de la dependencia a sustancias químicas* (Mexico City: 1979), 117–19. See also Guido Belasso, "Estrategias de prevención en farmacodependencia. Modelos de prevención y alternativas al consumo de drogas," presented at the V Congreso Nacional de Higiene Escolar, Acapulco, Guerrero, de 9 al 13 de Agusto de 1976. This conclusion was supported in Robert L. Bergman, "Navajo Peyote Use: Its Apparent Safety," 695–99. See also Heriberto García Salazar, "Drogadicción, etnología, y cambio social a Vuelo de Pajaro," *Annuario Antropológico* (Universidad Veracruzana) 1 (1970): 65–70.

11. Dr. y Gral. Demetrio Mayoral Pardo, "Toxicomania-Farmacodependencia," CEMEF Informe, 1:6 (1973), SSP-SP, 266.1, pl. 4–6. See also notes from a meeting of the Consejo de Administracion of the CEMEF, 4 October 1973, SSP-SP, 266.1. See also Alejandro Iñigo, "El Huichol, hermanado con el peyote casi desde que nace," *Excelsior,* 21 May 1970.

12. Notes from a meeting of the Consejo de Administración of the CEMEF, 4 October 1973, SSP, 266.1. See also 5 September 1972 joint memorandum from Guido Belsasso and John C Kramer, SSP-SP, caja 259.2; Navarro et al., *Drogadicción;* Segundo reporte.

13. Notes from a meeting of the Consejo de Administración of the CEMEF, 4 October 1973, SSP, 266.1. On the syphilis experiment, see Donald G. McNeil Jr., "Lapses by American Leaders Seen in Syphilis Tests," *New York Times,* 14 September 2011; Presidential Commission for the Study of Bioethical Issues, *"Ethically Impossible:" STD Research in Guatemala from 1946 to 1948* (Washington, DC, September 2011).

14. The larger critique was by the likes of Arturo Warman, Ricardo Pozas, and Guillermo Bonfil Batalla. Classics in the genre included Warman et al., *De eso que llaman antropología* (México: Ed. Nuestro Tiempo, 1968), and Pozas, *La antropología y la burocracia indigenista.*

15. See Warman, *De eso que llaman la antropología Mexicana.* See also Salomón Nahmad Sittón et al., *El peyote y los Huicholes;* Pozas, *La antropología y la burocracia indigenista,* 33–38; *¿Ha fracasado el indigenismo? Reportaje de una controversia* (13 September 1971 [Mexico, SEP, 1971]), 9–13. See also Guillermo Bonfil Batalla, "Las culturas autoctonas en Mexico," *Mexico Indigena* 1 (1989): 17–22.

16. The Declaration of Barbados is quite clear in this regard.

17. Nahmad Sittón, *El peyote.* Most of the material in the text had been previously published, and some was quite old. (Klineberg's essay was published in *American Anthropologist* 36 [1934]: 446–60. The Furst and Myerhoff essay appears in *Antropológica* 17 [1966]: 3–39.

18. Nahmad Sittón, *El peyote,* 7.

19. See Guillermo Bonfil Batalla, "Del indigenismo de la revolución a la antropología crítica."

20. Nahmad Sittón, *El peyote,* 24. The quote is from "Política indigenista en América Latina," *Anuario Indigenista* (Mexico: 1969): 26.

21. Otto Klineberg, "Notas sobre los Huicholes," in *El peyote y los Huicholes,* ed. Salomón Nahmad Sittón et al., 35.

22. See for example Agustín, *La contracultura en México,* 45–46.

23. See Bergman, "Navajo Peyote Use"; Calabrese, *A Different Medicine.*

24. See Yanna Yannakakis, *The Art of Being In-Between: Native Intermediaries, Indian Identity, and Local Rule in Colonial Oaxaca* (Durham: Duke University Press, 2008); Carmen Martínez Novo, "Managing Diversity in Postneoliberal Ecuador"; Andrés Guerrero, "The Construction of a Ventriloquist's Image."

25. This paper war was quickly put down when local authorities throughout the region disavowed any connection to the erstwhile rebels. See "Grupo Guerrillero 'Manuel Lozada,'" *Realidades de Nayarit,* 23 February 1994; INI, Nayarit, Expediente de la Delegación Estatal de Nayarit, Información Periodistica; *La Jornada,* 28 February 1994; "Confirmado: !Si hay guerrilla en Nayarit!," *Express* (Tepic), 1 March 1994; "Crece el movimiento armado en la sierra," *El Sol de Tepic,* 2 March 1994; "Un tal Doctor Molina es el autor de la 'Carta Guerrillera,'" *Diario del Pacifico,* 4 March 1994; "Marginación, miseria, y olvido oficial de las etnias nayaritas," *Realidades de Nayarit,* 2 March 1994. On 1 March the *ancianos* of Jesús Maria issued a declaration denying the whole rebellion, claiming that it was a fabrication and that the names that appeared on the declaration were forged. All materials were found in CDI, FD 18/0060.

26. That is the Partido Revolucionario Institucional, which governed Mexico from 1929 to 2000.

27. In July 1982 INI official Agustín Romano Delgado described the Programa Defensa y Desarrollo de las Culturas Autoctonos in Nayarit as a farce. It was managed in a paternalistic fashion, and they were undermining the authority of the *ancianos* by giving money to politically connected *comites.* See note of 8 July 1982 in Rescate Cultural, 1982 CDI, FD 18/009. See also Fondos de Solidaridad para la Promoción del Patrimonio Cultural de los Pueblos Indígenas, June 1991, FD 9/1304. See also Jeffrey Rubin, *Decentering the Regime;* Guillermo de la Peña, "Poder local, poder regional"; Dawson, *Indian and Nation in Revolutionary Mexico.*

28. Designed to save an endangered Indian, the INI's most significant effort in this regard was the Programa para el Desarrollo y Defensa de las Culturas Autoctonas (Program for the Development and Defense of Autoctonous Cultures), which was created in 1980. See Rescate Cultural, 1982 CDI, FD 18/009. See also INI, Evaluación del Programa "Desarrollo y Defensa de las Culturas Autóctonas," 1982, CDI, FD 9/36. On these types of projects more generally, see Elizabeth Povinelli, *The Cunning of Recognition;* Charles R. Hale, *Más que un Indio;* Nancy Postero, *Now We Are Citizens;* Martínez Novo, "Managing Diversity in Postneoliberal Ecuador." Peter Wade notes that one of the qualities of multiculturalism is that it tends to limit the spaces indigenousness and blackness can occupy. See Peter Wade, "Rethinking Mestizaje Ideology and Lived Experience," 255. On the paternalistic view of the Huichols, see in particular Negrin, *Colores mexicanos,* 12, 91. See also Courtney Jung, *The Moral Force of Indigenous Politics,* 219–20.

29. Ing. Rubén Sánchez Contreras to Severo Hernández Hernández (Sub-dir capatacion y organización, INI), 23 March 1983, CDI, FD 14/003; Arturo Moreno Chávez, chief, Dept. de Investigación Antropológica, to Enrique Valencia (INI), 17 January 1983, CDI, FD 14/003. See also a complaint signed by sixteen representatives from communities in the region, including Tuxpan de Bolaños, San Andrés, San Sebastian, Santa Catarina, and Ocota de la Sierra, presented by the Consejo Supremo Huichol, Zona Norte de Jalisco, Programa para la region indigena Huichol de la zona norte del Estado de Jalisco, 1982–1983, 11 November 1982; INI, Coordinadora Estatal de Nayarit, "Reunion de rescate cultural de la costumbres Wirraritari," 1996, CDI, FD 18/048. It was not until the early 1990s that the INI worked out the first of a series of accords with the mestizo campesinos who owned the lands along the sacred route of the pilgrimage, which called for the pilgrims to pass through these areas unmolested (Rosa Rojas, "Reactivarán sistema de vigilancia en Wirikuta para proteger el peyote," *La Jornada,* 17 April 2003).

30. Though often promoted as democratic and antiauthoritarian, in practice these institutions worked mainly as instruments of political control, and the CSH itself was dissolved in 1990 amid accusations of authoritarianism and corruption by its leader. The UCIH was created as a successor to the CSH in 1991 as an instrument to both foster community building and channel solidarity funds in the sierra. The UCIHJ was disbanded in 2001 when the CDI replaced the INI. See Unión de Comunidades Indígenas Huicholes de Jalisco (UCIHJ), "Programa de desarrollo Comunal de la Región Wixárika de Jalisco," 1995, CDI, FD 14/19; Negrín, *Colores mexicanos;* Paul Liffman, *Huichol Territory and the Mexican Nation,* 149.

31. Interview with Francisco López, 29 September 2009.

32. Interview with López, 29 September 2009.

33. Peter Furst and Stacy Schaefer, "Peyote Pilgrims and Don Juan Seekers," 510–12.

34. Completed in 1989, the dam flooded thirteen thousand hectares. More than 60 percent of those displaced by the dam were Wixárika.

35. In 1990 the governor was there to meet the cargo holders as they returned from Wirikuta (Stacy B. Schaefer, "The Cosmos Contained," 367).

36. Interview with Roteleo Carrillo, Zitakua, Tepic, Nayarit, 1 October 2009. See also Phil Weigand, *Ensayos sobre el Gran Nayar.* See also Comaroff and Comaroff, *Ethnicity, Inc.*

37. Only Tee'kata, in Santa Catarina, Jalisco, was in the sierra. INI, Dirección de Procuración de Justicia, Subdirección de Antropológica Jurídica, Departamento de Lugares Sagrados, Evaluación del Trabajo de Protección a Lugares Sagrados, compiled by Karen Frid, Diego Poliakoff, Ari Rajsbaum, Ramon Martínez (sometime between 1994 and 1995), CDI. FD 09/2310; INI, Notas para el Desarrollo Integral del Pueblo Wixárika de Jalisco, 2002, CDI, FD 14/045. See A. Ochoa, "Denician profanacion de sitios sagrados huicholes," *El Universal,* 3 October 2004; Vincent Basset, "New Age Tourism in Wirikuta."

38. Tatei Arama Tate Tatevari: Lugar Sagrado huichol-cora. See also article in *El Nacional,* 17 December 1990, and *El Universal,* 15 December 1990. All found in CDI, FD 18/18.

39. INI, Coordinadora Estatal de Nayarit, "Reunión de rescate cultural de la costumbres Wirraritari," 1996, CDI, FD 18/048; INI, Evaluación del Trabajo de Protección a lugares Sagrados, CDI, FD 09/2310.

40. INI, Coordinadora Estatal de Nayarit, "Reunion de rescate Cultural de la costumbres Wirraritari," 1996, CDI, FD 18/048.

41. Furst and Schaefer, "Peyote Pilgrims and Don Juan Seekers," 518–20. The area was later enlarged in 2000 as an "área natural protegida, bajo la modalidad de Reserva Estatal de Paisaje Cultural de Huiricuta, los Lugares Sagrados y la ruta histórico cultural del pueblo huichol."

42. See Ramón Vera Herrera, "Un lugar sagrado en peligro," *La Jornada,* 7 September 2002.

43. Basset, "New Age Tourism in Wirikuta," 199–203. See also Kali Argyriadis et al., eds., *Raíces en movimiento,* esp. 17–21.

44. Ramón Vera Herrera, "Un lugar sagrado en peligro," *La Jornada,* 7 September 2002; Rosa Rojas, "Reactivarán sistema de vigilancia en Wirikuta para proteger el peyote," *La Jornada,* 17 April 2003. In 2010 Dora Alicia Varela Martínez received a sentence of four years in prison and fifty days of the minimum salary as a fine for possession of twenty peyote plants and a vial of peyote extract. "Sentencian a mujer por posesión de peyote," *El Universal,* 22 April 2010.

45. This according to a June 2004 report by Alfredo Sánchez Azua, "Extranjeros se disfrazan y roban peyote mexicano," *El Siglo de Torreón,* 7 June 2004.

46. Azua, "Extranjeros."

47. In March 1998 a group of pilgrims from San Andrés Cohamiata were arrested and jailed by the army in Huejuquilla, el Alto, Jalisco, as they returned from Wirikuta, in Valparaíso, Zacatecas (Ramón Vera Herrera, "Un lugar sagrado en peligro," *La Jornada,* 7 September 2002). In November 2001 Mario Bautista Bautista and Guadalupe Lopez Bautista, Huichol community representatives on their way to a conference in San José del Cabo, Baja California, were arrested and jailed in Guadalajara for possessing peyote plants. Officials held them pending a determination that they were carrying the plants for "cultural reasons." "Huicholes arrested for transporting peyote plants," *Guadalajara Reporter,* 29 November 2001.

48. This is based on a 2004 agreement. Basset, "New Age Tourism in Wirikuta," 191–209.

49. "Asociación jaliciense acusa a policías de SLP de hostigar a la comunidad huichola," *La Jornada*, 28 February 2010. See also Basset, "New Age Tourism," 195.

50. "Asociación jalisciense acusa a policías de SLP de hostigar a la comunidad huichola," *La Jornada*, 28 February 2010.

51. Guillermina Guillén, "Retiran datos sobre exportación de peyote," *El Universal*, 3 June 2006; Guillermina Guillén, "La Semarnat autorizó 'por error' exportación de peyote," *El Universal*, 1 June 2006. Ramón Vera Herrera, "Se abre la puerta a la bioprospección en el desierto de Wirikuta," *La Jornada*, 22 September 2009. See also Rafael Díazbarriga Méndez, Acciones, Avances y Propuestas sobre Lugares Sagrados, CDI, FD CDI.91.01.0010.

52. It was signed by the government and the Unión Wixárika de Centros Ceremoniales de Jalisco, Durango y Nayarit A.C., and representatives of five states, the Senate and Chamber of Deputies, the CNDPI.

53. Pacto de Hauxa Manaka para la Preservación y Desarrollo de la Cultura Wixárika, 2008. On 6 June the governor of SLP Marcelo de los Santos Fraga signed a decree to create a plan to manage the Wirikuta reserve. It called for the protection of the water, land, flora, and fauna in this sacred site.

54. At the height of the controversies over Wirikuta, Hernan Vilchez, Paula Stefani, and a large cast of collaborators released a film titled *Huicholes: The Last Peyote Guardians,* which was screened in North America and Europe. Local activists in Mexico City organized Wirikuta Fest in May 2012 in the Foro Sol. Performers included Café Tacvba, Caifanes, Enrique Bunbury, and Calle 13 ("Confirman concierto 'Wirikuta Fest' en el Foro Sol," *El Proceso*, 30 April 2012).

55. Letter to the President of the United States of Mexico Felipe Calderón Hinojosa and to the People and Governments of the World, Mexico, D.F., 9 May 2011. See also Letter to Majestic Silver, 27 November 2014, from Guadalajara, signed by authorities from Santa Catarina Cuexcomatitlán (Minjares Valdez Bautista, Faustino González De la Cruz, and two others), Bancos de Calítique o Cohamiata, Estado de Durango (Sebastián Carrillo Carrillo and two others), Sebastián Teponahuaxtlán and Tuxpan of the municipalities of Mezquitic y Bolaños, state of Jalisco (Miguel Vázquez Torres J. Trinidad Chema Guzmán). See also Segunda Carta Urgente al Presidente de Mexico, Los Pueblos Gobiernos del Mundo, 8 February 8 2013. This type of practice is analyzed as a larger trope of indigeneity in Shepard Krech III, *Ecological Indian.*

56. In February 2012 opponents of the mines were granted an injunction in the Mexican courts while the case proceeded through the system. In early May (May 6) the CNDH recommended that the concessions be canceled because they were illegal. Boletín de Prensa: Wirikuta Lugar Sagrado Fundamental para la Supervivencia del Pueblo Wixárika y de la Humanidad, Ciudad de México, 7 February 2013.

57. Luis Santamaría, "La Iglesia Nativa Americana de México pide la legalización del consumo de peyote," *Infocatolica*, 28 November 2015.

58. Liffman, *Huichol Territory,* 37. Santamaría, "La Iglesia Nativa Americana de México"; Basset, "New Age Tourism," 191–209.

59. See Postero, *Now We Are Citizens;* Andrew Canessa, "New Indigenous Citizenship in Bolivia."

60. Interview with Scott Robinson, Mexico City, 26 July 2011. At the time of the interview Robinson, who made one of the early documentaries about Wirikuta, was an anthropologist affiliated with the UAM-Iztapalapa. He had a student who took up this practice.

61. As Paul Liffman notes, "such exits from a failed modernity belie the supposed homogeneity of the city and redress its alienation." He argues that la Nueva Mexicanidad actually offers Mexicans an opportunity to "rediscover senses of place, albeit diffusely." Liffman, *Huichol Territory,* 37. See also Argyriadis, et al., *Raíces en movimiento,* esp. 17–21.

62. Basset even argues that these voices have worked in favor of Wixáritari rights on a global stage. "New Age Tourism," 192.

63. Santamaría, "La Iglesia Nativa Americana de México"; Elio Masferrer Kan, "Los alucinógenos en las culturas contemporáneas, un patrimonio cultural," *Drogas Mexico* 10:59 (January–February 2003). In November 2016 the Mexican Supreme Court ruled in favor of the INAM, indicating that the SecGob could not take into account the beliefs of members of a church in deciding whether or not to authorize the church. At the time of writing, the INAM still lacks legal status in Mexico. The court did not rule on the constitutionality of section 245.1 of the Ley General de Salud, which outlawed peyote in Mexico. Víctor Fuentes, "Ampara la corte a 'Iglesia del Peyote,'" *Reforma,* 30 November 2016.

64. See Alejandro Camino, "El peyote: Derecho histórico des los Pueblos Indios."

CHAPTER TWELVE

1. Tom Soloway Pinkson, *The Shamanic Wisdom of the Huichol,* 125.

2. See in particular Stevens, *Storming Heaven;* Lattin, *The Harvard Psychedelic Club;* Jay Winter, *Dreams of Peace and Freedom.* The following discussion is also informed by Deloria's analysis and critique of narratives of indigeneity in the US. See Philip Deloria, "Counterculture Indians and the New Age"; Philip Deloria, *Indians in Unexpected Places.* Others who in some ways connect to this tradition would clearly include Aldus Huxley, Antonin Artaud, and Timothy Leary. See for example *Phantastica* (1924), *Les Tarahumaras* (1947), *and The Doors of Perception* (1954).

3. Franciso Silva López, "Los Huicholes," *El Heraldo de Mexico,* 14 July 1966. Central to this literature was Benítez, *En la tierra mágica del peyote.* The idea of existing out of time is critical to the narrative of the other here. See Johannes Fabian, *Time and the Other.*

4. Jaime Reyes Estrada, "'Que se cumplan las promesas,' pide el gobernador Huichol," *Excelsior,* 4 April 1972; Mariana Anguinao, "Supervivencia e ancestrales ritos y sistemas de gobierno entre los Huicholes," *Novedades,* 14 February 1971; Sergio Méndez, "La vida de los Huicholes," *Excelsior,* 27 June 1968.

5. Alfonso Villa Rojas, *Notas sobre los Huicholes* (México: INAH, CAPFCE, SEP, 1961), 20. See also Méndez, "La vida de los Huicholes."

6. Rosa María Roffiel, "El mundo alucinante de los Huicholes en fotos de tirado," *Excelsior,* 17 October 1973.

7. Ramón Morones, "Coras, Huicholes y Tepehuanes participaran de la vida nacional," *Excelsior,* 15 December 1970. See also Myerhoff, *Peyote Hunt,* 122, 132–36; Fernando Benítez, *En la tierra mágica del peyote,* 17, 19; Méndez, "La vida de los Huicholes."

8. Benítez would recount his experience among the Wixárika in a 1968 book, *En la tierra mágica del peyote.* It was translated and published in English in 1975. It is not clear who met Medina Silva first. Furst and Myerhoff started working with him in 1965. It appears that he started working with Benítez in 1967. See Medina Silva, "How One Goes on Being Huichol," 169–71.

9. Muriel Thayer Painter, *With Good Heart.*

10. See for example Robert Marshall, "The Dark Legacy of Carlos Castaneda."

11. Ageeth Sluis, "Journeys to Others and Lessons of Self."

12. All told, this and later books about his apprenticeship sold twelve million copies. *Time* magazine dubbed him the "Godfather of the New Age." See Carlos Castaneda, *The Teachings of Don Juan;* Carlos Castaneda, *A Separate Reality;* Carlos Castaneda, *Journey to Ixtlan.*

13. They were originally from Álica, near Tepic, and there is some dispute as to whether or not their neighbors would have considered them proper curers or shamans. Their community was founded by refugees from the Cristero revolt in the 1920s, and some anthropologists have suggested that their practices differed significantly from those found in the sierra.

14. These ceremonies with Don José at Esalen continued to the late 1970s. See Stanislav Grof, *When the Impossible Happens,* 76–80. Das later prepared the recording *Shamanic Pathways* with Halifax.

15. "Confessions of a Peyote Eater," 17. See also *Shamanic Pathways* by Joan Halifax and Prem Das (1992). See also Phil C. Weigand and Jay C. Fikes, "Sensacionalismo y etnografía: El caso de los Huicholes de Jalisco," 49–68.

16. See Larain Boyll, *Huichol Sacred Pilgrimage to Huiricuta* (Mill Valley, CA: Four Winds Circle, 1991), https://www.youtube.com/watch?v = Q3GKpy6Pj6w. See also Weigand and Fikes, "Sensacionalismo y etnografía."

17. http://worldnagualforum.yuku.com/topic/659/Interview-with-Ken-Eagle-Feather#.Vsd-hBjo2CQ; http://the-wanderling.com/ken_eagle_feather.html.

18. Eagle Feather describes meeting Matus in Ken Eagle Feather, *On the Toltec Path,* xi, 1. See also Ken Eagle Feather, *Toltec Dreaming.*

19. According to Jay Fikes and Phil Weigand, this story is a complete fabrication, and Secunda in fact was introduced to the Wixárika in 1982 when Prem Das passed through New York on a tour. Later that same year Das brought Secunda to the community of El Colorín, where he introduced him to Ríos, and Ríos agreed to be his teacher. Fikes and Weigand likewise insist that Secunda's narrative of thirteen years in the sierra simply makes no sense. Weigand and Fikes, "Sensacionalismo y etnografía".

20. Guy Trebay, "My Grandson the Shaman," *Village Voice,* 19 June 1990. See also www.shamanism.com/huichol-indians.

21. Comaroff and Comaroff argue that this represents an important shift in the way we view culture and is nested within neoliberal modernity. Brown

(2003) also addresses this issue at length. See Comaroff and Comaroff, *Ethnicity, Inc.*; Brown, *Who Owns Native Culture?*

22. See Diana Negrín da Silva, "El indio que todos quieren"; Negrín, *Colores mexicanos*, 122. See also www.shamangoods.net.

23. These comments appeared in response to a YouTube video featuring Secunda (https://www.youtube.com/watch?v = paBomgY2LYc).

24. La Barre to William B. Wing of the Smithsonian, 7 December 1970, NAA, Papers of Weston La Barre, Box 8.

25. This was Weston La Barre's description of the text in a book review that the *New York Times* declined to publish (Marshall, "The Dark Legacy of Carlos Castaneda"). See also Peter Furst and Stacy Schaefer, "Peyote Pilgrims and Don Juan Seekers," 507–508.

26. Jay Fikes and Phil Weigand (who are among Castaneda's harshest critics within academia), assert that, because they relied on Medina Silva, he, Myerhoff, and Furst created a distorted impression of Huichol shamanism. I use the term here both because it is the most common term deployed in this context and because of its capacity to signify a number of things, including curer, singer, (*cahuitero, mara'akáme*). See Jay Fikes, *Carlos Castaneda, Academic Opportunism and the Psychedelic Sixties*, 1–12; Jay Fikes, *Unknown Huichol*, 3–4. Edward H. Spicer is quoted in Noel indicating that Don Juan is a composite of many different shamans (Daniel C. Noel, ed.. *Seeing Castaneda*, 31–32). See also Sluis, "Journeys to Others," note 34; David Silverman, *Reading Castaneda*. Richard de Mille's *Don Juan Papers* is the most scathing critique of its veracity. He also published *Castaneda's Journey: The Power and the Allegory*. See also Robert Marshall, "The Dark Legacy."

27. Joan B. Townsend, "Individualist Religious Movements." See also Brett Hendrickson, *Border Medicine*, 165; Basset, "New Age Tourism."

28. See for example Judith Friedlander, *Being Indian in Hueyapan*; Philip J. Deloria, *Playing Indian*; Shari M. Huhndorf, *Going Native*; Fikes, *Carlos Castaneda*; Agustín, *La contracultura en México*, 45–46. At the very least their practices can be said to represent a superficial bricolage, or as Cristina Gutiérrez puts it, religion "a la carte." See Cristina Gutiérrez, *Nuevos movimientos religiosos*; Cristina Gutiérrez, *Congregaciones del éxito*.

29. This informs the critiques in Negrín, Fikes, and Weigand, among others. My approach is informed by Povinelli and Stephan Palmié. See Palmié, *The Cooking of History*, and "Mixed Blessings and Sorrowful Mysteries."

30. See for example Weigand, *Estudio histórico y cultural sobre los Huicholes*; Fikes, *Unknown Huichol*.

31. On more traditional rituals, see Fikes, *Unknown Huichol*; Weigand, *Ensayos sobre el Gran Nayar, México*; Weigand, *Estudio histórico y cultural sobre los Huicholes*.

32. Feinberg, *The Devil's Book of Culture*, 127–37, 188–90. See also Joralemon, "The Selling of the Shaman," 105–18; Michael Forbes Brown, "Shamanism and Its Discontents."

33. Basset, "New Age Tourism."

34. See for example Michael Taussig, *Shamanism, Colonialism, and the Wild Man*, 216–19.

35. The concept of appropriation has been used in a variety of ways by scholars over time to describe the way that one set of practices travels from one community to another. Roger Chartier, for instance, noted the way that literacy was appropriated and underwent multiple transformations as new collectivities took up something that had once rested with the powerful. Though not free of power (de Certeau would describe the scriptural economy as one managed from above through strategies but negotiated through tactics from below), appropriation in these instances allows for transformation without a claim to property that has been stolen. Michael Taussig notes too that cultures are continually appropriating practices from others without acknowledging them. See Roger Chartier, *The Order of Books;* Michel de Certeau, *The Practice of Everyday Life,* 132; Michael Taussig, *Mimesis and Alterity.*

36. Shortall, "Psychedelic Drugs," 187–206.

37. See Basset, "New Age Tourism."

38. Latour argues that modernity is based on a claim of man's separation from nature (Bruno Latour, *We Have Never Been Modern*). We might even think of their stories as "happily transgressive." See Micol Seigel et al., "The Spatial Politics of Radical Change, " 6. I also draw from Marisol de la Cadena, "Indigenous Cosmopolitics in the Andes."

39. Ben Feinberg notes that the narrative of immersion into indigenous culture requires a "prior clearly recognizable subject position within 'The West', which is somehow juxtaposed or transcended in the psychedelic Other." See Benjamin Feinberg, "Three Mazatec Wise Ones," 415.

40. I am thinking of Jean Baudrillard, *Simulacra and Simulation.* Sherry Smith's nuanced reading of the hippies in *Hippies, Indians, and the Fight for Red Power* is also useful here.

41. This is what Taussig argues in *Mimesis and Alterity.*

42. Boddy, "Spirit Possession Revisited," 424. See also Csordas, "Introduction: The Body as Representation and Being in the World," 8.

43. Scott Robinson describes his participation in a peyote ritual in similar terms (interview with Robinson, 26 July 2011). Others who use psychedelics in psychotherapy (Andrew Feldmar, for instance) believe that the empathic effect of these drugs plays a critical part in building trust between doctors and patients (interview with Andrew Feldmar, 11 May 2013).

44. See for example Angela Garcia, *The Pastoral Clinic Addiction and Dispossession,* 48–51.

45. Grof, *When the Impossible Happens,* 80. This is reminiscent of Walter Benjamin's notion of the mimetic faculty. See Walter Benjamin, "The Doctrine of the Similar." 69. See also Walter Benjamin, "On the Mimetic Faculty," 720–21; Anson Rabinbach, "Introduction to Benjamin's 'Doctrine of the Similar,'" 62.

46. Brant Secunda and Prem Das claimed to be adopted into Huichol families. Jay Fikes claimed to be adopted by Reuben Snake, a NAC ritual leader.

CONCLUSION

1. Much of this comes from an Interview with Eligio López, in Portero de la Palmita, 28 July 2011.

2. Interview with López, 28 July 2011.

3. "Experiencia de vida con los Huichols," *El Universal* 2011. http://archivo. eluniversal.com.mx/graficos/graficosanimados11/EU_destinos_huicholes/; http://blog.rivieranayarit.com/2014/10/discover-undiscovered-in-riviera-nayarit .html. Viridiana Ramírez, "Mundo Huichol: En la Sierra Nayarita habita una comunidad huichola que permite al viajero convivir con ella, apreciarla y descubrir sus tradiciones," *El Universal*, 17 July 2011; Myriam Navarro, "Distinguen a Huicholes por centro ecoturístico," *La Jornada*, 6 May 2012.

4. Navarro, "Distinguen a Huicholes."

5. The only available description we have of the church comes from Mrs. Maurice G. Smith, "A Negro Peyote Cult," *Journal of the Washington Academy of Sciences* 24:10 (15 October 1934): 448–53. From NARA RG 75, E 178, Office Files of Commissioner John Collier, 1933–1945.

6. See Circe Dawn Sturm, *Blood Politics*.

7. See Dawson, "Peyote in the Colonial Imagination," 43–62.

8. See Dawson, "Peyote in the Colonial Imagination," 43–62; Laura Lewis, *Hall of Mirrors*, 55, 118, 153; Aguirre Beltán, *Medicina y magia*, 20–35, 159; S. Alberro, *Del gachupín al criollo*, 342–43; Taussig, *Shamanism, Colonialism, and the Wild Man*; Cervantes, *The Devil in the New World*; S. Gruzinski, *Man-Gods in the Mexican Highlands*; S. Lipsett-Rivera, "Mira Lo Que Hace El Diablo."

9. On race in Oklahoma, and particularly the intersections of blackness and indigeneity, see Sturm, *Blood Politics*; Tim Madigan, *The Burning*; Alfred L. Brophy, *Reconstructing the Dreamland*.

10. The inclusive nature of the concept of mestizaje has long been disputed. See for example Agustín Basave, *México mestizo*; Guillermo Bonfil, *Mexico Profundo*; Dawson, *Indian and Nation*; Olivia Gall, "Identidad, exclusión y racismo"; C. C. Chorba, *Mexico, from Mestizo to Multicultural*; Saldívar, "'It's Not Race, It's Culture'"; Claudio Lomnitz, *Deep Mexico, Silent Mexico*; David Brading, *The Origins of Mexican Nationalism*; Rebecca Earle, *The Return of the Native*; A. M. Alonso, "Conforming Disconformity"; Knight, "Racism, Revolution, and Indigenismo," 71–113.

Bibliography

ARCHIVES
Mexico
Archivo General de la Nación (AGN)

  Inquisición
  Provincias Internas
  Comisión Nacional para el Desarrollo de los Pueblos Indígenas, Historical
    Archive (CDI)
  Presidentes
  Dirección Federal de Seguridad.

Secretaría de Salud Pública (SSP)
Biblioteca Miguel Lerdo de Tejada, Archivos Economicos
Bibilioteca Nacional
Papers of Norma Roquet (Cuernavaca Morelos)

Washington, DC
National Archives and Records Administration (NARA)
  NARA RG 75, E 764—Correspondence of the Chief Special Officer Relating
    to Peyote, 1908–1911, 1915–1918
  NARA RG 75 E 178, Office Files of Commissioner John Collier, 1933–1945

National Anthropological Archives (NAA)
Mooney
Slotkin
Weston La Barre
Sol Tax Papers

PUBLICATIONS

Aberle, David F. *The Peyote Religion among the Navajo.* Chicago: Aldine, 1982 (1966).

Agamben, Giorgio. *State of Exception.* Chicago: University of Chicago Press, 2005.

Aguirre Beltán, G. *Medicina y magia: El proceso de aculturación en la estructura colonial.* Mexico City: Instituto Nacional Indigenista, 1963.

Agustín, José. *La contracultura en México: La historia y el significado de los rebeldes sin causa, los jipitecas, los punks y las bandas.* Mexico City: Editorial Grijalbo, 1996.

Ahmed, Sara. "Happy Objects." In *The Affect Theory Reader,* edited by Melissa Gregg and Gregory J Seigworth, 29–51. Durham: Duke University Press, 2010.

Alberro, S. *Del gachupin al criollo: O de cómo los españoles de México dejaron de serlo.* Mexico City: El Colegio de México, 1992.

Alberro, S. *El aguila y la cruz: Origenes religiosos de la conciencia criolla. México, siglos 16–17.* Mexico City: Fondo de Cultura Economica/El Colegio de México, 1999.

Alonso, A. M. "Conforming Disconformity: 'Mestizaje,' Hybridity, and the Aesthetics of Mexican Nationalism." *Cultural Anthropology* 19 (2004): 459–90.

Anderson, Edward F. *Peyote: The Divine Cactus.* Tucson: University of Arizona Press, 1980.

Appadurai, Arjun. *The Social Life of Things: Commodities in Cultural Perspective.* Cambridge: Cambridge University Press, 1988.

Argyriadis, Kali, Renée de la Torre, Cristina Gutiérrez Zúñiga, and Alejandra Aguilar Ros, eds. *Raíces en movimiento. Prácticas religiosas tradicionales en contextos translocales.* Mexico City: COLJAL, CEMCA, IRD, CIESAS, ITESO, 2008.

Arlegui, Padre José. *Cronica de la provincia de Zacatecas.* Mexico City: Reimpresa por Cumplido, 1851 (1737).

Artaud, Antonin. *Les Tarahumaras.* Paris: Gallimard, 1987 (1947).

Artaud, Antonin. *México y viaje al país de los Tarahumaras.* Mexico City: FCE, 1995.

Assagioli, Roberto. *Psychosynthesis: A Manual of Principles and Techniques.* New York: Viking, 1965.

Astorga, Luis. *El siglo de las drogas.* Mexico City: Plaza Janes, 2004.

Basave, Agustín, *México mestizo: Análisis del nacionalismo mexicano en torno a la mestizofili.* Mexico City: FCE, 1992.

Basset, Vincent. "New Age Tourism in Wirikuta: Conflicts and Rituals." In *Peyote: History, Tradition, Politics, and Conservation,* edited by Bia Labate and Clancy Cavnar, 191–209. Santa Barbara, CA: Praeger, 2016.

Baudrillard, Jean. *Simulacra and Simulation*. Ann Arbor: University of Michigan Press, 1995.

Bayer, I., and H. Ghodse. "Evolution of International Drug Control, 1945–1995." *Bulletin on Narcotics* 51, nos. 1 and 2 (occasional papers 1999): 1–19.

Beasley-Murray, Jon. *Posthegemony: Political Theory and Latin America*. Minneapolis: University of Minnesota Press, 2011.

Bender, George. "Rough and Ready Research—1887 Style." *Journal of the History of Medicine and Allied Sciences* 23, no. 2 (1968): 159–66.

Benítez, Fernando. *En la tierra mágica del peyote*. Mexico City: Ediciones Era, 1968.

Benjamin, Walter. "On the Mimetic Faculty." In *Selected Writings, 1926–1934*. Translated by Rodney Livingstone et al. Edited by Michael W. Jennings et al., 720–21. Cambridge, MA: Belknap Press. 1986.

Benjamin, Walter. "The Doctrine of the Similar." *New German Critique*, no. 17 (Spring 1979): 65–69.

Bennett, Jane. *Vibrant Matter: A Political Ecology of Things*. Durham: Duke University Press, 2010.

Bergman, Robert L. "Navajo Peyote Use: Its Apparent Safety." *American Journal of Psychiatry* 128, no. 6 (1971): 695–99.

Beringer, Kurt. *Der Meskalinrausch*. Berlin: Julius Springer, 1927.

Berridge, Virginia, and Griffith Edwards. *Opium and the People: Opiate Use in Nineteenth-Century England*. New Haven: Yale University Press, 1987.

Bloom, A. D., J. V. Neel, K. W. Choi, S. Iida, and N. Chagnon. "Chromosome Aberrations among the Yanomamma indians." *Proceedings of the National Academy of Sciences (USA)* 66, no. 3 (1970): 920–27.

Boddy, Janice. "Spirits and Selves in Northern Sudan: The Cultural Therapeutics of Possession and Trance." *American Ethnologist* 15, no. 1 (1988): 4–27.

Boddy, Janice "Spirit Possession Revisited." *Annual Review of Anthropology* 23 (October 1994): 407–34.

Bonfil Batalla, Guillermo. "Del indigenismo de la revolución a la antropología crítica." In *De eso que llaman antropología mexicana*, edited by A. Warman et al., 39–65. Mexico City: Editorial Nuestro Tiempo, 1970.

Bonfil Batalla, Guillermo. *México Profundo: Reclaiming a Civilization*. Austin: University of Texas Press, 1996.

Boon, Marcus. *The Road of Excess: A History of Writers on Drugs*. Cambridge, MA: Harvard University Press, 2005.

Bourdieu, Pierre. *Outline of a Theory of Practice*. Translated by Richard Nice. Cambridge: Cambridge University Press, 1977.

Bowden, Charles. "Learning Nothing, Forgetting Nothing: On the Trail of Carl Lumholtz." *Journal of the Southwest* 49, no. 4 (2007): 357–68.

Brading, David. *The Origins of Mexican Nationalism*. Cambridge: Cambridge University Press, 1985.

Briggs, J. R. "'Muscale Buttons'—Physiological Effects—Personal Experience." *The Medical Register: A Weekly Journal of Medicine and Surgery* 1, April 1887, 276–77.

Brophy, Alfred L. *Reconstructing the Dreamland: The Tulsa Riot of 1921: Race, Reparations, and Reconciliation.* New York: Oxford University Press, 2002.

Brown, Michael Forbes. "Shamanism and Its Discontents." *Medical Anthropology Quarterly,* n.s., 2, no. 2 (1988): 102–20.

Brown, Michael Forbes. *Who Owns Native Culture?* Cambridge, MA: Harvard University Press, 2003.

Bruhn, Jan G., and Bo Holmstedt. "Early Peyote Research: An Interdisciplinary Study." *Economic Botany* 28, no. 4 (October–December 1974): 353–90.

Busch, Anthony K., and Walter C. Johnson. "LSD-25 as an Aid in Psychotherapy (Preliminary Report of a New Drug)." *Diseases of the Nervous System* 11, 1950, 241–43.

Cairns, Huntington. "A Divine Intoxicant." *Atlantic Monthly,* November 1929, 638–44.

Calabrese, John. "Spiritual Healing and Human Development in the Native American Church: Toward a Cultural Psychiatry of Peyote." *Psychoanalytic Review* 84, no. 2 (1997): 237–55.

Calabrese, John. *A Different Medicine: Postcolonial Healing in the Native American Church.* Oxford: Oxford University Press, 2014.

Camino, Alejandro. "El peyote: Derecho histórico des los Pueblos Indios." *México Indígena* 3, no. 15 (March–April 1987): 24–28.

Campos, Isaac. *Home Grown: Marijuana and the Origins of Mexico's War on Drugs.* Chapel Hill: University of North Carolina Press, 2014.

Campos, María del Rayo. "Cambio Social Huichol." Tepic, Nayarit: INI, 1993.

Canessa, Andrew. "New Indigenous Citizenship in Bolivia: Challenging the Liberal Model of the State and Its Subjects." *Latin American and Caribbean Ethnic Studies* 7, no. 2 (2012): 201–21.

Cárdenas de Ojeda, Olga. *Toxicomania y narcotrafic: Aspectos legales.* Mexico City: FCE, 1974.

Castaneda, Carlos. *The Teachings of Don Juan.* Berkeley: University of California Press, 1968.

Castaneda, Carlos. *A Separate Reality.* New York: Pocket Books, 1971.

Castaneda, Carlos. *Journey to Ixtlan.* New York: Simon and Schuster, 1972.

Centro Mexicano de Estudios en Farmacodependencia. *¿Cómo identificar las drogas y sus usarios? Programa nacional de combate a los problemas de drogas.* Mexico City: Secretaría de Educación Pública, 1976.

Cervantes, F. *The Devil in the New World: The Impact of Diabolism in New Spain.* New Haven: Yale University Press, 1994.

Chakrabarty, Dipesh. "Poscoloniality and the Artifice of History: Who Speaks for 'Indian' Pasts?" *Representations* 37, 1992, 1–26.

Chartier, Roger. *The Order of Books: Readers, Authors, and Libraries in Europe Between the Fourteenth and Eighteenth Centuries.* Palo Alto: Stanford University Press, 1994.

Chorba, C. C. *Mexico, from Mestizo to Multicultural: National Identity and Recent Representations of the Conquest.* Nashville: Vanderbilt University Press, 2007.

Clifford, James. *Routes: Travel and Translation in the Late Twentieth Century.* Cambridge, MA: Harvard University Press, 1997.

Clifford, James. "Indigenous Articulations." *Contemporary Pacific* 13, no. 2 (Fall 2001): 467–90.

Clifford, James. "Varieties of Indigenous Experience: Diasporas, Homelands, Sovereignties." In *Indigenous Experience Today*, edited by Marisol de la Cadena and Orin Starn, 197–223. New York: Berg, 2007.

Clough, Patricia. "The Affective Turn: Political Economy, Biomedia, and Bodies." In *The Affect Theory Reader*, edited by Melissa Gregg and Gregory J. Seigworth, 206–27. Durham: Duke University Press, 2010.

Comaroff, Jean, and John Comaroff. *Ethnicity, Inc.* Chicago: University of Chicago Press, 2009.

Conzatti, Cassiano. "Las plantas heróicas mexicanas: el peyote, el ololiuhqui y el toloache." *La Farmacia* 4, 1926.

Coronil, Fernando. "Beyond Occidentalism: Toward Nonimperial Geohistorical Categories." *Cultural Anthropology* 11, no. 1 (1996): 51–87.

Coulter, J.M. "Preliminary revision of the North American Species of Cactus, Anhalonium, and Lophophora." *Contributions from the U.S. National Herbarium* 3, 1894, 91–132.

Courtwright, David T. *Forces of Habit: Drugs and the Making of the Modern World*. Cambridge: Harvard University Press, 2001.

Crewe, R. "Brave New Spain: An Irishman's Independence Plot In Seventeenth-Century Mexico." *Past and Present* 207, no. 1 (2010): 53–87.

Csordas, Thomas J. "The Rhetoric of Transformation in Ritual Healing." *Culture, Medicine, and Psychiatry* 7, no. 4 (1983): 333–75.

Csordas, Thomas J. "Medical and Sacred Realities: Between Comparative Religion and Transcultural Psychiarty." *Culture, Medicine, and Psychiatry* 9, 1985, 103–16.

Csordas, Thomas J. "Embodiment as a Paradigm for Anthropology." *Ethos* 18, no. 1 (1990): 5–47.

Csordas, Thomas J. "The Psychotherapy Analogy and Charismatic Healing." *Psychotherapy: Theory, Research, Practice, Training* 27, no. 1 (1990b): 79–90.

Csordas, Thomas J. "Word from the Holy People: A Case Study in Cultural Phenomenology." In *Embodiment and Experience: The Existential Ground of Culture and Self*, edited by Thomas J. Csordas. Cambridge: Cambridge University Press, 1994.

Csordas, Thomas J. "Introduction: The Body as Representation and Being-in-the-World." In *Embodiment and Experience: The Existential Ground of Culture and Self*, edited by Thomas J. Csordas, 1–24. Cambridge: Cambridge University Press, 1994b.

Csordas, Thomas J. "Ritual Healing and the Politics of Identity in Contemporary Navajo Society." *American Ethnologist* 26, no. 1 (February 1999): 3–23.

Cueto, Marcos. "Appropriation and Resistance: Local Responses to Malaria Eradication in Mexico, 1955–1970." *Journal of Latin American Studies* 37, no. 3 (August 2005): 533–59.

Das, Prem. "Initiation by a Huichol Shaman." In *Art of the Huichol Indians*, edited by K. Berrin, 129–41. New York: Harry Abrams, 1978.

Dawson, Alexander. *Indian and Nation in Revolutionary Mexico*. Tucson: University of Arizona Press, 2004.

Dawson, Alexander. "El peyote y la autodeterminación a lo largo de la frontera entre Estados Unidos y México, desde Pátzcuaro hasta Avándaro." In *La ambivalente historia del indigenismo: Campo interamericano y trayectorias nacionales, 1940–1970*, edited by Laura Giraudo and Juan Martín Sánchez, 159–90. Lima, Peru: Instituto de Estudios Peruanos, 2011.

Dawson, Alexander. "Salvador Roquet, María Sabina, and the Trouble with Jipis." *Hispanic American Historical Review* 95, no. 1 (2015): 103–33.

Dawson, Alexander. "Peyote in the Colonial Imagination." In *Peyote: History, Traditions, Politics, and Conservation*, edited by Beatriz Caiuby Labate and Clancy Cavnar, 43–62. Santa Barbara CA: Praeger, 2016.

de Certeau, Michel. *The Practice of Everyday Life*. Berkeley: University of California Press, 1984.

de la Cadena, Marisol. "Indigenous Cosmopolitics in the Andes: Conceptual Reflections beyond 'Politics.'" *Current Anthropology* 25, no. 2 (2010): 334–70.

de la Peña, Guillermo. "Poder local, poder regional." In *Poder regional en México*, edited by Jorge Zepeda Patterson. Mexico City: El Colegio de México, 1986.

de la Peña, Guillermo. "Apuntes sobre los indigenismos en Jalisco." In *Estudios del hombre 13 y 14, Jalisco al cierre del siglo 20. Lecturas antropológicas*, 95–118. Guadalajara: Universidad de Guadalajara, 2002.

de la Peña Páez, Ignacio. "El estudio formal de la herbolaria mexicana y la creación del Instituto Médico Nacional: 1885–1915." In *La investigación científica de la herbolaria medicinal mexicana*, edited by Mercedes Juan et al. Mexico City: Secretaría de Salud, 1993.

Deleuze, Gilles. *Essays Critical and Clinical*. Minneapolis: University of Minnesota Press, 1997.

Deloria, Philip J. *Playing Indian*. New Haven: Yale University Press, 1998.

Deloria, Philip J. "Counterculture Indians and the New Age." In *Imagine Nation: The American Counterculture of the 1960s and 70s*, edited by Peter Braunstein and Michael William Doyle, 159–88. New York: Routledge, 2001.

Deloria, Philip J. *Indians in Unexpected Places*. Lawrence: University of Kansas Press, 2004.

de Mille, Richard. *Castaneda's Journey: The Power and the Allegory*. Santa Barbara, CA: Capra Press. 1976.

de Mille, Richard, ed. *The Don Juan Papers.*, 2nd ed. Belmont, CA: Wadsworth, 1990.

Dixon, Walter E. "A Preliminary Note on the Pharmacology of the Alkaloids Derived from the Mescal Plant." *British Medical Journal* 2, no. 1971 (8 October 1898): 1060–61.

Douglas, M. *Purity and Danger: An Analysis of Concepts of Pollution and Taboo*. London: Routledge, 1966.

Dyck, Erika. *Psychedelic Psychiatry: LSD from Clinic to Campus*. Baltimore: Johns Hopkins University Press, 2008.

Dyck, Erika. "Peyote and Psychedelics on the Canadian Prairies." In *Peyote: History, Tradition, Politics, and Conservation*, edited by B. C. Labate and C. Cavnar, 151–70. Santa Barbara, CA: ABC-CLIO/Praeger, 2015.

Eagle Feather, Ken. *On the Toltec Path: A Practical Guide to the Teachings of Don Juan Matus, Carlos Castaneda, and Other Toltec Seers.* 2nd ed. Rochester, VT: Bear and Company, 2006.

Eagle Feather, Ken. *Toltec Dreaming: Don Juan's Teachings on the Energy Body.* 2nd ed. Rochester, VT: Bear and Company, 2007.

Earle, Rebecca. *The Return of the Native.* Durham: Duke University Press, 2007.

Earle, Rebecca. "'If you eat their food . . .': Diets and Bodies in Early Colonial Spanish America." *American Historical Review* 115, no. 3 (2010): 688–713.

Earle, Rebecca. "Indians and Drunkenness in Spanish America." *Past and Present*, (2014, supplement 9): 81–99.

Ellis, Havelock. "A Note on the Phenomena of Mescal-Intoxication." *Lancet* 1 ,1897, 1540–42.

Ellis, Havelock. "Mescal: A New Artificial Paradise." *Contemporary Review* 73, January–June 1898.

Enciso, Froylán. *Nuestra historia narcótica: pasajes para (re) legalizar las drogas en México.* Mexico City: Debate, 2015.

"End the Ban on Psychoactive Drug Research." Editorial, *Scientific American* 310, no. 2 (2014): 1–2.

Epps, Garrett. *Peyote vs. the State: Religious Freedom on Trial.* Norman: University of Oklahoma Press, 2009.

Estrada, Álvaro. *María Sabina: Her Life and Chants.* Translated by Henry Munn. Santa Barbara, CA: Ross-Erikson, 1981.

Estrada, Álvaro. *Huautla en tiempo de hippies.* México City: Grijalbo, 1996.

Estudio relativo al peyote. Instituto Médico Nacional, Mexico, 1913.

Ewell, E. E. "The Chemistry of the Cactaceae." *Journal of the American Chemical Society* 18, 1896, 624–43.

Fabian, Johannes. *Time and the Other: How Anthropology Makes Its Object.* New York: Columbia University Press, 1983.

Faliba, Alfonso. *Los Huicholes de Jalisco.* Mexico City: INI, 1959.

Faudree, Paja. "Tales from the Land of Magic Plants: Textual Ideologies and Fetishes of Indigeneity in Mexico's Sierra Mazateca." *Comparative Studies in Society and History* 57, no. 3 (2015): 838–69.

Feeney, Kevin. "The Legal Basis for Religious Peyote Use." *Psychedelic Medicine: New Evidence for Hallucinogenic Substances as Treatments* 1, 2007, 233–50.

Feeney, Kevin. "Peyote, Race, and Equal Protection in the United States." In *Prohibition, Religious Freedom, and Human Rights: Regulating Traditional Drug Use*, edited by B. C. Labate and C. Cavnar, 65–88. Berlin: Springer-Verlag, 2014.

Feinberg, Benjamin. "Three Mazatec Wise Ones and Their Books." *Critique of Anthropology* 17, no. 2 (1997): 411–37.

Feinberg, Benjamin, *The Devil's Book of Culture: History, Mushrooms, and Caves in Southern Mexico.* Austin: University of Texas Press, 2003.

Fernberger, Samuel W. "Observations on Taking Peyote (Anhalonium Lewinii)." *American Journal of Psychology* 34, no. 2 (April 1923): 267–70.

Fernberger, Samuel W. "Further Observations in Peyote Intoxication." *Journal of Abnormal and Social Psychology* 26, 1932, 367–78.

Fikes, Jay C. *Carlos Castaneda, Academic Opportunism, and the Psychedelic Sixties.* Victoria, BC: Millenia Press, 1993.

Fikes, Jay C. *Unknown Huichol: Shamans and Immortals, Allies against Chaos.* Lanham, MD: Rowman and Littlefield Publishers, 2011.

Fikes, J. C., P. C. Weigand, and A. García, eds. *La mitología de los Huicholes.* Zamora: El Colegio de Michoacán, El Colegio de Jalisco y la Secretaría de Cultura del Estado de Jalisco, 1998.

Fitz, Henry. "The Last Hurrah of Christian Humanitarian Indian Reform: The Board of Indian Commissioners, 1909–1918." *Western Historical Quarterly* 16, no. 2 (1985): 147–62.

Frazier, Lessie Jo, and Deborah Cohen. "Defining the Space of Mexico '68: Heroic Masculinity in the Prison and 'Women' in the Streets." *Hispanic American Historical Review* 83, no. 4 (2003): 617–60.

Freud, S. *Totem and Taboo: Some Points of Agreement between the Mental Lives of Savages and Neurotics.* New York: W.W. Norton, 1989 (1913).

Friedlander, Judith. *Being Indian in Hueyapan.* Rev. ed. New York: Palgrave Macmillan, 2006.

Furst, Peter T. "To Find Our Life: Peyote among the Huichol Indians of Mexico." In *Flesh of the Gods: The Ritual Use of Hallucinogans,* edited by Peter T. Furst, 184–236. New York: Praeger, 1972.

Furst, Peter T., ed. *Flesh of the Gods: The Ritual Use of Hallucinogens.* New York: Praeger, 1972.

Furst, Peter T. *Hallucinogens and Culture.* San Francisco: Chandler and Sharp, 1976.

Furst, Peter T. "Myth as History, History as Myth." In *People of the Peyote: Huichol Indian History, Religion, and Survival,* edited by Stacy B. Schaefer and Peter T. Furst, 26–60. Albuquerque: University of New Mexico Press, 1996.

Furst, Peter T., and Stacy B. Schaefer. "Peyote Pilgrims and Don Juan Seekers." In *People of the Peyote: Huichol Indian History, Religion, and Survival,* edited by Stacy B. Schaefer and Peter T. Furst, 503–22. Albuquerque: University of New Mexico Press, 1996.

Gall, Olivia. "Identidad, exclusión y racismo: Reflexiones teóricas y sobre México Revolucionario." *Revista Mexicana de Sociología* 66, no. 2 (April–June 2004): 221–59.

Gamio, Manuel. *Forjando Patria (pro nacionalismo).* Mexico City: Librería de Porrúa Hermanos, 1916.

Garcia, Angela. *The Pastoral Clinic Addiction and Dispossession along the Rio Grande.* Berkeley: University of California Press, 2010.

García Carrera, Juan. *La otra vida de María Sabina.* Mexico City: Talleres Esfuerza, 1986.

García Vallejo, Juan Pablo. "Breve historia de la legislación de drogas en México, in the Gaceta Cannábica" 13 August 2010 (http://gacetacannabica.blogspot.ca/2010/08/breve-historia-de-la-legislacion-de.html).

Gilman, Alfred, et al. *Goodman and Gilman's the Pharmacological Basis of Therapeutics.* 10th ed. New York: McGraw-Hill Professional, 2001.

Gitlin, Todd. *Years of Hope, Days of Rage.* New York: Bantam, 1987.

Gitlin, Todd . "On Drugs and Mass Media in America's Consumer Society." In *Youth and Drugs: Society's Mixed Messages,* edited by Hank Resnik et al., 31–52. Washington, DC: US Dept. of Health and Human Services, Public Health Service, Alcohol, Drug Abuse, and Mental Health Administration, Office for Substance Abuse Prevention, 1990.

Goode, Erich. "Moral Panics and Disproportionality: The Case of LSD Use in the Sixties." *Deviant Behavior* 29, no. 6 (2008): 533–43.

Goode, Erich, and Nachman Ben-Yehuda. *Moral Panics: The Social Construction of Deviance.* Oxford: Blackwell, 1994.

Goodman, Jordan, Paul E. Lovejoy, and Andrew Sherratt, eds. *Consuming Habits: Drugs in History and Anthropology: Global and Historical Perspectives on How Cultures Define Drugs.* 2nd ed. London: Routledge, 2007.

Gootenberg, Paul. *Andean Cocaine: The Making of a Global Drug.* Chapel Hill: University of North Carolina Press, 2008.

Gootenberg, Paul. "Cocaine's Long March North, 1900–2010." *Latin American Politics and Society* 54, no. 1 (Spring 2012): 159–80.

Gootenberg, Paul, and Isaac Campos. "Toward a New Drug History of Latin America: A Research Frontier at the Center of Debates." *Hispanic American Historical Review* 95, no. 1 (2015): 1–35.

Gould, Jeffrey L. "Solidarity under Siege: The Latin American Left, 1968." *American Historical Review* 114, no. 2 (2009): 348–75.

Grof, Stanislav. *When the Impossible Happens: Adventures in Non-Ordinary Realities.* Sounds True, 2006.

Gruzinski, S. *Man-Gods in the Mexican Highlands: Indian Power and Colonial Society, 1520–1800.* Palo Alto: Stanford University Press, 1989.

Gruzinski, S. *Images at War: Mexico from Columbus to Blade Runner (1492–2019).* Durham: Duke University Press, 2001.

Guerrero, Andrés. "The Construction of a Ventriloquist's Image: Liberal Discourse and the 'Miserable Indian Race' in Late Nineteenth-Century Ecuador." *Journal of Latin American Studies* 29, no. 3 (October 1997): 555–90.

Gutiérrez, Cristina. *Nuevos movimientos religiosos.* Guadalajara: Ed. El Colegio de Jalisco, 1996.

Gutiérrez, Cristina. *Congregaciones del éxito: interpretación socio-religiosa de las redes de mercadeo en Guadalajara.* Guadalajara: Ed. El Colegio de Jalisco-Universidad de Guadalajara, 2005.

Guttmann, Erich. "Artificial Psychoses Produced by Mescaline" *Journal of Mental Science* 82, no. 338 (May 1936).

Guttmann, E., and W. S. Maclay. "Mescalin and Depersonalization." *Journal of Neurology and Psychopathology 16, no. 63 (*January 1936):193–212.

Hagan, William T. *Quanah Parker, Comanche Chief.* Norman: University of Oklahoma Press, 1993.

Hale, Charles R. *Más que un Indio: Racial Ambivalence and Neoliberal Multiculturalism in Guatemala.* Santa Fe: NM: School of American Research Press, 2006.

Heath Dwight B. "Drinking Patterns of the Bolivian Camba." *Quarterly Journal of Studies on Alcohol* 19, no. 3 (1958): 491–508.

Hendrickson Brett. *Border Medicine: A Transcultural History of Mexican American Curanderismo.* New York: New York University Press, 2014,

Hernandez Díaz, M. Angél. *Región Huicot: Diagnostico sociodemografico.* 1995.

Hernández González, Rafael, *El Peyote en la Nueva España (un viaje hasta nuestros dias).* Thesis for Licenciado en Historia, UNAM, 2000.

Hiatt, Nathaniel J. "A Trip Down Memory Lane: LSD at Harvard." *Harvard Crimson,* 23 May 2016.

Highmore, Ben. "Bitter Aftertaste: Affect, Food, and Social Aesthetics." In *The Affect Theory Reader, edited by Melissa Gregg and Gregory J. Seigworth,* 118–137. Durham: Duke University Press, 2010.

Hrdlicka, Ales. "Physiological and Medical Observations among the Indians of the Southwestern United States and Northern Mexico." *Smithsonion Institution, Bureau of American Ethnology, Bulletin* 34, 1908, 250–1.

Huhndorf, Shari M. *Going Native: Indians in the American Cultural Imagination.* Ithaca, NY: Cornell University Press, 2001.

Huxley, Aldous, *The Doors of Perception and Heaven and Hell.* New York: Perennial Library, 1990.

Joralemon, Donald. "The Selling of the Shaman and the Problem of Informant Legitimacy." *Journal of Anthropological Research* 14, no. 2 (1990).

Joe-Laidler, Karen, Geoffrey Hunt, and Molly Moloney. "'Tuned Out or Tuned In': Spirituality and Youth Drug Use in Global Times." *Past and Present,* 2014, supplement 9, 62–80.

Jung, Courtney. *The Moral Force of Indigenous Politics.* Cambridge: Cambridge University Press, 2008.

Kahan, Fannie. *Culture's Catalyst: Historical Encounters with Peyote and the Native American Church of Canada.* Erica Dyck, ed. Winnipeg: University of Manitoba Press, 2016.

Kapadia, Govind J., and M. B. E. Fayez. "Peyote Constituents: Chemistry, Biogenesis, and Biological Effects." *Journal of Pharmaceutical Sciences* 59, no. 12 (1970): 1699–1727.

Kirsch, Thomas. "Restaging the Will to Believe: Religious Pluralism, Anti-Syncretism, and the Problem of Belief." *American Anthropologist* 106, no. 4 (2004).

Klüver, Heinrich. "Mescal Visions and Eidetic Vision." *American Journal of Psychology* 37, no. 4 (October 1926): 502–15.

Knauer, Awyn W., and William Maloney, "A Preliminary Note on the Psychic Action of Mescalin, with Special Reference to the Mechanism of Visual Hallucination." *Journal of Nervous and Mental Disease* 40, 1913, 425–36.

Knight, Alan. "Racism, Revolution, and Indigenismo: Mexico 1910–1940." In *The Idea of Race in Latin America, 1870–1940,* edited by Richard Graham, 71–113. Austin: University of Texas Press, 1990.

Kovecses, Zoltan. *Metaphor and Emotion: Language, Culture, and Body in Human Feeling.* Cambridge: Cambridge University Press, 2000.

Krebs, Teri S., and Pål-Ørjan Johansen. "Lysergic Acid Diethylamide (LSD) for Alcoholism: Meta Analysis of Randomized Controlled Trials." *Journal of Psychopharmacology* 26, no. 7 (2012): 994–1002.

Krech, Shepard III. *Ecological Indian: Myth and History*. New York: Norton, 2000.

La Barre, Weston. "Primitive Psychotherapy in Native American Cultures: Peyotism and Confession." *Journal of Abnormal and Social Psychology* 42, no. 3 (July 1947): 294–309.

La Barre, Weston. *The Peyote Cult*. Norman: University of Oklahoma Press, 2012 (1938).

Latour, Bruno. *We Have Never Been Modern*. Translated by Catherine Porter. Cambridge, MA: Harvard University Press, 1993.

Lattin, Don. *The Harvard Psychedelic Club: How Timothy Leary, Ram Dass, Huston Smith, and Andrew Weil Killed the Fifties and Ushered in a New Age for America*. New York: Harper, 2011.

Leighton, Alexander, and Dorothea Leighton. "Elements of Psychotherapy in Navaho Religion." *Psychiatry: Interpersonal and Biological Processes* 4, no. 4 (1941): 515–23.

Lewin, Louis. *Phantastica*. Rochester, NY: Park Street Press, 1998 (1924).

Lewis, Laura. *Hall of Mirrors: Power, Witchcraft, and Caste in Colonial Mexico*. Durham: Duke University Press, 2003.

Liffman, Paul. *Huichol Territory and the Mexican Nation: Indigenous Ritual, Land Conflict, and Sovereignty Claims*. Tucson: University of Arizona Press, 2011.

Lipsett-Rivera, S. "Mira Lo Que Hace el Diablo: The Devil in Mexican Popular Culture, 1750–1856." *The Americas* 59, no. 2 (2002): 201–19.

Lomnitz, Claudio. *Deep Mexico, Silent Mexico: An Anthropology of Nationalism*. Minneapolis: University of Minnesota Press, 2001.

Long, Carolyn N. *Religious Freedom and Indian Rights: The Case of Oregon v. Smith*. Lawrence: University of Kansas Press, 2000.

López-Muñoz, Francisco, Ronaldo Ucha-Udabe, and Cecilio Alamo., "The History of Barbiturates a Century after Their Clinical Introduction." *Neuropsychiatric Disease and Treatment* 1, no. 4 (December 2005): 329–43.

Low, Sehta M. "Embodied Metaphors: Nerves as Lived Experience." In *Embodiment and Experience: The Existential Ground of Culture and Self*, edited by Thomas J. Csordas, 139–62. Cambridge: Cambridge University Press, 1994.

Lozoya, Xavier. *La herbolaria en México*. Mexico City: Consejo Nacional para la Cultura y las Artes, 1998.

Ludwig, Arnold M. "Patterns of Hallucinogenic Drug Abuse." *Journal of the American Medical Association* 191, no. 2 (11 January 1965).

Lumhotlz, Carl. *Unknown Mexico: A Record of Five Years' Exploration among the Tribes of the Western Sierra Madre; in the Tierra Caliente of Tepic and Jalisco; and among the Tarascos of Michoacan*. 2 vols. New York: Scribner's and Sons, 1902.

Lyttle, Thomas. "Drug Based Religions and Contemporary Drug Taking." *Journal of Drug Issues* 18, no. 2 (1988): 17–23.

Madigan, Tim. *The Burning: Massacre, Destruction, and the Tulsa Race Riot of 1921*. New York: St. Martin's Press, 2001.

Manzano, Valeria. "'Rock Nacional' and Revolutionary Politics: The Making of a Youth Culture of Contestation in Argentina, 1966–1976." *The Americas* 70, no. 39 (2014): 393–427.

Marks, Harry M. *The Progress of Experiment: Science and Therapeutic Reform in the United States, 1900–1990.* Cambridge: Cambridge University Press, 1997.

Maroukis, Thomas C. *The Peyote Road: Religious Freedom and the Native American Church.* Norman: University of Oklahoma Press, 2012.

Marshall, Robert. "The Dark Legacy of Carlos Castaneda." *Salon,* 12 April 2007, http://www.salon.com/2007/04/12/castaneda/.

Martínez, Maximo. *Las plantas medicinales de México.* 3rd ed. Mexico City: Ediciones Botas, 1944.

Martínez Novo, Carmen. *Who Defines Indigenous? Identities, Development, Intellectuals, and the State in Northern Mexico.* New Brunswick, NJ: Rutgers University Press, 2006.

Martínez Novo, Carmen. "Managing Diversity in Postneoliberal Ecuador." *Journal of Latin American and Caribbean Anthropology* 19, no. 1 (March 2014): 103–25.

Mata Torres, Ramón. *Los peyoteros.* Guadalajara: Kérigma, 1976.

Matt, Susan J., and Peter Stearns. *Doing Emotions History.* Champaign: University of Illinois Press, 2014.

McCleary, James A., Paul S. Sypherd, and David L. Walkington. "Antibiotic Activity of an Extract of Peyote (Lophophora Williamii [Lemaire] Coulter)." *Economic Botany* 14, no. 3 (July–September 1960.

McKenzie, F. A. *"Pussyfoot" Johnson.* London: Rodder and Stoughton Limited, 1921.

Medina Silva, Remón. "How One Goes on Being Huichol." In *People of the Peyote: Huichol Indian History, Religion, and Survival,* edited by Stacy B. Schaefer and Peter T. Furst, 169–205. Albuquerque: University of New Mexico Press, 1996.

Mills, K. *Idolatry and Its Enemies: Colonial Andean Religion and Extirpation, 1640–1750.* Princeton: Princeton University Press, 1997.

Miranda, Juan. *Curanderos y chamanes de la Sierra Mazateca.* Mexico City: Gaturperio Editores, 1997.

Mitchell, S. Weir. "Remarks on the Effects of Anhelonium Lewini (The Mescal Button)." *British Medical Journal* 2, no. 1875 (5 December 1896): 1625–29.

Mithoefer, Michael C., Mark T. Wagner, Ann T. Mithoefer, Lisa Jerome, Scott F. Martin, Berra Yazar-Klosinski, Yvonne Michel, Timothy D. Brewerton, and Rick Doblin. "Durability of Improvement in Post-traumatic Stress Disorder Symptoms and Absence of Harmful Effects or Drug Dependency after 3,4-Methylenedioxymethamphetamine-Assisted Psychotherapy: A Prospective Long-term Follow-up Study." *Journal of Psychopharmacology* 27, no. 1 (2013): 28–39.

Mooney, James. "The Mescal Plant and Ceremony." *Therapeutic Gazette* 12, no. 1 (1896): 7–11.

Moreno, Roberto. "La Inquisición para Indios en la Nueva España, siglo 16 a 19." In *Chicomoztoc* no. 2, UNAM, México, 1989, 7–20.

Moses, L. G. *The Indian Man: A Biography of James Mooney.* Urbana: University of Illinois Press, 1984.

Mount, Guy. *The Peyote Book: A Study in Native Medicine.* Arcata, CA: Sweetlight Books, 1987.

Myerhoff, Barbara. *Peyote Hunt: The Sacred Journey of the Huichol Indian.* Ithaca: Cornell University Press, 1974.

Nahmad Sittón, Salomón, Otto Klineberg, Peter T. Furst, and Barbara Myerhoff, eds. *El peyote y los Huicholes.* Mexico City: SepSetentas, 1972.

Nahmad Sittón, Salomón. "Some Considerations of the Indirect and Controlled Acculturation in the Cora-Huichol Area." In *Themes of Indigenous Acculturation in Northwest Mexico,* edited by Thomes Hinton and Phil C. Weigand, Anthropological Papers, no. 38, University of Arizona Press, 1981, 4–8.

Nahmad Sittón, Salomón. "Huichol Religion and the Mexican State: Reflections on Ethnocide and Cultural Survival." *People of the Peyote: Huichol Indian History, Religion, and Survival,* edited by Stacy B. Schaefer and Peter T. Furst, 471–502. Albuquerque: University of New Mexico Press, 1996.

Nathan, Peter E., Mandy Conrad, and Anne Helene Skinstad. "History of the Concept of Addiction." *Annual Review of Clinical Psychology* 12, 2016, 29–51.

Negrín, Diana Michele. *Colores Mexicanos: Racial Alterity and the Right to the Mexican City.* PhD diss., University of California, Berkeley, 2014.

Negrín, Juan. *Acercamiento histórico y subjectivo al Huichol.* Guadalajara: Universidad de Guadalajara, 1985.

Negrín da Silva, Diana. "El Indio que todos quieren: El consumo de lo 'Huichol' tras la batalla por Wirikuta." *Sociedad y Ambiente* 1, no. 8 (July–October 2015): 54–74.

Nelson, Diane. *A Finger in the Wound: Body Politics in Quincentennial Guatemala.* Berkeley, CA: University of California Press. 1999.

Nesvig, Martin. "Peyote, Ever Virgin: A Case of Religious Hybridism in Mexico." In *A Linking of Heaven and Earth: Studies in Religious and Cultural History in Honor of Carlos M .N. Eire,* edited by Scott K. Taylor et al., 175–90. London: Routledge, 2012.

Neurath, Johannes, *Las fiestas de la Casa Grande.* Guadalajara: CONACULTA (Coordinación Nacional de Antropología y el Consejo Nacional de Ciencia y Tecnología) and the Instituto Nacional de Antropología e Historia, Universidad de Guadalajara, 2002.

Ngai, Sianne. "Merely Interesting." *Critical Inquiry,* no. 4 (Summer 2008): 777–817.

Nichols, David E. "Differences between the Mechanism of Action of MDMA, MBDB, and the Classic Hallucinogens: Identification of a New Therapeutic Class: Entactogens." *Journal of Psychoactive Drugs* 18, no. 4 (1986): 305–13.

Noel, Daniel C., ed. *Seeing Castaneda: Reactions to the "Don Juan" Writings of Carlos Castaneda.* New York: Putnam, 1976.

Noel, Daniel C. *The Soul of Shamanism.* New York: Continuum, 1997.

Noriega, Juan Manuel. "Curso de historia de drogas." *Anales del Instituto Médico Nacional,* 1902, 2–14.

Nutt, David. "A Brave New World for Psychology." *The Psychologist* 27, September 2014, 658–61.

Opler, Morris E. "The Use of Peyote by the Carrizo and Lipan Apache Tribes." *American Anthropologist* 40, no. 2 (April–June 1938): 271–85.

Opler, Morris E. "A Description of a Tonkawa Peyote Meeting Held in 1902." *American Anthropologist* 41, no. 3 (July–September 1939): 433–39.

Oram, Matthew. "Efficacy and Enlightenment: LSD Psychotherapy and the Drug Amendments of 1962." *Journal of the History of Medicine and Allied Sciences* 69, no. 2 (2012): 221–49.

Ortega, J. *Historia del Nayarit, Sonora y ambos Californias*. Mexico City: Tipogradia de E Abadiano, 1887 (1754).

Ortíz Pinchetti, Francisco. *La operación Condor*. Mexico City: Proceso, 1981.

Osmond, H., and J. Smythies. "Schizophrenia: A New Approach." *Journal of Mental Science* 98, no. 411 (April 1952): 309–15.

Osmond, Humphry. "Peyote Night." *Tomorrow* magazine 9, no. 2 (1961).

Ots, Thomas. "The Angry Liver, the Anxious Heart, and the Melancholy Spleen: The Phenomenology of Perceptions in Chinese Culture." *Culture, Medicine, and Psychiatry* 14, no. 1 (1990): 21–58.

Pahnke, Walter N., et al. "The Experimental Use of Psychedelic (LSD) Psychotherapy" *Journal of the American Medical Association* 212, no. 11 (1970): 1856–63.

Painter, Muriel Thayer. *With Good Heart: Yaqui Beliefs and Ceremonies in Pascua Village*. Tucson: University of Arizona Press, 1986.

Palacios, Agustin, Santiago Ramirez, and Gregorio Valmer. *Psicoanálisis, la técnica,* Mexico City: Editorial Pax, 1964.

Palmié, Stephan. "Other Powers: Tylor's Principle, Father Williams's Temptations, and the Power of Banality." In *Obeh and Other Powers: The Politics of Caribbean Religion and Healing*, edited by Dian Paton and Maarit Forde, 316–40. Durham: Duke University Press, 2012.

Palmié, Stephan. *The Cooking of History: How Not to Study Afro-Cuban Religion*. Chicago: University of Chicago Press, 2013.

Palmié, Stephan. "Mixed Blessings and Sorrowful Mysteries: Second Thoughts about 'Hybridity.'" *Current Anthropology* 54, 2013, 1–20.

"Paradise or Inferno." *British Medical Journal* 1, no. 1936 (5 February 1898): 390.

Peele, Stanton. "Addiction as a Cultural Concept." *Annals of the New York Academy of Sciences* 602, 1990, 205–20.

Pensado, Jaime M. *Rebel Mexico: Student Unrest and Authoritarian Political Culture during the Long Sixties*. Palo Alto: Stanford University Press, 2013.

Pensado, Jaime M. "'To Assault with the Truth': The Revitalization of Conservative Militancy in Mexico during the Global Sixties." *The Americas* 70, no. 3 (2014): 489–521.

Perabeles, Alfonso. "Salvador Roquet: ¿Médico tira? ¿Loco? ¿Genio? ¿Revolucionario?" *Piedra Rodante* (Mexico City), 15 November 1971.

Pérez Montfort, Ricardo. "El veneno 'faradisiaco' o el olor a tortilla tostada: Fragmentos de historia de las drogas en México, 1870–1920." In *Hábitos, normas y escándalo: Prensa, criminalidad y drogas durante el porfiriato tardío,* edited by Ricardo Pérez Montfort, Alberto del Castillo Yurrita, and Pablo Piccato, 143–210. Mexico City: Plaza y Valdéz, 1997.

Pérez Montfort, Ricardo. *Yerba, goma, y polvo: Drogas ambientales y policías en México, 1900–1940.* Mexico City: Ediciones Eras, 1999.

Pérez Montfort, Ricardo. "Historias primigenias." *Nexos,* 1 March 2000.

Pérez Montfort, Ricardo. "Sustancias alucinógenas durante los años 30 y 40." In *Drogas, política y cultura,* September 2015, http://drogasmexicobrasil. mx/blog/2015/09/14/sustancias-alucinogenas-durante-los-anos-30-y-40/.

Perrine, Daniel M. "Visions of the Night, Western Medicine Meets Peyote 1887–1899." *Heffter Review of Psychedelic Research* 2 (2001): 6–52.

Petrullo, Vincenzo. *The Diabolic Root: A Study of Peyotism, the New Indian Religion, among the Delawares.* Philadelphia: University of Pennsylvania Press, 1934.

Peyote: An Abridged Compilation from the Files of the Bureau of Indian Affairs. Prepared by Dr. Robert E. L. Newbern, chief of medical service under the direction of Chas. H. Burke, commissioner. Lawrence, KS: Haskell Institute, 1922.

"Peyotes: Datos para su estudio." *Anales del Instituto Médico* 4, 1899, 203–14.

Piccato, Pablo. *City of Suspects: Crime in Mexico City, 1900–1931.* Durham: Duke University Press, 2001.

Piñeiro, Juanjo. *Psiconautas: Exploradores de la conciencia.* Barcelona: La Liebre de Marzo, 2000.

Pinkson, Tom Soloway. *The Shamanic Wisdom of the Huichol: Medicine Teachings for Modern Times.* 2nd ed. Merrimac, MA: Destiny Books, 2010.

Pred, Allan. *The Past Is Not Dead: Facts, Fictions, and Enduring Racial Stereotypes.* Minneapolis: University of Minnesota Press, 2004.

Prentiss, D. W., and Francis Morgan. "Anhalonium Lewinii." *Therapeutic Gazette* 9, 16 September 1895, 577–85.

Postero, Nancy. *Now We Are Citizens: Indigenous Politics in Postmulticultural Bolivia.* Palo Alto: Stanford University Press, 2007.

Povinelli, Elizabeth. *The Cunning of Recognition: Indigenous Alterities and the Making of Australian Multiculturalism.* Durham: Duke University Press, 2002.

Pozas A., Ricardo. *La antropología y la burocracia indigenista.* Mexico City: Editorial Tlacuilco (Cuaderno para trabajadores, 1), 1976.

Probyn, Elspeth. "Writing Shame." In *The Affect Theory Reader,* edited by Melissa Gregg and Gregory J Seigworth, 71–92. Durham: Duke University Press, 2010.

Rabinbach, Anson. "Introduction to Benjamin's 'Doctrine of the Similar.'" *New German Critique,* Spring 1979.

Ramírez, José. "Lectura de turno—El Peyote." *Anales del Instituto Médico Nacional* 4, no. 12 (1900): 233–50.

Ramírez, José. "Peyote."*Anales del Instituto Médico Nacional,* 1908.

Reddy, William. *The Navigation of Feeling: A Framework for the History of Emotions.* Cambridge: Cambridge University Press, 2001.

Reed, Karen. *El INI y los Huicholes.* Mexico City: Secretaría de Educación Pública; Instituto Nacional Indigenista, 1972.

Reko, B. P. "Alcaloides y glucósidos en plantas mexicanas." In *Memorias y revista de la sociedad científica "Antonio Alzate"* 49 (1928): 379–419.

Robles, Clemente. "Acción fisiológica del clorhidrao de peyotina." *Anales del Instituto de Biologia*, Mexico, 1931.

Rodiles, Janine. *Una terapia prohibida. Biografía de Salvador Roquet, 1920–1995*. Mexico City: Grupo Editorial Planeta, 1998.

Rojas, Beatriz. *Los Huicholes en la historia*. CEMCA, El Colegio de Michoacán and INI, 1993.

Roquet, Salvador, and Pierre Favreau. *Los alucinógenos: De la concepción indígena a una nueva psicoterapia*. Mexico City: Ediciones Prisma, 1981.

Roquet, Salvador, Pierre Favreau, M. Rubén Ocaña, and Marcela Ruiz de Velasco. "The Existential through Psychodisleptics: A New Psychotherapy." Paper presented at Humanistic Psychology of the Americas sixth international conference, Association for Humanistic Psychology, Cuernavaca, Mexico, 19–21 December 1975.

Rosemblatt, Karin. *The Science and Politics of Race in Mexico and the United States, 1910–1950*. Chapel Hill: University of North Carolina Press, 2018.

Rouhier, Alexander. *Le peyotl: Suivi des plantes divinatoires*. Paris: Gaton Daoin, 1927.

Rubin, Jeffrey. *Decentering the Regime: Ethnicity, Radicalism, and Democracy in Juchitán, Mexico*. Durham: Duke University Press, 1997.

Rusby, H. H. "Mescal Buttons." *Bulletin of Pharmacy 8,* 1894, 306.

Safford, W. E. "Narcotic Plants and Stimulants of the Ancient Americans." *Annual Report of the Smithsonian Institution for 1916* (1917): 387–424.

Saldaña-Portillo, María Josefina. *Indian Given: Racial Geographies across Mexico and the United States*. Durham: Duke University Press, 2016.

Saldívar, Emiko. "'It's Not Race, It's Culture': Untangling Racial Politics in Mexico." *Latin American and Caribbean Ethnic Studies* 9, no. 1 (2014).

Sayer, Derek. "Everyday Forms of State Formation: Some Dissident Remarks on 'Hegemony.'" In *Everyday Forms of State Formation: Revolution and the Negotiation of Rule in Modern Mexico,* edited by Gilbert Joseph and Daniel Nugent, 377–87. Durham: Duke University Press, 1994.

Schaefer, Stacy B. "The Cosmos Contained: The Temple Where Sun and Moon Meet." In *People of the Peyote: Huichol Indian History, Religion, and Survival,* edited by Stacy B. Schaefer and Peter T. Furst, 332–76. Albuquerque: University of New Mexico Press, 1996.

Schaefer, Stacy B. "The Crossing of Souls: Peyote, Perception, and Meaning among the Huichol Indians." In *People of the Peyote: Huichol Indian History, Religion, and Survival,* edited by Stacy B. Schaefer and Peter T. Furst, 138–68. Albuquerque: University of New Mexico Press, 1996.

Schaefer, Stacy B. "The Peyote Religion and Mescalero Apaches." In *Big Bend's Ancient and Modern Past,* edited by Bruce Glasrud and Rober J. Malouf. College Station: Texas A&M University Press, 2013.

Schaefer, Stacy B. *Amada's Blessings from the Peyote Gardens of South Texas*. Albuquerque: University of New Mexico Press, 2015.

Schaefer, Stacy B., and Peter T. Furst. "Introduction." In *People of the Peyote: Huichol Indian History, Religion, and Survival,* edited by Stacy B. Schaefer and Peter T. Furst, 1–25. Albuquerque: University of New Mexico Press, 1996.

Schiebinger, Londa. *Plants and Empire: Colonial Bioprospecting in the Atlantic World.* Cambridge, MA: Harvard University Press, 2007.

Schiebinger, Londa. "West Indian Abortificants and the Making of Ignorance." *Agnotology: The Making and Unmaking of Ignorance,* edited by Robert N. Proctor and Londa Schiebinger, 149–62. Palo Alto: Stanford University Press, 2008.

Schievenini Stefanoni, José Domingo. "La prohibición de la marihuana en México, 1920–1940." MA thesis, Universidad Autónoma de Querétaro, 2012.

Schivelbusch, Wolfgang. *The Tastes of Paradise.* New York: Vintage, 1992.

Schultes, Richard Evans. "Peyote—An American Indian Heritage from Mexico." *El Mexico Antiguo* 4, no. 5/6 (April 1938).

Schultes, Richard Evans. "The Appeal of Peyote (Lophophora Williamsii) as a Medicine." *American Anthropologist,* n.s., 40, 1938b.

Scott, James. *Seeing Like a State.* New Haven: Yale University Press, 1998.

Seigel, Micol, Lessie Jo Frazier, and David Sartorius. "The Spatial Politics of Radical Change, an Introduction." *Journal of Transnational American Studies* 4, no. 2 (2012): 1–19.

Shelton, Anthony. "The Girl Who Ground Herself: Huichol Attitudes Towards Maize." In *People of the Peyote: Huichol Indian History, Religion, and Survival,* edited by Stacy B. Schaefer and Peter T. Furst, 451–467. Albuquerque: University of New Mexico Press, 1996.

Shonle, Ruth. "Peyote—Giver of Visions." *American Anthropologist* 27, no. 1, 1925.

Shortall, Sarah. "Psychedelic Drugs and the Problem of Experience." *Past and Present,* 2014, supplement 9, 187–206.

Siff, Stephen. *Acid Hype: American News Media and the Psychedelic Experience.* Champaign: University of Illinois Press, 2015.

Silverblatt, I. *Modern Inquisitions: Peru and the Colonial Origins of the Civilized World.* Durham: Duke University Press, 2004.

Silverman, David. *Reading Castaneda.* New York: Routledge, 1975.

Slotkin, J. S. "Peyotism, 1521–1891." *American Anthropologist,* n.s., 57, no. 2, part 1 (April 1955): 202–23.

Sluis, Ageeth. "Journeys to Others and Lessons of Self: Carlos Castaneda in Camposacape." *Journal of Transnational American Studies* 4, no. 2 (2012).

Smith, Huston, and Reuben Snake, eds. *One Nation under God: The Triumph of the Native American Church.* Santa Fe: Clear Light Publishers, 1996.

Smith, Sherry L. *Hippies, Indians, and the Fight for Red Power.* New York: Oxford University Press, 2012.

Soto Laveaga, Gabriela. "Shadowing the Professional Class: Reporting Fictions in Doctors' Strikes." *Journal of Iberian and Latin American Research* 19, no. 1 (2013): 30–40.

"Statement on Peyote." *Science* 114, no. 2970 (30 November 1951): 582–83.

Stephens, Michele M. *Under the Eyes of God: The Huichols and the Mexican State, 1810–1910.* PhD diss., University of California at Los Angeles, 2012.

Stephens, Michele M. "'... As Long as They Have Their Land': The Huichol of Western Mexico, 1850–1895." *Ethnohistory* 62, no. 1 (January 2015): 39–60.

Stevens, Jay. *Storming Heaven: LSD and the American Dream.* New York: Grove Press, 1998.

Stewart, David P. "Internationalizing the War on Drugs: The UN Convention against Illicit Traffic in Narcotic Drugs and Psychotropic Substances." *Denver Journal of International Law and Policy* 18, no. 3 (Spring 1990): 387–404.

Stewart, Omer C. *Peyote Religion: A History.* Norman: University of Oklahoma Press, 1987.

Stewart, Omer C., and David Aberle. *Peyotism in the West.* Salt Lake City: University of Utah Press 1984.

Stuart, R. "Entheogenic Sects and Psychedelic Religions." *MAPS* 12, no. 1, 2002.

Sturm, Circe Dawn. *Blood Politics: Race, Culture, and Identity in the Cherokee Nation of Oklahoma.* Berkeley: University of California Press, 2002.

Taussig, Michael. *Shamanism, Colonialism, and the Wild Man: A Study in Terror and Healing.* Chicago: University of Chicago Press, 1987.

Taussig, Michael, *Mimesis and Alterity.* New York: Routledge, 1993.

Townsend, Joan B. "Neo-Shamanism and the Modern Mystical Movement." In *Shaman's Path: Healing, Personal Growth, and Empowerment,* edited by Gary Doore. Boston: Shambala, 1988.

Townsend, Joan B. "Individualist Religious Movements: Core and Neo-Shamanism." *Anthropology of Consciousness* 15, no. 1 (2004): 1–9.

Tsing, Anna Lowenhaupt. "From the Margins." *Cultural Anthropology* 9, no. 3 (August 1994): 279–97.

Turner, Bryan. "The Body in Western Society: Social Theory and Its Perspectives." In *Religion and the Body,* edited by Sarah Coakley, 15–41. Cambridge: Cambridge University Press, 1997.

United Nations Division on Narcotic Drugs, *Bulletin on Narcotics* 11, no. 2 (April–June 1959).

Urbina, Manuel. "El peyote y el ololiuhqui." *Anales del Museo Nacional de Mexico* 7, 1903, 25–48.

Valadéz, Susana. "Dreams and Visions from the Gods: An Interview with Ulu Temay, Huichol Shaman." *Shaman's Drum* 6, 1986, 18–23.

Villa Rojas, Alfonso. *Notas sobre los Huicholes.* Mexico City: INAH, CAPFCE, SEP, 1961.

Villoldo, Alberto. "An Introduction to the Psychedelic Psychotherapy of Salvador Roquet." *Journal of Humanistic Psychology* 17, 1977.

Voekel, Pamela. *Alone before God: The Religious Origins of Modernity in Mexico.* Durham: Duke University Press, 2002.

Wade, Peter. "Rethinking Mestizaje Ideology and Lived Experience." *Journal of Latin American Studies* 37, no. 2 (May 2005): 239–57.

Warman, Arturo Margarita Nolasco, Guillermo Bonfil, Mercedes Olivera, and Enrique Valencia. *De eso que llaman la antropología mexicana.* Mexico City: Editorial Nuestro Tiempo, 1970.

Weigand, Phil C., and Jay C. Fikes. "Sensacionalismo y etnografía: El caso de los Huicholes de Jalisco." *Relaciones. Estudios de historia y sociedad* 25, no. 98 (Spring 2004): 49–68.

Weigand, Phil C. *Ensayos sobre el Gran Nayar, México.* INI, El Colegio de Michoacán y CEMCA, 1992.

Weigand, Phil. *Estudio histórico y cultural sobre los Huicholes.* Guadalajara: Universidad de Guadalajara, 2002.

Weil, Andrew. "The Strange Case of the Harvard Drug Scandal." *Look* magazine, 5 November 1963.

Wertham, F., and M. Bleuler. "Experimental Study of the Influence of Mescalin on the Rorschach Test." *Archives of Neurology and Psychiatry* 27, 1932, 52.

Winter, Jay. *Dreams of Peace and Freedom: Utopian Moments in the Twentieth Century.* New Haven: Yale University Press, 2008.

Yensen, Richard. *Hacia una medicina psiquedélica: Reflexiones sobre el uso de enteógenos en psicoterapia.* Barcelona: Los Libros de la Liebre de Marzo, 1998.

Zaehner, Robert Charles. "The Menace of Mescalin." *New Blackfriars* 35, no. 412-13 (1954): 310–23.

Zimmerman, Nadya. *Counterculture Kaleidoscope: Musical and Cultural Perspectives on Late Sixties San Francisco.* Ann Arbor: University of Michigan Press, 2008.

Zingg, Robert. *The Huichols: Primitive Artists, Contributions to Ethnography.* New York: G. E. Stechert, 1938.

Zolov, Eric. *Refried Elvis: The Rise of the Mexican Counterculture.* Berkeley: University of California Press, 1999.

Zolov, Eric. "Mexico's Rock Counterculture (La Onda) in Historical Perspective and Memory." In *New World Coming: The Sixties and the Shaping of Global Consciousness,* edited by Karen Dubinsky et al., 379–87. Toronto: Between the Lines, 2009.

Index

www.ingramcontent.com/pod-product-compliance
Lightning Source LLC
Chambersburg PA
CBHW020659270326
41928CB00005B/196